Map courtesy Gordon Rushton

(not to scale)

With fires made up and regulator wide open Earl of Merioneth *leaves Tan-y-bwlch for Dduallt on 23rd August 1968.*

Brian Jones

Immortal Rails

VOLUME 2

1964–1983

Peter Johnson

The Story of the Closure and Revival of the Ffestiniog Railway

1939 - 1983

Published in the 50th Anniversary year of the operation of the first trains on the revived Ffestiniog Railway

ISBN 1-900622-09-2 (Hardback)

British Library Cataloguing in Publication Data

A catalogue record for this book
is available from the British Library
Catalogue Reference No.385.5'2'0942925

Publishing, Typesetting and Design by:
RailRomances, PO Box 85,
Chester CH4 9ZH

Special Graphics by:
John Milner
J.C. Sreeves

Endpaper Maps by:
Gordon Rushton

Bureau Services by:
Lazertype, Laurel Bank,
Gresford, Wrexham LL12 8NT

Printed by:
The Amadeus Press Ltd,
Ezra House, West 26 Business Park,
Cleckheaton BD19 4TQ

Prelude

Immortal Rails Volume 1 described three aspects of the Festiniog Railway's history. Firstly, how the railway, badly run down, had apparently come to the end of its natural life and was closed, to passengers in 1939 and completely in 1946. Secondly, how the railway became derelict whilst the company tried find a way to abandon its responsibilities legally and realise its assets for the benefit of the shareholders, and enthusiasts sought a way to take control of the railway and to restore it. Thirdly, how the railway was reopened and the difficulties that had to be surmounted to keep it running. Using material from government files, the Festiniog Railway Company Board's minutes, general manager Allan Garraway's weekly reports to the Company Board and other contemporary sources the tale was brought up to the end of 1963, with trains running to Tan-y-bwlch, passenger numbers increasing, the loco position invariably critical, the purse strings always tight and the railway determined to secure compensation from the CEGB for the breach in the route that prevented a straightforward restoration of the line to Blaenau Ffestiniog. An Interlude described the railway's relationship with the Ministry of Transport's officials responsible for ensuring that the railway was run safely.

Volume 2 continues the story until 1983, when George Thomas MP, speaker of the House of Commons, performed the official opening of Blaenau Ffestiniog station and Allan Garraway retired. The railway had been extended to Dduallt (1968), Llyn Ystradau (1977) and Tanygrisiau (1978), finally reaching its new terminus in 1982. During the period the railway expanded its fleet of locomotives and rolling stock to cater for expanding passenger numbers but was always on a financial knife-edge, despite the award of grants from the the Wales Tourist Board and other public bodies. An Interlude describes how the impasse with the CEGB over the deviation route was resolved, and how its construction was funded.

Highlights of the period since 1983, outlined in a Postscript, demonstrate that the Ffestiniog Railway has not rested on its laurels and continues to progress, not always in the expected direction. It is certainly clear that the Railway has just an exciting future ahead of it as it has had an eventful past.

Leicester
January 2005

Contents

Prelude 5
Chapter 7 – Onwards to Dduallt 1964–1968 7
Chapter 8 – After Dduallt 1969–1975 47
Chapter 9 – On to Tanygrisiau ~ the Deviation Years 1976–1978 85
Interlude 2 – The Electricity Board and the Deviation 1952–1978 103
Chapter 10 – Back to Blaenau ~ the Final Years 1979–1983 151
Postscript – 1983–2005 185
Appendix 11 – Alternative proposals for crossing the dam at Tanygrisiau 206
Appendix 12 – Summary of tickets issued; eight weeks 1970–1971 207
Appendix 13 – Winter Programme 1969–1970 208
Appendix 14 – Grant Applications to the Wales Tourist Board 1973–1993 208
Appendix 15 – Estimate included with 1972 LRO Application 209
Appendix 16 – Extract from drawings LRO Amendment 1968 210
Appendix 17 – Financial details to end of May 1972 211
Index 212

Conventions

Circa 1973 the town of Portmadoc was renamed Porthmadog. The railway was called the 'Festiniog Railway' by its 1832 Act of Parliament and in 1979 the name 'Ffestiniog Railway' was adopted for marketing purposes.

The spellings of Tan-y-bwlch, Tanygrisiau and Blaenau Ffestiniog have been adopted as such throughout the text regardless of how they were spelled in quoted documents.

An omission from a quoted document is indicated by (. . . .) and an editorial insertion by the use of square brackets ([]). In order to avoid excessive use of [sic] in quoted documents spellings have been corrected and in some cases a modicum of punctuation introduced.

Chapter 7

Onwards to Dduallt

1964 ~1968

Despite all the best intentions, the period of consolidation after reaching Tan-y-bwlch in 1958 lasted but five years before plans for expansion became prominent. Without doubt the railway was in much better condition but there were still many weaknesses. The steady increase in passenger numbers put great pressure on the infrastructure, the old carriages were wearing out more quickly than new ones could be built to replace them, the Fairlies were effectively at the limit of their working lives, the Penrhyn locos were good substitutes for *Prince* but not for the articulated machines, which were still needed during the peak. Then the desire to convince the CEGB that the FR was serious in its intent to return to Blaenau Ffestiniog, to construct $2^1/_2$ miles of new railway to bypass the CEGB's power station and reservoir, put great demands on a railway that, in all honesty, had neither resources nor finances to deal with it.

1964 started with Allan Garraway discussing the carriage-building programme with Fred Boughey along with Alan Heywood and John Dobson, the latter two *'our main guards'*. They had formed the opinion that following construction of the first carriage it should be followed by the 'one-off' observation car before starting the series production of more composite saloons. To do so would be immediately financially advantageous, because of the additional first-class seats. Having two such vehicles would provide cover if one became *hors de combat*. It would also resolve the shortage of van and buffet storage space on the second train set. The new observation car would operate coupled next to No. 14, the buffet car, giving visual continuity; No. 11, with its low roof contour and short length, looked odd behind No. 14 with its roof profile designed to accommodate the late-20th century physique.

Bill Broadbent had prepared a report on the state of the locomotive fleet late in 1963. Produced in connection with an examination of the Company's requirements when the services were restored to Blaenau Ffestiniog, it is undated:

> 'Merddin Emrys – *Will require major boiler overhaul or renewal within next four years. Mechanical condition fair, and after detail attention to cylinders and axlebox bearings will not require other major repairs for some years.*
>
> Earl of Merioneth – *Boiler in fair condition. A good deal of mechanical repair and modification has been recently carried out on this loco, which will not require another general overhaul for some years.*
>
> Prince – *Newly boilered in 1955, recently mechanically overhauled and fitted with new cylinders. This loco is in good order for many years to come.*
>
> Linda – *Purchased from Penrhyn Quarry, Bangor in 1963. Boiler in fair condition, and mechanical condition greatly improved after FR modifications recently completed.*
>
> Blanche – *Purchased from Penrhyn Quarry, Bangor in 1963. Not yet at Portmadoc, but known to have a new (five years old only) boiler and mechanical condition believed to be sound. Similar modifications as carried out on* Linda *required, but these can be implemented within the forthcoming year.*
>
> Volunteer – *Built in 1944 by Messrs Peckett Ltd, Bristol. Repairs required on firebox, otherwise boiler in good condition. Mechanically excellent, but it is intended to reduce driving axle loadings by the addition of a pony truck and tender, which work is likely to be programmed in 1965/6.*
>
> *This resumé of the motive power position indicates the current availability of four steam*

locomotives, three having a tractive effort in excess of 7,000lbs. Blanche *will shortly be delivered to us and will require only minor modifications to make her immediately available for service.*

By 1965 we should be clear to tackle the conversion of Volunteer *from an 0-6-0 saddle-tank to a 2-6-0 tender engine, which work can be phased in with the firebox repairs. This work can be completed by the end of 1966.*

In 1967 we are likely to face the reboilering of Merddin Emrys, *but this will involve less labour and time than the previous major boiler overhaul undertaken four years ago and could be completed by the running season of 1968.*

In brief, we can plan our motive power maintenance programme, now that we have secured Linda *and* Blanche, *to give us six steam locos available for traffic by 1968's operating season, plus three standby diesels. Obviously we shall require on average one steam loco out of traffic for washout, periodical or mileage examination as a matter of routine for a day or two each week, but this can be diagrammed in the normal way.'*

On the staff front, Paul Dukes' engagement, to local girl Ann Sands, had been announced and he had said he was looking for work with better pay and prospects, perhaps at the Wylfa nuclear power station, about to be constructed on Anglesey. Garraway said of him:

'In the five years he has been with us he has proved a very useful worker in several spheres, particularly in the changeover on PW work from the old patching methods to thorough relaying. At Boston Lodge he has proved his versatility and is very adept at fabrication, in which sphere he will mostly be missed, but he is not a steam man. . . .'

At the 27th January Board meeting Broadbent had news from Penrhyn, where the quarry was willing to sell the two locomotives and the rail as a single transaction. The Board therefore committed the Company to expenditure of £10,925 (locomotives – £3,000, less rent on account of £75, rail £8,000) and authorised issuing a cheque for 30% of that amount, £3,187 10s (£3,187.50), immediately. Both of the locomotives were, of course, already on FR property.

The observation car proposal was approved. To provide more undercover accommodation a second-hand steel-framed shed was to be erected at Boston Lodge with assistance from the Royal Engineers, Southern Command; Francis Wayne was authorised to sign an indemnity to the War Department. It was expected that the work would start in March. Located in front of the existing carriage shed the 'new' building would provide accommodation for four bogie vehicles.

Vulcan Foundry personnel had been at Boston Lodge during the winter, working on the fireboxes of *Linda* and *Merddin Emrys*, removal of *Prince*'s tubes

Members of 483 Port Maintenance Troop, Royal Engineers, erecting steel work for the carriage workshop in March 1964.

D.W. Ronald
Collection John Alexander

The Society's White Rose group was responsible for the acquisition of the Hunslet diesel locomotive Tyke *in 1964. It was delivered on 9th March and photographed on 16th May. Despite having been overhauled before delivery it saw very little use and was out of service by 1970.*

John Alexander

and riveting on *Earl of Merioneth*. *Merddin Emrys*'s motion had been repaired, requiring a complete strip-down. One of *Moelwyn*'s fly cranks had broken for the second time; it was being welded as a temporary measure, whilst a new one was made. At the end of January *Blanche*'s wheels were sent to the Hunslet Engine Company for re-gauging.

Other work on *Linda* included fitting a steam brake, modifying the cab and drawgear, fabricating and fitting new sandboxes, building a tender, fitting a whistle from an ex-Great Central Railway J11 and repainting in the standard FR green livery.

David Rouse left the railway to work at Cookes' explosive plant in Penrhyndeudraeth. He went on to become involved in the preservation of ex-GWR 0-6-0 3205 and a driver at the West Somerset Railway.

Preliminary work on the redevelopment of the South Snowdon wharf next to Harbour station saw the FR's layout modified, by agreement, by the developer's contractor in March. The water tank and coal road were relocated and the three-way stub point replaced; it was relocated in Glan-y-mor yard during August. Relations with the developer were not always so smooth.

At the beginning of March the Royal Engineers (483 Port Maintenance Troop) arrived to erect the carriage shed extension, the task taking three weeks under the command of a Society member, David Ronald. The steelwork was delivered by the White Rose group, together with a small 1941-built Hunslet diesel locomotive called *Tyke*; Garraway paid tribute to Eddie Jones and the group for the part played in these acquisitions, asking for a letter of appreciation to be sent by Alan Pegler.

Garraway hoped that five steam locomotives would be available during the year, starting with *Merddin Emrys*, *Linda* and *Prince*, with *Blanche* joining the fleet after Easter and possibly *Earl of Merioneth* during the summer. With its wheels re-gauged *Blanche* would be running substantially in Penrhyn condition, the only other modifications being injectors and vacuum brake gear. A temporary tender would be used, as with *Linda* the previous year. A policy of regular manning was introduced, with Garraway himself on *Linda*, Evan Davies on *Merddin Emrys* and Bill Hoole allocated to *Blanche*; *Prince* was to be the standby.

The bodyside sections of the new coach, No. 24, had been trial assembled in Birkenhead, with delivery to Boston Lodge expected by Easter. The underframe would be fabricated in-house, possibly at the expense of work on *Earl of Merioneth*. Completion of the new underframe for No. 23 or 26 had been deferred due to a shortage of labour.

Miss Langsdale, it was reported to the Board on 19th February, was still in residence at No. 2 Boston Lodge. Pegler offered to visit her.

The Wales Tourist Board had awarded the railway a

certificate of merit, with a presentation in Cardiff on 18th March. Every effort was made to extract publicity from the event, with Pegler and Trevor Bailey arranging a *Flying Scotsman*-hauled special train complete with the FR crest on the headboard and '*Festiniog Railway Special*' boards mounted on the carriages.

The thefts from Boston Lodge resulted in the Board, on 25th April, imposing a ban on visitors to the works and a requirement that Society members should seek permission before entering.

An anonymous donation of £1,500 for a 'specified objective' was allocated to the new observation car. Some gifts were made in kind, as the offer of an automatic telephone exchange, which was accepted with appreciation. Once again the meeting was held on the Society AGM special train bound for Portmadoc, the meeting spanning the journey between Glyndyfrdwy, near Llangollen, and Dyffryn Ardudwy, on the Cambrian coast; 492 people travelled on the FR.

No. 24's underframe was ready for its body during May; assembly made such good progress that some interior fitting out was possible before the month's end. Underframe manufacture started for the new observation car, No. 13, at the same time; the number was actually allocated although Garraway's report contains the only reference to it seen so far.

Traffic at Easter had been poor but had picked up during the spring, exceeding the 1963 figures by the end of May. On 1st June the 2.20pm, five coaches, *Linda*-hauled, was delayed due to slipping and problems with the sanders, which had not been used previously. *Prince* went to the rescue but even the two locomotives together did not find it easy keeping their feet.

A special train run on 11th June for a party, including Garraway, participating in performances of Gilbert & Sullivan's '*HMS Pinafore*' in Blaenau Ffestiniog. In place of the usual buffet fare the passengers were offered tomato soup, chicken salad, trifle and coffee, the most ambitious buffet car venture so far attempted.

The Board was concerned, at its meeting on 15th June, about the 'heavy' purchase of goods for resale, otherwise the financial position was under control. Broadbent was given responsibility for names of locomotives and rolling stock. Passenger coach livery was discussed, with reference to the policy of 26th November 1956; Broadbent was given authority to arrange for one of the new vehicles to be varnished experimentally, on the understanding that, if desirable, it would be repainted in the usual colours.

The railway's impact on the local economy was brought home with a letter from Portmadoc UDC that expressed the Council's appreciation of the Company's contribution to the tourist industry. The Council intended to take out life membership of the Society therefore; in response the Council's clerk was to be sent a first class free pass.

Blanche was steamed for the first time during June, having a double regulator fitted before being used on ballast workings and a trial empty passenger train working. Its first run in traffic took place on 24th June, when it took the 10.45am. *Merddin Emrys* had coped well with an eight-car train on 23rd June, demonstrating the benefit of work carried out to steam pipes and valve gear, reported Garraway.

At the end of the month a large party from the London area group celebrated 10 years of working parties; on the evening of 27th June the party had a special train that ran beyond Tan-y-bwlch to the Garnedd tunnel; Garraway organised a cake decorated with a marzipan *Prince* and lettered '***10 years hard labour***'. Also on that day the Midland group delivered the four-wheeled van it had built as a homework project. The group also delivered the bogies from van No. 3, which it had started overhauling for use with No. 24.

At Boston Lodge, fitter John 'Borth' Roberts finished on medical advice, his position being taken by Bob Harris, previously a volunteer with the Welshpool & Llanfair Light Railway. In July Fred Howes joined as a platelayer and Peter Wood as a fireman/platelayer.

By a resolution carried at the 21st July Board meeting the Company's registered office was transferred to Portmadoc from 12 Grosvenor Place, London SW1.

No. 24 made its first journey up the line during the evening of 19th August but one of the axleboxes ran hot. In response to a demand for more accommodation

Opposite: Blanche *arrives at Tan-y-bwlch with the non-stop 'Y Cymro' in 1964, painted black and equipped with a temporary tender. The Croesor wagon in the foreground is lettered for the use of loco ash, presumably the material ballasting the new siding.*

Author's collection

Prince *as running in 1964, with straight frames. A Kylchap cowl and brick arch fitted in 1963 had improved draughting and steaming; although considered a 'loco of last resort' and only to be rostered on light trains, driver Bill Hoole had caused surprise by keeping time with six cars in May 1964, one of the benefits of the roller bearings fitted to No. 14. The loco was seen with Hoole at the controls during shunting on 24th June 1964.*

A.G. Ellis, FR Archives

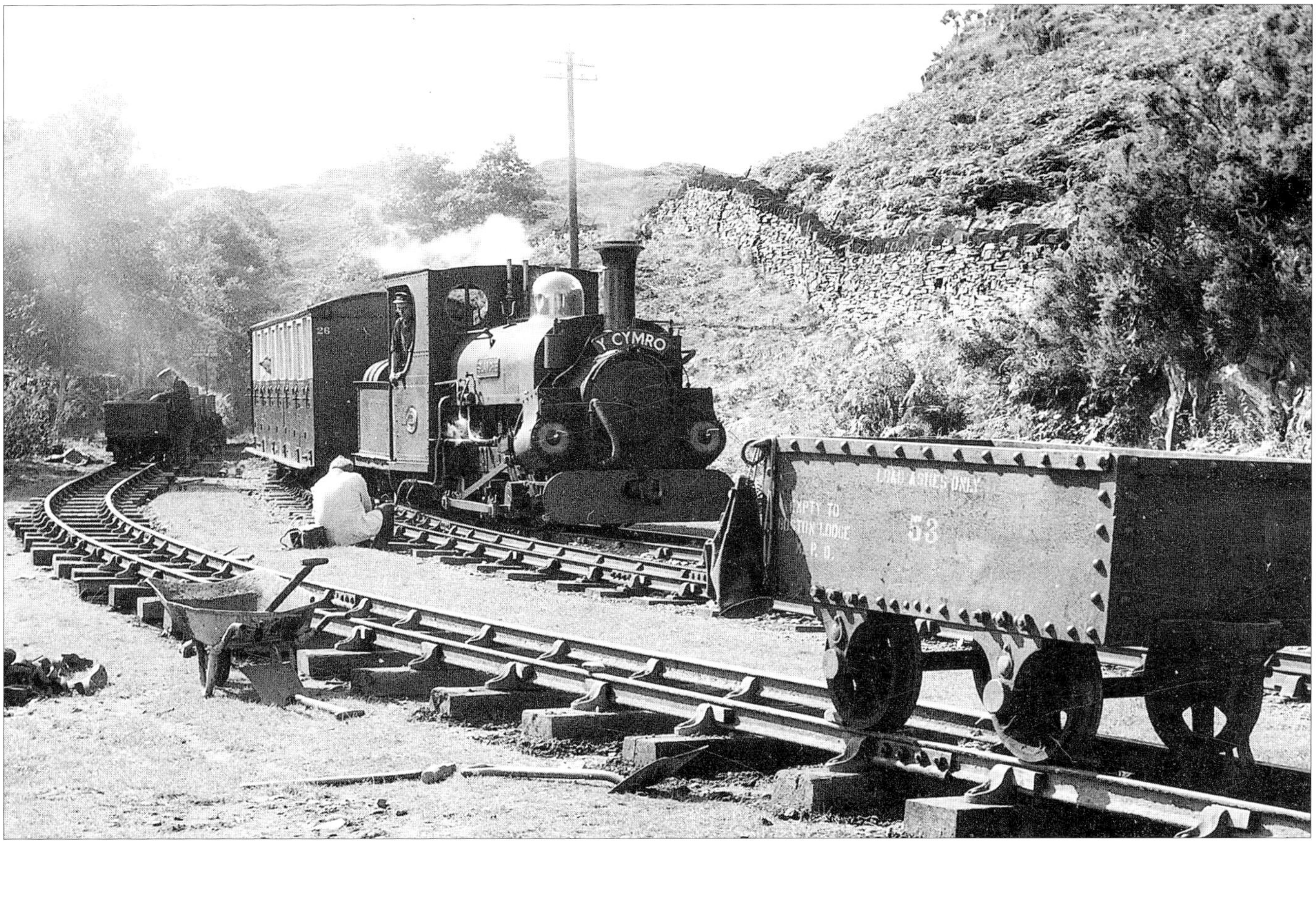

Harbour station on 11th August 1964. Linda *waits to take the train which has the Midland Group's No. 1 van, then recently delivered, attached to its rear.* Princess *is on display in the siding on the left; the land behind the railings was subsequently acquired to make room for additional carriage storage.*

Alan Bowler

from the operators it entered service on 25th August; during that week 6,533 bookings were made.

On the publicity front, Pegler commissioned Terence Cuneo to produce an FR painting. Waterlow & Co. agreed to print 3,000 copies as posters for £978 and BR agreed to display 400 copies. The remainder were to be put on sale at 10s (50p) each, at which price, the Board noted on 16th September, 2,000 copies sold would mean they would cost the railway nothing.

Following communication with Miss Langsdale's solicitor the Board agreed to steps being taken to move her from No. 2 Boston Lodge for her own safety.

In order to assess the viability of the varnished carriage livery, introduced with No. 24, the Board agreed that it should be applied to the next two new coaches, Nos. 100 and 101, and the buffet car No. 14. They also agreed that these vehicles be run as a train during the off-peak season in order to assess whether or not all new stock should be varnished rather than be painted. This is the first reference to vehicles being numbered in the 1xx series.

At Boston Lodge work resumed on the 30ft underframe, now allocated to No. 26, and work started on assembling No. 100's body during October. Wagon repairs were put in hand ready for the winter's track programme.

The Board was informed, at its 27th October meeting, that Miss Langsdale had agreed to move to No. 4 Boston Lodge; however, as Fred Boughey was living there now the Board agreed to purchase a house for her in Penrhyn that could later be suitable for occupation by a crossing keeper.

In a change of policy, the varnished carriage livery

should be applied only to new carriages, the Board agreed. No. 14 was to be labelled the '*Snapper Bar*', in recognition of the location from which it was recovered, but in small letters. Roller bearings, obtained at a 'special price' from manufacturer SKF, had been fitted to its bogies in March.

Dennis Evershed and Ken Thorne had agreed to donate four acres of land needed by the railway for the first part of the spiral at Dduallt; in recognition of this generosity the Board awarded them free passes.

Ffestiniog UDC had asked for clarification of the railway's intentions in the town; the FR had planned to terminate at either the former Great Western station site or at Duffws, both in the town centre and with land available for car parking. As the severance of the FR's property by the CEGB's access road and the standard gauge link line rendered fulfilment of this ambition unlikely, the Board decided, without prejudice to any claims, to limit passenger services to the North Western exchange site provided that adequate facilities for a terminus and car parks were made available there, and providing there was adequate connection with any quarries still operating.

On 1st November Garraway produced a list of items sold with revenue/profit generated, observing that no allowance had been made for losses or overheads. The best-selling item was Whitbread's beer, turning over £865, of which 40% was profit. This was followed by coloured postcards, £634 with 100% profit, and locomotive badges, £642 with 46%. Whisky made £5 profit on sales of £39, whilst gin made £2 profit on sales of £19. He commented that a guidebook produced for the railway by Ian Allan Ltd had not sold as well as those produced in-house.

During the month Gerald Fox completed reconstruction of the Cei Mawr parapet and made a start on preliminary works for the deviation.

Recovery of the old Penrhyn rail became problematical, as the first contractor that was approached to give a quote for lifting it wanted £9,000! By the 9th December Board meeting this amount, presumably from a different contractor, had been reduced by one-third. To pay for the transport, however, required the Company to take extended credit from Penrhyn, a move which had that organisation's approval; some existing rail would be sold for scrap to offset the expenditure. The intention was to acquire five miles of rail, two for the existing line and three for the deviation.

A close-up view of the van built by the Society's Midland Group and delivered to the railway in 1964. In addition to its brake compartment it had a nominal seating capacity of eight. After an overhaul in 1987 the vehicle was transferred to the civil engineering department.

Author's collection

Blanche *receives attention from admirers whilst running round at Portmadoc on 11th August 1964. Apart from the temporary tender it is still in Penrhyn Quarry Railway condition.*

Alan Bowler

A new charitable trust was registered on 10th November, taking over the name and assets of the old one. The Company had circulated shareholders, asking them to donate their holdings to the Trust. A total of 49 had become untraceable since C.E. Davies had written to them in 1950. By February 1965 the position was:

	Ordinary stock	5% pref	$4\frac{1}{2}$% pref	Debentures
FR Trust	£51,922	£24,230	£6,180	£15,496
FR Society		£1,000		
Untraced	£17,468	£9,420	£2,110	£2,787
Others	£16,795	£8,390	£1,710	£9,517
Total	£86,185	£43,040	£10,000	£27,800

On 9th December the Board reviewed progress of the carriage-building programme and agreed that the observation car should be numbered 100 in celebration of the centenary of passenger services, due in 1965, and carry a side-board lettered '*Observation Car 100*'. A named train called '*The Centenarian*' could be run, especially if made up of four-wheeled stock. No. 25 should be completed in 1965. It was agreed to defer completion of the Glan-y-mor carriage shed in favour of constructing a two-road awning at Harbour station. The projects were of equal value, £500, but the awning would provide shelter for passengers as well as carriages. It was also agreed to purchase and refurbish Tyddyn-y-bwlch, near Penrhyn crossing, for Miss Langsdale now and a crossing keeper later. The cost would be £1,600.

Reporting on heavy rain that had caused landslides at Rhiw Plas and Boston Lodge on 12th December, Garraway noted that the situation could have been a lot worse; the same rains had damaged the Welshpool & Llanfair Light Railway's Banwy bridge, '*a serious disaster for them*', which indeed it was.

No. 26 was placed on its new underframe during December and was fully operational again. Shortly afterwards 'old No. 1 van', which had been replaced by the Midland group's 'new No. 1 van', had its running gear removed so that the body could be used as a permanent way hut.

Operationally, the year ended on 19th December, when Santa was once again delivered to Portmadoc. After the Christmas break, on 2nd January 1965, without the benefit of either planning permission or an LRO, Michael Lewis turned the Deviation's first sod at Dduallt.

Back at Boston Lodge, Jack Owen completed a mobile generator, comprising an Austin 7 engine and a DC dynamo, which was mounted on a slate wagon flat; *Moelwyn* received a new fly crank; *Blanche*'s new tender and a pair of bogies for No. 24 were started; and *Prince* was stripped down to investigate a suspected broken firebox longitudinal stay – they were all found to be bent and serving no useful purpose!

At Minffordd, the CEGB's activities were beneficial to the railway. Plant access for a new transmission pylon was required at Bron Turnor crossing and Garraway negotiated that the FR would relay the crossing without charge, providing the CEGB would install wider gates and restore the fencing without charging the railway. As, Garraway joyfully told the Board, one of the gates was only a few rotten timbers and the fence was not too good, he felt the railway had got a fair deal that satisfied both parties!

Trains loaded with materials for the Deviation were taken up to Dduallt in February, with *Prince* steamed for the purpose.

On 24th February the Board considered the draft accounts for 1964. Subject to audit the gross receipts had increased to £28,051, from £24,097, with operating profit increased by £700. Whilst this was satisfactory cash resources would be strained by the purchase of rails and other equipment for the deviation; especially with no compensation having been paid. It was agreed to settle a solicitors' account for £600 and to increase the Portmadoc – Tan-y-bwlch fares: first class, single 6s 0d (30p), return 10s 0d (50p); third class, single 3s 6d (17½p), return 6s 6d (32½p).

At the end of the month Garraway reviewed the track situation, noting that there were no lengths

Observation saloon No. 100 entered service in 1965, when it was photographed. It had seating for 18, 10 in the observation saloon and eight in a saloon that was equipped with Pullman armchairs and tables.

Author's collection

without new sleepers between Penrhyn and Tan-y-bwlch. The largest concentrations of old sleepers were to be found around Penrhyn station, Minffordd weighhouse, Gwyndy bank, Rhiw Goch and Bryn Mawr. The new sleepers were, of course, second-hand standard-gauge sleepers purchased from BR and not always of consistent quality. There was still much to do to bring the track up to anything approaching present-day standards, he observed. At the end of March he was hoping to obtain spent ballast from the Bala – Blaenau Ffestiniog branch near Trawsfynydd, £100 for 3,000 tons or 15s (75p) per ton delivered, and sleepers from Africa.

It required a lot of effort to bring *Blanche* to operating condition. The frame stretchers were loose and required strengthening; the cylinders were attached to the smokebox and that component was not attached to the frames as it should have been. A new smokebox saddle was designed, incorporating a stronger means of holding the cylinders. There was some wastage on the tubeplate, caused by leaking tubes; the boiler inspector approved a repair by replacing half of the tubeplate. It was at first intended to send the boiler to the Vulcan Foundry's Newton-le-Willows premises but that company was not able to take on the work, so arrangements were made to have the work done by a qualified welder at Boston Lodge. Over the same period *Linda* received a new ash hopper and ashpan and steamchest drain cocks. Several tubes were replaced.

Four carriage bogies were put in hand during the winter, two each for No. 24 and No. 100. Based on the Lynton & Barnstaple Railway design, they included roller bearings and Metalastik suspension. The first bogie was not completed until early March due to the time taken to manufacture jigs to aid the construction of further examples.

An unfortunate incident occurred on 11th March, when a woman was knocked down on the Cob by *Moelwyn*. It seems she had not heard the locomotive and ran after her dog. She was taken to hospital and found to have broken both legs.

There had been, Garraway and Broadbent informed the Board on 12th April, very few comments, adverse or otherwise, on the varnished carriage livery. Therefore, it was decided, any carriages that needed repainting during the summer would be varnished; the policy would be reviewed in the autumn.

Garraway had arranged for Leeds Metal Traders to lift the Penrhyn rail for £4,000, payable in four monthly instalments after completion of lifting to Penrhyn's satisfaction. By 12th May LMT was lifting 30 lengths a day and hoped to complete the work in two months.

New wheels for No. 24 were received on 30th April and the vehicle returned to service the next day, coinciding with the Society's AGM.

The Board considered the cash position on 12th May. The lowest balance during the early season would be £300, after payment of all debts; this was in line with past performance and expectations. No allowance had been made for completing the Penrhyn rail purchase, for which deferment had been agreed, or its transportation. In view of the commitment to pay LMT £4,000, the Board foresaw that the cash position might be restricted during the next winter. It also agreed to find out more about the revenue possibilities of issuing railway letter stamps by consulting the Talyllyn Railway, which had started such a service in 1957.

No. 100 was launched at a passenger centenary event on 24th May and entered service the next day. Accommodation was for 10 passengers on swivel chairs in the observation saloon, eight on Pullman armchairs in a first-class saloon, the two separated by an entrance vestibule, and two prams in the brake compartment, accessed by wide sliding doors. A corridor connection gave access to buffet service. Garraway commented that it was instantly much more popular than No. 11.

Following the entry of No. 100 into traffic, both Nos. 11 and 12 received attention to improve the riding qualities of their bogies. No. 12 also had a dynamo fitted and was wired to run a refrigerator and No. 11 had one of its guards' doors modified to open inwards, the second set was similarly modified in July.

Signs that further attempts to involve the military in the Railway's restoration were coming to fruition appeared in Garraway's report of 20th June, when he noted the visit of two representatives from 16 Railway Training Regiment, based at Longmoor, Hampshire. Following agreement that an exercise would be carried out on the railway in September a further reconnaissance was carried out in August.

The possibility that changes in ownership of land adjacent to the railway might affect it became apparent during the same week. The locomotives had been priming, a problem eventually traced to the Tan-y-bwlch water supply, in turn caused by peat getting into the stream that fed it. It turned out that new landowners, the Economic Forestry Group, had been

Seen when new in 1964, No. 24 had seated 32 3rd class passengers in two saloons separated by a 1st class compartment seating four.

Geoff Hall, FR Archives

No. 100 was so identified to mark the centenary of official passenger services and launched on 24th May 1965. Principal guest was Sir Reginald Wilson of the British Transport Commission; his wife performed the ceremony.

FR Archives

Blanche *approaches Penrhyn crossing on 2nd June 1966.*

C.W. Hughes

ditching above Creau and caused the problem. Trials to assess a suitable level of water treatment were conducted the following week.

A leaking washout plug on *Merddin Emrys'* firebox was traced to a poorly welded bush installed before the war. The failed weld was spotted before it could fail under pressure and a new bush was made and fitted using electric welding techniques.

On *Blanche* the boiler repairs were completed and the boiler put in the frames by 18th July. The steam brake, smokebox and lagging were completed and the cylinders and motion were being fitted up before the month ended.

Following the downgrading of Minffordd BR to halt status, from 19th October 1964, and an announcement that it would be opened only when the FR was operating, the installation of electric lighting, Garraway noted on 18th July, was *'just a typical example of BR absurdity'*! An agency arrangement was made, whereby the FR sold tickets to BR passengers, initially at Minffordd but later at Portmadoc. By the end of the year turnover from this source had reached £148, producing a profit of £8 for the FR; over the years the agency developed into a substantial travel business.

The 10th anniversary of reopening was duly commemorated on 23rd July, and coincided with the carriage of the year's 50,000th passenger; Oswald Thomas presented a life pass to Leslie Barraclough of Brighouse.

No. 26 re-entered service on 9th August, looking very smart in varnished livery; the fitting of full-height doors, making it weatherproof, had permitted the use of upholstered seats obtained from old buses. At the same time Garraway expressed his concern about the condition of No. 22, saying that it needed repairs nearly every time it went out and would have to be withdrawn at the end of the season; it was questionable if it could be made fit for even occasional use, he commented. The four-wheelers were being

The first Garratt, K1, arrived from Beyer, Peacock & Company on 23rd March 1966.

FR Archives

The Simplex, always referred to by Allan Garraway as 'Simplex', had become known as Mary Ann, *as evidenced by this 8th April 1966 photograph showing it with a painted name, perhaps applied unofficially, at Boston Lodge. The origin of the name is unknown; Ann Dukes, long-time resident at Minffordd station house and wife of Paul Dukes, told the author it was nothing to do with her. The name was not applied officially until 1971.*

Stephen Evans, FR Archives

Colonel Campbell's private siding under construction at Dduallt during 1966.

FR Archives

Blanche*'s boiler and saddle tank in Glan-y-mor yard in 1965. The erstwhile long shed is on the left and the frame of the carriage workshop behind. The bolster wagon set in the foreground was built at Boston Lodge in 1875.*

Geoff Hall, FR Archives

Blanche*'s tender under construction during 1965.*

Geoff Hall, FR Archives

Below: Earl of Merioneth *raising steam in the long shed.*

John Hunt

On 23rd October 1966, Prince *departs with Allan and Moyra Garraway's wedding train.*

John Neville

Blanche *and* Linda *in August 1966; the green and ivory carriage livery had started to give way to varnished mahogany.*

John Alexander

overused in consequence and the bowsiders were deteriorating badly. He went on to say:

'I am afraid that a very considerable sum of money will have to be spent on getting outside assistance on the maintenances of these vehicles within the next year or two, if they are to be maintained in a safe and fit condition for traffic. At the present time I am ashamed of some of them, which really do look extremely scruffy. With the ever-increasing traffic we are carrying and the greater number of coaches in service, the maintenance problem is increasing. We have been having considerable discussions between the two guards, Fred Boughey and myself, as to the future programme and there is no doubt that on a long-term basis we have got to push forward with building the new stock as fast as ever we can, but at the same time we must keep the existing stock going and shall have to use outside labour, which it seems we may now be able to get as we have done on [No.] *26.* [No.] *26 now being closed in does partly compensate for the loss of* [No.] *22 and if* [No.] *23 is similarly dealt with, things will not be quite so bad. The point is that open Welsh Highlands cannot be used for coach party reservations and although they are popular in fine weather with some people, there are many who do object to them.*

[Nos.] *17, 18 and 20 all more or less equally need heavy repair work and if only one is done per year there is still going to be another two seasons to keep one of them running, but more important still, I do want you to appreciate that a considerable amount of money will be necessary on this side of the business in the*

future, if we are to continue to carry even the same amount of traffic.'

To add to the problems *Merddin Emrys* failed on 10th August, losing a valve cotter and damaging both an intermediate valve rod and valve spindle. It was patched up and kept going for the rest of the week with assistance from *Prince* on the heavier trains. *Linda* worked the 2.15pm, but unfortunately a slight shower of rain produced greasy conditions and even with continual sanding it lost nearly half an hour and *Prince* following lost a few more minutes. This was, however, mostly recovered in time to make the 6.08pm connection. On arrival at Tan-y-bwlch the left driving wheel axlebox was found to be warm due to being full of water from a leaking saddle tank. The engine was kept going by keeping the box syringed out.

This was not all, as on the Thursday *Linda* broke a spring on its return to Portmadoc on the 2.06pm; it was changed under the water column at Portmadoc in 20 minutes causing no more than ten minutes delay to the 3.00pm non-stop. That night *Linda*'s tank was attended to and over the weekend *Merddin Emrys*' bogie was taken out and the motion straightened and sorted out. On 10th August, *Blanche* took a 5.45pm special and got to Tan-y-bwlch satisfactorily, but on starting away to return an eccentric seized, breaking the strap, bending the rod and also breaking the eccentric pulley itself.

Blanche's tender had a half-cab, improving crew accommodation considerably. It was painted matt black, a temporary scheme that lasted only until the autumn, when it received the standard FR locomotive livery.

Garraway didn't see much future for *Merddin Emrys*, on 22nd August commenting:

'ME continues to give trouble due to the blow-through at the bottom end and I am afraid that my remarks regarding coach No. 22 apply similarly to this locomotive, which I am afraid can only be patched up as a standby for the future.'

Opposite: *Before the summer of 1965 was over* Blanche *was sufficiently complete to be returned to traffic albeit in advance of a visit to the paint shop. The loco is seen leaving Tan-y-bwlch; tree growth has long-since eliminated the view of Llyn Mair.*

Geoff Hall, FR Archives

Following the end of the peak season, on 5th September, Garraway reviewed the year's achievements, driving home his message about the state of the locomotives and rolling stock. In six weeks an average of over 11,000 journeys had been made and a total of 72,500 passengers carried, once again illustrating that the railway was carrying over half its traffic in this short period. Garraway was of the opinion that the heavy traffic now being carried did require more coaches and more and larger locomotives. *Merddin Emrys* was decidedly the worse for wear and had been very troublesome; the absence of *Blanche* earlier on had also been worrying. Consequently train delays were more numerous and the only saving grace was that the improved track had enabled time to be regained more easily.

Garraway emphasised the point that everyone was talking about increasing traffic and their eyes were all set on the exciting ultimate goal of reaching Blaenau, without giving sufficient thought as to how the extra traffic was going to be carried or hauled. The essential factor was that unless a very good train service was maintained in the summertime to bring in the revenue, then there was no hope of ever expanding the railway, he said. As an example, during a period of seven days in the summer more than 1,400 people per day had been booked on the line plus an average of another 200 from outside and other coach tours. Garraway made his point:

'To operate such an extremely heavy commuter service as we are doing requires equipment that is in fair condition and is suitable for this task. Historical and interesting items are all right only if they are really suitable for the purpose. The varied assortment of four-wheeled vehicles that we have to press into service is not at all popular with the general public and from an operating standpoint is extremely slow to handle. No. 22 is literally tied together with various bits of wood and metal to keep it usable and next year, at the best it can only be used in dire emergency.'

The bright side of the picture was the fact that the increased traffic plus the fare increase had already given the railway more money during this short period than it had altogether during the previous year.

In an attempt to keep *Merddin Emrys* operational during the army's visit several tubes were replaced, a joint on the bottom-end fireman's-side cylinder was remade and a fracture of the firebox wrapper was welded up.

A traditional view of a train, this one hauled by Earl of Merioneth, *on Cei Mawr. Since the picture was taken the view has been lost to the trees.*

FR Archives

Changing tokens at Minffordd, 1968.

Rodney Weaver, FR Archives

Earl of Merioneth *being serviced at Portmadoc in 1968.*

Richard C.A. King

Linda *arrives at Dduallt towards the end of the season in 1968.*

Rodney Weaver, FR Archives

An S&T working party gravitates through Garnedd tunnel, probably before the line was extended to Dduallt in 1968.

John Neville

The self-propelled permanent way trolley was inherited from the 'old' railway and appears to have received very little notice. It was used for a while by the deviationists before being withdrawn, perhaps on safety grounds. Tan-y-bwlch, 19th September 1966.

G.E. Baddeley, FR Archives

Getting a compressor to the deviation proved to be quite a saga, then when it was en route on 19th September 1967 it derailed at Garnedd.

S. Sutcliffe, FR Archives

The army set up camp at Minffordd on 15th September, toured the line the next day and started their exercise 'Shish Kebab' on 17th September. With 150 personnel participating, it was a major logistical operation for both parties. During the next three weeks tasks carried out included relaying the track between Tan-y-bwlch and Garnedd tunnel, using Penrhyn rail, installing two turnouts in Glan-y-mor and preparing the *Earl of Merioneth*'s boiler for hydraulic testing and overhauling a compressor at Boston Lodge.

During the course of the exercise the army played its part in railway operation, too, but not everything went according to plan. On 23rd September *Blanche* derailed at Gysgfa when hauling a ballast train. Garraway commented that no obvious reason had been detected. The track had been relaid in 1958/9 and was in satisfactory condition although it tended to get out of alignment because the ground was '*soggy*'. For this reason a caution had been imposed on the location the day before but there was no evidence of speeding and the train was stopped within 50ft of the derailment occurring. The only damage sustained was a broken spring; the army rerailed the locomotive.

Miss Langsdale's tenancy at Boston Lodge continued to exercise the Board at its 13th October meeting; her annual rent of £15 12s 0d (£15.60) barely covered the rates. Les Smith was to agree a 'reasonable' increase with her; £1 per week was subsequently negotiated. In the meantime mortgage arrangements for the purchase of Tyddyn-y-bwlch at Penrhyn had been completed.

Garraway was the centre of attention on 23rd October, when he married Moyra McMillan at St Mary's church in Tremadoc. A suitably decorated *Prince*-hauled train conveyed the couple on the first stage of their journey to a honeymoon in Scotland, the railway's pranksters ensuring that the gates at Lottie's Crossing were locked! The Company adapted the first floor of the Harbour station to become their home.

A new locomotive was being considered during November. The Manchester-based locomotive builder, Beyer, Peacock & Company, was in the throes of being wound up and offered the Company the first Garratt locomotive, 0-4-0+0-4-0 *K1*, built in 1909 for the Tasmanian Government Railway. The company had reacquired the locomotive in 1947 and was now offering it to the FR for £1,000. *K1* had been offered to the Narrow Gauge Railway Museum Trust at Tywyn on permanent loan, sometime after the Museum had acquired the BP & Company works locomotive 0-4-0WT *Dot*. The offer had been subject to the Museum being able to display it under cover. This was not feasible at the time and the matter was left in abeyance. Garraway went to see the locomotive on 5th November; he recommended its acquisition, saying it would be suitable for the FR although it would require a lot of work, and money spending on it, to adapt it. He went on to say that looking to the future, with trafficincreasing, the opportunity of getting a suitably large locomotive was too good to miss. The Board, on 24th November, decided that its purchase should be deferred until there were fewer demands on cash!

The limited future of *Merddin Emrys*' boiler was highlighted when the boiler inspector visited Boston Lodge, also on 5th November. It was reported that a certain amount of staying and replacement of rivets, as well as re-tubing, would be required if it was to run the following year. If it were to run for another two to three years it needed about 60 stays replacing.

Also at Boston Lodge work was in hand on building a new underframe for No. 23 and on an underframe for new carriage No. 25. Contractors had started dismantling No. 19. Having two handbraked vehicles in a train, as occurred following No. 14's entry to traffic, turned out to cause unexpected problems – No. 14's wheels needed turning after it had been run with its brake on; the following January the brake was modified to leak the vacuum when turned on to prevent a repetition.

The cash balance of £6,200 on 24th November, together with anticipated donations from the Society, was expected to be sufficient to meet the railway's financial obligations during the winter, including transport of the Penrhyn rail; payment was not required for the rails and locomotives for at least another year.

Garraway's 1966 budget was considered at this meeting. The Board thought his estimate of £26,000 income, with no allowance made for donations or sale of scrap, a reasonable basis on which to work. However, it also thought some expenditure could only be made if there was additional income, as much as £7,000, from other sources. In the absence of this extra income items such as the awning for the Harbour station, the purchase of the Garratt and part of the carriage construction programme would have to be deferred. Expenditure on the deviation was to be treated as advances to be set against any compensation received from the CEGB.

A new register of shareholders had been created

Blanche *and the* Earl of Merioneth *at Boston Lodge in April 1968.*

Jack Patience

Linda *at Bakehouse crossing, Penrhyn; the 'ski jump' termination of the headshunt is on the left and the up home colour light signal visible above the loco.*

Geoff Hall, FR Archives

Earl of Merioneth *and train seen from Campbell's platform, 31st August 1968.*

John Alexander

with untraced holdings listed separately. At this point the Trust held nearly 75% of each class of stock. Pegler's £12,000 debenture was also held by the Trust; it had originally been issued to secure a bank loan of £11,480. The Board resolved to credit £520 to the loan account so that the resulting balance of £12,000 could be treated as satisfied by the debenture and the loan account closed. No interest on the loan had been paid since 1954.

Minffordd goods shed had been re-roofed in October for the benefit of the permanent way department. Its advantage was manifest in December when wet weather forced the gang indoors; the wagonload of chaired sleepers assembled there helped to speed relaying at Cei Mawr when the weather abated.

A hard lesson was learnt following the army's relaying in the autumn. The use of unsorted Penrhyn rail proved to be most unsatisfactory because the wear was unmatched. When more Penrhyn rail was earmarked for use upwards from Highgate crossing at Penrhyn in January 1966 the time was taken to sort it, giving a much more satisfactory result. Later batches were marked in situ before lifting and some substantial lengths were laid exactly as they had been on the PQR.

The need for volunteer accommodation was discussed at the board meeting held on 24th January 1966. The Society wished to renovate Penrhyn station and use it as a hostel at a budgeted cost of £3,200. Initially the Board agreed to consider the matter but by the time of its 28th March meeting it felt that the money could be better spent on other objectives of both Company and Society, such as locomotives and the carriage programme. In any event it felt that volunteer accommodation could be provided more cheaply, perhaps by use of sectional buildings or a 'scrap' sleeping car and dining car located in Minffordd yard. Having said that, the minute concludes *'In general however, the board considered the matter most sympathetically and would be prepared to assist any agreed scheme by granting a peppercorn lease for 7/14/21 years during the validity and in pursuance of the agreement between the Company and the FR*

Trackwork in progress at Portmadoc during the winter of 1966/7.

John Neville

Rhoslyn bridge under construction, 1969.

Geoff Hall, FR Archives

You can help
TO RESTORE
THE WORLD'S PREMIER
NARROW GAUGE RAILWAY
JOIN THE
FESTINIOG RAILWAY SOCIETY
SEND A YEAR'S SUBSCRIPTION NOW
TO
£1
R. H. R. GARRAWAY
35 HOLMWOOD ROAD · CHEAM · SURREY
10/-
UNDER 18

Society.' What a change in position!

Back on 24th January Broadbent reported that he had given a verbal indication to Beyer, Peacock & Company of the Company's intention to buy *K1*. It was unloaded at Portmadoc on 24th March, when a successful appeal to raise £1,500 to pay for it was launched. He had arranged to sell scrap rail, made surplus by the Penrhyn material, to John Summers at £11 10s 0d (£11.50) per ton; it was expected that the Penrhyn rail would be used between Tan-y-bwlch and Blaenau Ffestiniog. The carriage-building programme was confirmed as one vehicle per year in addition to the renovation of Nos. 17, 18 and 23 during 1966 and No. 15 in 1967. No. 23 was completed in February.

Relaying through Penrhyn continued into March. In February the Thermit welding of rails was used for the first time. The first rails so treated were in the station area, gaining experience for the main point of the exercise, to avoid having joints located within the level crossing. In April more rails were welded for use at Rhiw Goch.

A new boiler inspector paid a two-day visit to Boston Lodge at the end of March, leaving Garraway very concerned that the new man was much stricter than the old. Following representations to the insurance company the latter's chief engineer paid a visit on 21st April and restored the status quo! Garraway said of him '*He was trained in the proper manner by the right company at Stratford!*'

An ongoing task during the Spring was the installation of a cable duct across the Cob by the GPO. Part of the agreement was that the FR would have use of it for its own communications purposes.

Trevor Bailey resigned from the Company Board with effect from 26th April, citing '*heavy pressure of other work*' according to the minute. No explanation was given in his letter to Pegler.

In May Garraway visited the Isle of Man in company with the Talyllyn Railway's Bill Faulkner and John Bate. Invited by the Isle of Man Steam Railway Society, they were to advise on the 3ft gauge line. Garraway thought the railway reminiscent of the FR in the 1930s, the workshops having strong affinities with Boston Lodge too. Saying that the FR and TR flags were kept flying in the island he boasted '*They definitely prefer the Festiniog style of set-up.*'

Traffic at Whitsun, the last weekend in May, was, in Garraway's word, '*phenomenal*'. 6,466 passengers spent £1,605 10s 8d (£1,605.53) to make 11,523 journeys and a further £587 18s 2d (£587.91) in the shop and on refreshments during the week. On three days there had been over 1,000 bookings. Operating the peak summer service was an advantage in dealing with the traffic and might have helped attract passengers, too, Garraway felt.

Bookings the following week amounting to 2,840, but these were marred by a derailment on 9th June.

Palmerston *stabled at Portmadoc to prevent the wharf developer from attempting to make a crossing over the railway, 6th January 1968.*

John Alexander

A Prince*-hauled ballast train approaches Tan-y-bwlch on 12th April 1968. The wagons were built by Robert Hudson in Leeds and obtained from the RAF.*

Stephen Evans, FR Archives

Linda broke a spring hanger at Rhiw Goch and continued to Penrhyn at slow speed. When reversing into the loop the leading wheels derailed; limited breakdown equipment was taken to site by road and with a modicum of packing the loco managed to pull itself back on. It was later established that the hanger was the third on the Penrhyn locos to have broken since the FR had been operating them, although there was evidence of problems in the past. An inspection programme was put in hand, along with a modification to mitigate any further fractures. Garraway took care to record that the incident was reported using the 'appropriate form'.

Following completion of its interior painting, No. 17 returned to traffic during June, when workshop attention was transferred to No. 23. Garraway received a request from the Narrow Gauge Railway Museum at Towyn for the loan of the iron horse dandy, a move he supported, although it was supplied without a horse. The museum managed to source a stuffed one, which completed the display.

Even as late as 3rd July Garraway thought it unlikely that the *Earl of Merioneth* would be ready for the start of the peak summer service so *Merddin Emrys* was prepared as standby. Ten tubes were replaced and the bottom-end eccentric, which was loose, was attended to. He thought it would be good for a few days' work if required. In the event the *Earl of Merioneth* missed the season completely and *Merddin Emrys* stayed cold until 29th August when it appeared twice daily for two weeks and then again before the end of September.

He considered the numbering of the new carriages on 3rd July, obviously in the light of remarks that had been made to him. As the observation car, No. 100, had been numbered out of series because of the passenger centenary, he suggested the other new carriages should be numbered in the same series – No. 24 to be No. 101 and No. 25, under construction, to be No. 102. In the event No. 24 became No. 104 and No. 25 became No. 105; Garraway referred to the latter by its new number for the first time on 4th September.

A special train ran on 22nd July for the Llanfrothen & Penrhyndeudraeth District committee supporting the National Eisteddfod to be held in Bala in 1967; 350 passengers travelled in 12 coaches hauled by *Prince* and *Linda*. The organisers paid £6 to cover the direct costs and sold the tickets; the FR took over £20 in buffet car sales and unspecified amounts at the termini. Seven passengers joined the Society and the organisers promised a donation to the Garratt fund. One of the organisers commented that the ride was much smoother than he remembered pre-war – perhaps because he was jammed in and couldn't move!

A programme for adapting Penrhyn station as a volunteer hostel was agreed by the Board on 25th July, following a meeting with the Society; the latter would undertake the work. *'It was agreed that anything in this direction should be warmly encouraged.'*

Good news from the local authorities came on two fronts. The railway's rateable value had been reduced from £495 to £160 and Deudraeth RDC had become a corporate member of the Society. In recognition of the latter Wayne was asked to send a first-class free pass for the use of the Council.

A Mr. B.J. Blackburn had asked if he could take over, restore and operate the railway between Tanygrisiau and Blaenau Ffestiniog until such time as the Company had need of this section. The request was approved provided it was carried out within the ambit of the Company's organisation and Ministry of Transport regulations were observed. This was rather an odd decision as Blackburn had been in correspondence with Garraway and had already given up because he was unable to provide the bus link that Garraway had told him was essential. At the same time he had told Garraway that he felt the FR was not sufficiently preservation minded and that the policy of building new rolling stock would turn passengers away.

Whilst the overdraft was £2,300 and declining it was forecast that the cash balance in December would be lower than that of the previous year, unless any compensation cash was received; Garraway reported that the passenger journeys were up 12,300 at the same time. Major Charles Walker made an interest-free loan to the Company, a gesture that was rewarded by the gift of one of the Society's silver medals. Broadbent was investigating the possibility of realising the scrap value of *Palmerston*'s copper firebox if it could be extracted without destroying the locomotive.

The week ended 21st August coincided with 1965's record week and produced nearly identical results. Monday, however, was the quietest August day for several years, with only 771 bookings, whilst Wednesday set a new record, with 1,863 bookings and many passengers unable to travel on the afternoon trains, although having 100 passengers on the 5.45pm suggests that a good number were prepared to wait for a later departure. An extra train had been introduced to run at 10.10am, relieving the 10.40am, which it crossed at Tan-y-bwlch. Minor adjustments were made to the timetable later in the day to take account of its return path.

The Economic Forestry Group was responsible for

Earl of Merioneth *leaves Portmadoc with the first train for Dduallt on 6th April 1968.*

R.G. Roscoe, FR Archives

delays on 31st August, when a tree was felled across the line at Llechwedd Coed just before the 4.10pm ex-Tan-y-bwlch was due. A party of 'Tadpoles' from Chace School at Plas Halt heard the noise and saw the telephone wires moving violently so one its leaders ran up the line to stop the train.

An innovation on the track was introduced in September, when a flange lubricator was installed at Whistling Curve. Its use was to establish if side cutting of the rails and wheel-flange wear would be reduced. In Minffordd yard a start was made on building a roadway to the ballast chutes so ballast taken in by road could be loaded directly into wagons. No. 105 entered traffic on 22nd September. It was similar to No. 104 except that three third-class seats were lost to make space for a toilet compartment. Straight away contractors started work on stripping and rebuilding No. 18.

At its 26th September meeting the Board set 1968 as the target for extending train operating to Dduallt. It was recorded that the cash balance would be £3,000 after the payment of outstanding accounts. Fares revenue during the summer had been that amount up on the previous year. A £4,000 payment on account was due from the CEGB. In contrast with the forecast at the start of the year it was now thought that the overdraft at Whit 1967 would be less than in 1966. On the strength of this financial performance Garraway had already been authorised to obtain components for two more coaches; production of underframes was put in hand, with a further one for No. 22.

Plans were being drawn up, it was reported, to increase the covered accommodation for carriages; a second platform was also under consideration at Portmadoc. Ron Lester and Fred Howes were to spend a week with a Southern Region permanent way gang in the Purley region to gain experience on track maintenance techniques.

On the personnel front, local member Harold Creamer was to be asked to deputise for Garraway in the event of his unavoidable absence or leave; Garraway was ill and did little more than light office work over the next two months. It was December before he returned to full-time work. He continued to submit his reports most weeks but on a reduced scale.

Tony Massau, who had joined the permanent way department two years earlier, left the Company's employ on 1st October and was replaced on 22nd November by Paul Anderson, a volunteer and railwayman.

Gales early in December damaged most of the railway's roofs, particularly at Minffordd station and the long shed at Boston Lodge. The doors of Minffordd goods shed were also damaged and needed replacement. As a result the Board agreed to seek consequential loss insurance of £26,000 for two years at a premium of £80.

Work on rebuilding the line to Dduallt continued during the autumn, reaching Coed-y-bleiddiau by Christmas; progress was delayed by a shortage of the carriage screws used to screw down the rail chairs as Penrhyn screws were ½in shorter than the adopted FR standard; a new supply arrived in the new year. Alongside this extension activity track was relaid in the main line at Portmadoc.

In addition to the carriage construction work at Boston Lodge there was progress on the reconstruction of *Earl of Merioneth*, *Moelwyn* was re-engined and 'peculiar wear' on one of No. 17's bogies investigated; the latter was found to be caused by one of the axles being ½in out of parallel.

When the Board met on 30th January 1967 most of the business conducted related to the Deviation. Regarding the outstanding payment due for the Penrhyn material it was hoped that Penrhyn would agree to the final payment being deferred until the compensation was received from the CEGB; doing so would limit the closed-season overdraft to £5,000.

Further gales on 14th February brought down the trident signal post on the Cob, saving the task of removing it because of rot.

A disagreement over the use of Tremadoc Estate land for car parking at Portmadoc was initiated by the developer of the adjacent South Snowdon wharf during March; it transpired that he had obtained planning permission for a development that made use, for the access road, of some of the land, including that occupied by the gents' toilets, leased by the railway from the estate. The railway was accused of trespass and told it would be held responsible if the development scheme failed because of alleged non-cooperation.

Graham Bourne, the developer, was a local man who also owned the Greenacres caravan site at Borth-y-gest; it transpired that half of the development was owned by the builder. Bourne's engineering consultant was Major S.L. Richards, who had rented a room in the station during the war. Garraway later learned that in planning terms the long lease

The layout at Tan-y-bwlch was realigned to provide an island platform during the first part of 1968, the work still incomplete after services were resumed to Dduallt on 6th April. John Harrison waits to exchange tokens with Earl of Merioneth's *fireman.*

Norman Gurley, FR Archives

by which the station land was occupied meant that the railway was considered to be the owner rather than occupier and should have been notified of the planning application; unfortunately this procedural failure did not render the application invalid. It also transpired that the Tremadoc Estate sold land occupied by the railway, on both long and short leases, without disclosing the Company's interest. The surprising feature of this case is that it seems that no one took the trouble to look at the planning application when it was advertised to see what impact it might have had on the railway.

Despite the efforts made to return *Earl of Merioneth* to service in 1966 it was only completed just in time for Easter 1967, but there were still problems with it. The steamchest casting at the bottom end was cracked whilst that at the top end had a blowhole; these faults were repairable but in the meantime the locomotive moved around in clouds of steam! It was 22nd April before Garraway considered the locomotive to be in satisfactory condition.

The end of Bill Hoole's footplate career came on 27th March, when he had a seizure whilst at home. Garraway noted that his absence would make the railway's driver position 'more acute'. *Blanche* had hauled the first train of the season but by early April was found to have a serious crack in its left cylinder: the better one, remarked Garraway. The crack was repaired by patching, a temporary measure, leaving him to suggest that fitting new cylinders would be a task for the next winter.

An addition to the locomotive fleet was in prospect at the Board's 8th May meeting. John Ransom, then a Society director, had offered the Company his Alco 2-6-2PT in exchange for £500 in preference shares. The locomotive had been built in 1917 as part of the war effort and shipped to France, where it had remained in service at Pithiviers. The tramway on which it operated had closed in 1964 and Ransom acquired the locomotive to secure its preservation in 1966, thinking it would be of use to any narrow gauge passenger-carrying railway, not necessarily the FR. A transfer agreement was agreed, which gave Ransom the right of first refusal if the locomotive ever became surplus to requirements. The issue of fifty 5% preference shares was approved on 13th September and the locomotive was delivered to the FR on 16th October.

The overdraft had reached £3,500, with Penrhyn agreeing to repayment at the rate of £100 per month, without payment of interest, a generous gesture.

Following consideration of a report by Francis Wayne on profit-sharing schemes Garraway was to propose a means of implementing a 10% pay increase for staff from June; he had already proposed a 2% bonus based on traffic revenue. The need for a Company pension fund was also highlighted.

The newest carriage, No. 105, was derailed at Trwyn-y-Garnedd on 17th May whilst on the evening train. The cause was initially attributed to excessive twist in the track on reverse curves coupled with '*a*

John Ransom's Alco 2-6-2T stopped for a press call in Birmingham on 14th October 1967.

Cater's News Agency, FR Archives

certain rigidity in the bogies peculiar to this vehicle'. It was later discovered that a new batch of springs was slightly longer than previous supplies, reducing clearances under the kingpins.

Poor weather over the spring bank holiday weekend brought record numbers to ride on the FR. On Sunday the summer Sunday service was operated with an extra at 12.05pm attracting 150 passengers. The 2.30pm was fully loaded by 2.20pm and was despatched early; thereafter trains were despatched without regard to the timetable, the last leaving Portmadoc at 6.15pm. At the end of the day six trains had carried 874 passengers! This was a record for a Sunday; 1,044 were carried on six trains the next day.

Traffic remained buoyant through the season and by 9th July, when the Board met, was 20% up on 1966. Even this excitement did not inhibit Garraway from describing the week ending 6th August as '*quite fantastic*'. All afternoon trains were crowded, he said, with passengers being prepared to stand in the new carriages, more than 50 on some occasions, rather than be left behind. 8,933 bookings generated 16,811 passenger journeys, £2,317 7s 4d (£2,317.37) in fares and £938 6s 2d (£938.31) in sales.

No. 22 returned to service on 10th August, giving a further 56 seats to spread the load, although traffic that week was more evenly spread. With 9,188 bookings, journeys 17,457, revenue increased by £72 and sales to £1,012 9s 10d (£1,012.59). Continued improvements were attributed partially to a BBC-TV broadcast on 19th August. By 3rd September traffic was 26% up, although at the expense of overcrowding and passenger complaints.

Whilst the sales were good, stock levels were blamed for stretching the Company's finances. Possibly in an attempt to address this, and to further increase sales, it was agreed, on 13th September, to appoint Maurice Bolton as sales manager on a salary of £500 plus 1% of miscellaneous sales.

The future terminus in Blaenau Ffestiniog came up for discussion on the same date. The Council had again expressed the wish that the FR would terminate at the site of the former GWR goods yard. The Board agreed that this was its preferred site provided that the Council, and the other bodies with which the railway had outstanding compensation claims, would bear the cost of extending the railway beyond Glan-y-pwll. Extension of the operating railway to Dduallt was still anticipated to occur during 1968, with Smith reporting that the station site should be ready for its run-round loop to be laid in February.

Other aspects of the railway's infrastructure were discussed, with agreement reached to arrange for expert inspection of the '*higher embankments and retaining walls*' and for someone from Maenofferen Quarry to advise on improving clearances in the Garnedd tunnel. BR had asked for £44 2s 4d (£44.12) to maintain the connection at Minffordd, Pegler and Broadbent to follow up, later securing a reduction to £22 1s 2d (£22.06); with the FR still receiving coal and ballast by rail the connection was essential to its continued operation.

Miss Langsdale was still in residence at Boston Lodge but the house at Penrhyn, Tyddyn-y-bwlch, obtained for her was nearly ready for occupation; it was to be offered to her via her solicitor.

Developer Bourne's activities had had an impact on car parking revenues, down to 5,736 tickets issued in 1967 from 10,032 issued in 1966, despite a 20% increase in traffic. Allegedly he would harangue the car park attendant and discourage prospective users. The Company put the loss resulting at £250. Smith was to try and get a longer lease for the land from the Tremadoc Estate.

The sum of £500 was allocated to be distributed between staff as a bonus, Garraway being set the task of devising a scheme for Pegler's approval. £495 had been distributed before the next Board meeting in October. In addition Garraway was given a bonus of £100 and had his salary increased to £1,100.

Fares for 1968 were set at: Portmadoc – Dduallt return, 1st class 14s (70p), 3rd class 9s (45p); Portmadoc – Tan-y-bwlch return, 1st class 12s (60p), 3rd class 7s (35p). The observation car supplement was to be 2s 6d (12½p) for the up journey only, and the 24-hour clock was to be adopted.

The high level of traffic during September was responsible for Garraway deciding to continue with a weekend service until 22nd October. It had become clear that there were increasing numbers taking weekend breaks in the area '*so long as the weather is not treacherous*'.

On 17th October, following a review of forecast income and expenditure to 30th June 1968, the Board agreed to the recruitment of two joiners, or others, to enable three coaches to be completed in 1968, noting that '*this would probably involve some financial bridging operation, details of which would be considered later*'; the vehicles concerned were composite No. 106, buffet car No. 103, half built, and observation car No. 101. With these vehicles operational the railway would be able to operate three six-coach train sets, each with an observation car and a buffet car. Garraway was asked to explore the possibility of obtaining a development grant in respect of them and the extension of passenger services to Dduallt. Broadbent and Wayne would inquire into the possibility of an investment grant.

The saga of Miss Langsdale came to an end with the recording of her death, still in residence at Boston Lodge some nine years after her position there was first considered! No. 2 Boston Lodge was offered to John Halsall and Tyddyn-y-bwlch to the Davies family, the latter with a tenancy tied to operation of the crossing gates. Will and Bessie Jones had given notice of their intention to vacate Tan-y-bwlch station house in February 1968. Wayne was asked to notify the Ministry of Transport of the railway's intention to operate passenger trains to Dduallt from 6th April 1968.

Towards the end of October a profile gauge was made so the manager from Maenofferen could inspect Garnedd tunnel. He saw no difficulty in giving the railway the required clearances and arranged a further inspection with one of his rockmen. The work was carried out during November.

Initial examination of the Alco in October resulted in its wheels and axleboxes receiving priority. It was steamed again on 4th November, taking six coaches to Tan-y-bwlch satisfactorily, although steaming performance was less than ideal, probably due to its blastpipe being out of alignment. In comparing the locomotive's performance with that of the Penrhyn

Hunslets, Garraway referred to the latter as the '*ladies*' for the first time in writing; it became a popular soubriquet.

When the Board met on 13th/14th November, the minutes provide no explanation for the meeting being held over two days. Although there was no quorum, Pegler and Routly reported on their meeting with railway inspectors Colonel McMullen and Colonel Robertson on 25th October. On the subject of a civil engineering inspection the advice given was to secure the services of a civil engineer of a standing comparable with a railway chief engineer; Livesey & Henderson (L&H) had already indicated willingness to conduct the survey. Of the extension of services to Dduallt the inspectors required sketches of track layouts, especially of terminal arrangements, details of the tightest clearances and of proposed signalling arrangements.

Financially, the railway was expected to remain in credit until late January, when the use of the overdraft facility would be avoided only by receipt of cash from the Society or grants. On the latter, Garraway had consulted with Welsh Office officials at Colwyn Bay; he was to pursue a grant of £2,000 and improvement grants from Deudraeth RDC in respect of No. 2 Boston Lodge and Tyddyn-y-bwlch.

Pen Cob and Pen-y-bryn halts were little used, it was reported, so were summarily closed with immediate effect. Members' travel privileges were to be withdrawn from the three busiest trains during the 1968 peak season.

Volunteer support fell away during December, discouraged from travelling by an outbreak of foot-and-mouth disease. The permanent staff continued working on the track and the Maenofferen gang on Garnedd.

Relations with the developer, Bourne, reached their lowest point at the end of November, when Garraway and Harold Creamer found his workmen demolishing the boundary fence near the water tower; Bourne wished to build a level crossing over the railway to provide adequate access to the development. Following representations the fence was restored only to be demolished again three days later. Garraway arranged for the construction of a temporary siding along the boundary line and parked several wagons of scrap and *Palmerston* on it. During the month Bourne had part of the railway's car park dug up and had the fence removed once more. By holding its position the railway forced Bourne to build a bridge across a corner of the harbour to secure his access.

1968 began with a serious shortage of volunteers due to the combined effects of bad weather and the foot-and-mouth disease outbreak inhibiting travel. A group from Bristol did manage to get to Portmadoc for the first weekend in January by plotting a route that avoided infected areas. It was February before agreement was reached with the National Farmers' Union over a modus operandi for the resumption of volunteer visits.

A small reshuffle of the Board occurred at its 17th January meeting, held at the English Speaking Union, Charles Street, London W1. Gerry Fiennes (Gerard Francis Gisborne Twistleton-Wykeham-Fiennes in full, a career railwayman who had parted company with BR following publication of his outspoken observations on the way the national network was managed) was elected a director and Viscount Garnock elected to the newly created post of Company President for a two-year period.

A joint meeting held with the Society Board, the first, was held on the same day, following which the Company agreed not to demolish the old Tan-y-bwlch station building without prior consultation, whilst observing that the state of the building did not justify any expenditure on either restoration or preservation.

The Company also agreed that it would welcome loans from Society members; however it would not encourage loans, to ensure that it did not become over-extended. A joint committee was to be set up to identify structures or rolling stock worthy of preservation, such items not to be destroyed without notification unless safety was involved.

The next Company Board meeting, on 17th February, was significant in being the first held on Company property, at Harbour station. It was arranged thus to coincide with a leaving party held to mark the retirement of Will and Bessie Jones; the Company presented them with a television set.

At the meeting it was recorded that Tan-y-bwlch station house would be offered rent-free to John Harrison* on the basis that his wife, Nell, would run the shop there. Ffestiniog UDC provided a grant to rehabilitate the property, the first stage of the work being completed in November.

The proposed 6th April opening to Dduallt had become doubtful in consequence of the loss of $2^1/_2$ months' work at Dduallt by the foot-and-mouth disease outbreak; the run-round loop would be incomplete. It was possible, though, that operation could be started if a lay-over locomotive was stabled in the siding.

John Routly and Wayne had met the bank manager that morning; he was to obtain approval for a £5,000 overdraft without guarantees. However, it appeared that the Company would require a further £3,000 by the end of May. Leslie Stephenson, of T. Stephenson & Sons Ltd, the firm that did most of the Company's printing for many years, had made a temporary loan of £2,500, although it was repayable at short notice. The financial position was considered reasonable in view of the value of the Company's buildings, many of which had been improved, the annual turnover of nearly £50,000 and Society membership exceeding 4,000.

With the extension of services to Dduallt in prospect the future of Tan-y-bwlch was considered. To make the goods shed suitable as a sales outlet expenditure of £2,000 was anticipated, half in the current year as the minimum work necessary would be carried out to conserve cash. Later Garraway raised the issue of passenger safety when trains were crossing, his concerns leading to construction of the island platform and, later, the footbridge. A second water tank was to be installed to cater for double-headed trains. Clough Williams Ellis, of Portmeirion, was asked to advise on landscaping.

A five-year forecast of expenditure on locomotive overhauls was listed and was later followed by examination, when the Board met in London on 12th March, of an expenditure forecast for rolling stock:

Locomotives		**Rolling Stock**	
1968	£11,500	1969	£9,600
1969	£5,000	1970	£3,000
1970	£7,000	1971	£6,000
1971	£2,000	1972	£6,000
1972	£4,000	1973	£4,000

The 1968 figure for locomotives included £8,000 for *Merddin Emrys*'s boiler but the £11,500 was not included in the year's budget. The 1969 rolling stock figure also included £6,000 for *Merddin Emrys*.

It was agreed that departments must submit cash flow forecasts in future, and to launch an appeal to Society members. At this meeting Smith was nominated to replace Wayne as the Company's nominee on the Society Board, the change to take effect from the Society's AGM on 27th April.

On 31st March the line between Tan-y-bwlch and Dduallt was inspected by the chief inspector of railways, Colonel J.R.H. Robertson, himself. Subject to certain works being completed he gave approval for its opening on 6th April. Deadlines for other outstanding work were set as 1st May and 1st June.

The Easter weekend was very busy, adding to the excitement of the opening to Dduallt. Four trains ran on the Saturday and five each on the Sunday and Monday; all the carriages were used. Garraway reported that the average fare paid per passenger was almost identical to that of 1967; many were just making a short journey between Tan-y-bwlch and Dduallt. Nevertheless, takings were nearly three times those of the previous Easter.

The railway was subjected to some vicious vandalism in the Tan-y-bwlch area during April. A ballast train was derailed at Llechwedd Coed after a rail chair had been placed on the track; the chair concerned had not been taken from the nearby cache and its source was unknown. The next day, 11th April, John Harrison, newly moved in to Tan-y-bwlch station house, accosted some youths who had been walking along the line and was attacked; Garraway did not report the nature of any injuries sustained. During an inspection obstructions were found in the checkrails below Tan-y-bwlch bridge.

At its 7th May meeting the Board had a resolution of the car park dispute in sight. It had claimed £590 from the Tremadoc Estate in respect of loss of income in 1967 and 1968 because it had been denied the use of the car park in accordance with its tenancy agreement. It told the Estate that if agreement was reached with Bourne over the area previously occupied by the toilets, and if the estate accepted that claim, it would not pursue a further claim against it. It had also suggested that the railway bought the Estate land it occupied, offsetting the £590 claim against the agreed valuation. It had also reached an accord with Bourne, subject to legal agreement.

In search of improving locomotive reliability Garraway had obtained a quote from Andrew Barclay of £5,985 for a new 'standard' boiler or £5,685 each for two; he hoped that Hunslet would quote less. A new firebox for *Linda* was approved at a cost of about £1,500, to be delivered in August 1969 and paid for out of that year's budget.

* For further details of John Harrison and his background see *Rails Through the Sand* by John Milner ~ RailRomances 1996.

The overdraft had reached £1,766 at 4th May, in addition to the £2,500 loan from Leslie Stephenson. Professional fees amounting to £1,800 in respect of the LRO were outstanding. Stephenson's personal loan was to be replaced by a loan from his Company on receipt of personal guarantees from the directors, £1,000 from Routly, £500 each from Pegler, Smith, Wayne, Garnock, Broadbent and the Society's Norman Pearce; in the event he left his loan in place, eliminating the overdraft.

The loop at Dduallt was brought into operation on 20th May, bringing to an end the use of a second loco to shunt and release the train. Realignment of the tracks at Tan-y-bwlch to provide an island platform was completed five days later.

An indication of the regard in which the railway was coming to be held by the outside world was demonstrated on 23rd May, when it was visited by Dr Hastings Banda, President of Malawi, accompanied by Lord Snowdon and George Thomas MP, Secretary of State for Wales. The party travelled by special train from Minffordd to Tan-y-bwlch. Whilst inspecting *Blanche* after the journey, Snowdon promised to return one day, with his family.

The spring bank holiday week, when the peak summer service was operated, was incredibly busy with 1,166 passengers carried on the bank holiday, 26th May. The heavy traffic continued into the following week, when Garraway reported 1,985 bookings and £616 revenue on 3rd June; at one stage the booking office queue stretching across the car park; an extra train was run at 17.45 to '*mop up latecomers and get everyone back to Portmadoc who needed to get back*'.

The next day was so busy that the timetable was abandoned and trains got away as soon as they were loaded. The nominal 17.45 left Portmadoc at 17.00! On 5th June, Thursday, a 45-minute interval timetable was operated, with trains crossing at Penrhyn and Tan-y-bwlch; despite the firemen having to operate the token instruments at Minffordd this ad hoc timetable ran smoothly enough to demonstrate its practicability on other busy occasions.

Garraway foresaw, however, that a 45-minute interval service would only be really practical if improvements were made to the layout at Penrhyn, a proposition that would be of limited value as further carriages became available and train lengths increased. He therefore proposed building a loop at Rhiw Goch and encouraged the Board to acquire additional land for carriage storage at Portmadoc.

Commercially, he reported that fare revenue was increased by 73% and sales by 70%, the latter largely attributable to a new shop that had been built in the booking hall during the winter; it had already paid for itself, said Garraway.

By the 20th June meeting, held at Portmeirion, the credit balance had topped £2,000 and outstanding loans '*would be cleared shortly*'. Passenger receipts were reported as 78% higher than in 1967; in May, when journeys had reached 17,250, compared to 9,763 the previous year, Garraway had described the situation as '*almost embarrassing*'.

Hunslet had quoted to build two Fairlie boilers for £5,200 each, 10% payable on delivery and 10% every four months for three years. Andrew Barclay's price had been reduced to £4,235, payable on delivery. The Board agreed to order from Barclay but with a request for payment to be spread over twelve months. Whilst the Society was to be asked for supporting guarantees if necessary the Board accepted that the Company might need to finance an additional £12,000 by the end of May 1969 because of this expenditure.

Tan-y-bwlch goods shed was brought into use as a tearoom on 6th July. The kiosk, known as the bunny hutch, that had previously served there was moved to Dduallt later in the month. Dry weather in August caused problems at Tan-y-bwlch; there was no drinking water for 10 days and great care was taken to conserve the locomotive water supply.

Although Garraway did not comment on it at the time, the new buffet car No. 103 entered service on 21st July, the last vehicle to receive the varnished livery. The peak three-train service started the same day. No. 103 combined a large kitchen with a small saloon and had a hatch from which refreshments were served whilst the train was stationary at Dduallt. In common with previous new vehicles and restorations it was returned to Boston Lodge in the evenings, for finishing off, for several weeks.

A new and distinctive feature of the carriage fleet appeared shortly afterwards that went unrecorded at the time despite having a marked effect on the railway's appearance, for it was the first vehicle to appear in what became the standard cherry livery. There had been no (written) debate about this but the varnished livery was proving unsatisfactory because of uneven wear, with no two vehicles looking the same. The Board inspected and approved the new livery on 6th August.

Trains crossing at Tan-y-bwlch after the island platform was completed in 1968.

Arthur Lambert, FR Archives

Below: *Dduallt loop had just been completed when the White Rose group ran an excursion on 26th May 1968.*

Adrian Taylor, FR Archives

The carriage concerned was No. 16, approaching the end of a lengthy restoration led by Ron Jarvis. The inspection was part of a peripatetic Board meeting held at Portmeirion but which also included a visit to Dduallt to meet the deviationists.

In the light of the increased traffic receipts an interim bonus of £10 payable to staff, together with a letter of appreciation, was approved.

The John Player tobacco company of Nottingham had offered to fund a footbridge for Tan-y-bwlch station, it was reported; a decision on acceptance was deferred until Les Smith could comment on it. On 10th September the Board agreed to proceed with the erection of the bridge as soon as possible.

The Board had an opportunity to influence the development of railway-inspired tourism in Merioneth, because Merionethshire County Council had informed the Company of its proposal to acquire the standard gauge trackbed between Glyndyfrdwy and Morfa Mawddach in order that part of it, between Bala and Llanuwchllyn, could be used for a narrow gauge railway, soliciting the Company's view. After some discussion on the optimum gauge – 15in was the original proposal – the Board agreed to welcome the scheme on the basis that more railways would bring more tourists; however, the council was to be informed of the economic pitfalls of operating and maintaining a service without voluntary labour.*

The army, in the form of 275 Railway Squadron, returned to the railway from 17th–25th September, arrangements being made at short notice due to the unit's intended venue on the Isle of Man becoming unavailable. In addition to taking part in train operation the unit was put to work in Minffordd yard, relaying the tracks towards the coal drops.

* John Wilkins, who owned the Fairbourne Railway, was also in discussion with British Railways with a view to taking over the Dolgellau – Morfa Mawfach stretch of the line.

On 11th November 1968 the standard gauge crane at Minffordd was used to load Linda's *boiler for despatch to Leeds, for a new firebox to be fitted. The crane had seen very little service and this might have been the last occasion it was used.*

Norman Gurley, FR Archives

On 10th September Broadbent reported that an order had been placed with Hunslet for two Fairlie boilers for £4,250 each for delivery in March 1969. Payment was to be £4,250, plus £1,500 for *Linda*'s new firebox, in March followed by £4,250 plus £100 interest in August. (*Linda*'s boiler was sent to Hunslet by 11th November.)

The accountant, Martin Barradell, reported that the cash balance slightly exceeded £23,500 and calculated that it would be enough to get the railway through to May 1969 without resorting to an overdraft. The calculations included reducing the Penrhyn debt by £1,000 in addition to the £100 payments being paid monthly. By 3rd November, when Barradell presented a revised forecast, the cash balance was £19,000. Taking into account £3,000 anticipated from the Society, £100 monthly payments to Penrhyn and paying £4,000 for the boilers in March and June, he expected a shortfall of £7,500 at the end of May with a cash balance restored by July. Penrhyn had asked for payment of £5,437 10s (£5,437.50) outstanding; Broadbent was to negotiate an increased monthly payment.

The Board agreed to pay a £200 bonus to Garraway and a £1,000 bonus to the other staff, including the £10 payment already made. Sales Manager Bolton's commission was increased to 2%. Looking ahead, the Board agreed that the 1969 budget should include Deviation expenditure of either £500 or £1,000. Fares were to be increased, Garnock and Garraway to agree the details.

The question of increasing capacity was discussed, with Garraway pointing out that a loop between Penrhyn and Tan-y-bwlch would allow trains to be run at 30-minute intervals and be equivalent to five extra coaches. Budr was considered the optimum site and Garraway was to investigate further, to the point of producing a draft contract for the land required and estimates for the civil engineering work.

At its 3rd November meeting the Board considered staff benefits after increasing Garraway's salary to £1,300 plus the £200 bonus and pension provision of 10% of salary. A 'death in service dependent's income' insurance policy was to be established. It would pay out half pay until the age of 60 of the deceased; the Company would hold any proceeds in trust for dependent(s) as the Board saw fit. Wayne was to initiate a retirement benefits pension scheme by spring 1969. These benefits would be available only to '*top-grade salaried staff*', a category that consisted only of Garraway.

Broadbent proposed that the Alco should be named *Mountaineer*, a name carried by one of the railway's England locomotives. It had been the subject of work to get it fit for FR service all through the summer; steam tests were carried out during November, when it needed much tweaking to get it to steam satisfactorily but reached Dduallt with a test train, and seven fare-paying passengers, on 17th November, a non-operating day. Afterwards steaming was further improved by use of *Linda*'s chimney. Its cab was incomplete at this stage.

Garraway reported that for the week ending 3rd November sales revenue amounted to:

Main shop	£7,913
Tea bar	£2,517
Railwayana shop (in museum)	£959
Minffordd	£57
Penrhyn	£17
Tan-y-bwlch kiosk (bunny hutch)	£342
Tan-y-bwlch café (goods shed)	£3,215
Dduallt	£1,298
No. 14	£3,152
No. 12	£990
No. 103 (from 21st July)	£922

He thought these figures justified the expenditure at Tan-y-bwlch and also commented that as No. 103 had taken over from No. 14 and the latter from No. 12 in the roster he expected on-train revenue to grow.

Autumn permanent way work included the recovery of rail from Duffws as the lease was due to be surrendered to the Newborough Estate; although not specified this would have been the land alongside the original station building, last used by Maenofferen to access the LNWR yard. Some land adjacent to the GW station site in Blaenau Ffestiniog was to be sold to the local authority.

Following various repairs *Earl of Merioneth* was steamed for a test run on 24th November. Arising from the previous week's trial with the Alco the train was advertised, attracting 14 passengers, mostly members, and £5 in revenue. Further Sunday test runs in December, locomotive unspecified but probably the Alco, brought in another £15.

Another loco that appeared from Boston Lodge after some thorough attention around this time was the diesel, *Upnor Castle*. It had appeared on the main line in August, shunting carriages at Portmadoc and working a test train to Dduallt on 17th of that month. Its brake gear, from a BR Hunslet diesel locomotive, was fitted during the autumn.

During November, No. 22 was spray-painted in cherry red by the East Anglian group members; Garraway was doubtful of the benefits but the group was keen to do the work and to he recognised that the speed of application would be an advantage in the future.

So, in 1968 the FR returned to Dduallt. In 13 years $9^1/_2$ miles of railway had been reopened, three original steam locomotives had been restored and five others acquired, of which three were capable of working trains, and five four-wheeled and 10 bogie carriages had been restored and two others obtained and put into service. In the face of rapidly expanding passenger numbers it was committed to re-boilering the Fairlies and had built five new bogie carriages in its own workshops. It had also taken the first steps of the leap into the unknown quantity that was the Deviation, starting to build $2^1/_2$ miles of new railway using volunteer labour when the result of the compensation claim for the appropriated trackbed was still outstanding.

Blanche *and train en route for Portmadoc near Hafod-y-llyn, below Tan-y-bwlch, on 26th May 1969. The train formation is rather unusual, there being no brake vehicle next to the locomotive, as usually occurs on the down journey. No. 14, the carrriage made from Lynton & Barnstaple Railway components, is third from the loco; the quarrymen's coach was one of the first vehiicles to be painted red.*

Cyril Perrier

Chapter 8

After Dduallt

1969~1975

Having reopened to Dduallt the FR was faced with the dual challenges of funding and building the Deviation whilst keeping its locomotive and carriage fleets fit enough to carry increasing numbers of passengers safely. The Railway was much changed by the restoration and the expectations of expanded tourist traffic brought new pressures. With the locomotive and carriage fleets expanded to meet demand, attention turned to the facilities at Harbour station and Boston Lodge.

1969 was the year of the investiture of the Prince of Wales at Caernarfon. For some time the Board had been keen that it would provide an opportunity to secure a royal visit to the Railway; its ambitions in this direction suffered a setback with the news that the Prince's intended 14-day tour of the principality had been reduced to a four-day event. On 11th February it was decided that *Prince* should be taken to Blaenau Ffestiniog and placed where Prince Charles would see it. Allan Garraway, however, present at the meeting, reminded the Board that the loco was stripped down for repairs. It had low priority due to an earlier decision to concentrate on having both Fairlies in traffic; using a contractor to do the work would cost about £600. In the light of this information, and the locomotive's limited traffic potential, it was agreed that the expenditure could not be countenanced.

A public relations company, Bullock & Turner Ltd, had been asked to advise on promotion. Arising from that company's report 1969 was to be 'Fairlie year', with a launch on Easter Monday, 7th April. Lord Garnock was to be asked to devise a scheme whereby dignitaries staying at Portmeirion during the investiture would be introduced to the FR, preferably by means of a special train rather than reserved accommodation. In the event it proved impossible to make special arrangements so an open invitation was issued instead.

The Board had discovered that the Company had been affiliated to the Transport Trust without approval by Michael Seymour, the archivist. It decided that affiliation could be advantageous and should be regularised. It seems that the Board was concerned that the Railway should not be seen as a preservation organisation lest it would prejudice its position with the CEGB. It transpired that Garnock, who was absent, had previously agreed that Seymour should enrol on the basis of him being responsible for records and preservation. Garnock did not intend that the operating Railway should be involved with the Trust and subsequently apologised.

Accountant Martin Barradell presented a cash-flow forecast to 30th June, showing a likely cash requirement for £6,500 during May and June. It was expected that, based on previous experience, the bank would advance £5,000 without security but that guarantees would be needed for any excess above that figure. Following discussion on the Penrhyn debt it was agreed to increase the monthly repayment to £200, backdated to December 1968.

Changes in land ownership adjacent to the Railway had brought with them new attitudes towards fires that might be started by the locomotives. Garraway reported on discussions held with Laidlaw Drew Ltd on the provision of oil-firing equipment for the locomotives. The Board approved expenditure of £350 for the supply and commissioning of a trial unit; this was additional to the budget.

By the end of the month Garraway reported that four carriages were complete in the new red livery; he did not identify them but they were Nos. 11, 12, 15 and 22. Vans Nos. 1 and 2 had also been repainted; No. 19 was completed by Easter. Other carriage work included modifying the guards' doors on No. 100 to match No. 101, the latter under construction, and overhauling No. 14's kitchen compartment.

The refurbishment of No. 2 Boston Lodge was completed by the end of March and John and Katy Halsall moved in.

The Prince of Wales with Alan Pegler and Viscount Garnock in Blaenau Ffestiniog on 2nd July 1969. Princess *just makes it into the picture.*

FR Archives

The week before Easter Hunslet's subjected Linda's boiler, with new firebox, to a hydraulic test. The superheater elements could not be fitted due to a design fault but the boiler was returned to Boston Lodge by the end of the month.

The Fairlie event on Easter Monday, supported by Portmadoc Women's Institute members in traditional dress, made the Daily Telegraph, the Liverpool Daily Post and two appearances on television. A total of 7,438 journeys were made during the week, all but double the previous week's 3,398.

By 8th April, when the Board met at Harbour station, the forecast overdraft requirement was reduced to £5,500, largely because the first instalment for the Fairlie boilers was not now due until May. The bank had agreed an overdraft limit of £7,000 until July, with reluctance according to Barradell.

The Board approved Garraway's recommendation that Alan Heywood be appointed Traffic Manager with effect from 24th May. The appointment would relieve Garraway of administrative work and allow Alan Skellern to spend more time on S&T activities. They went on to agree, in principle, that '*within the limits of policy laid down by the Board, executive authority should be vested in the General Manager rather than individual Directors, and, that relations with the deviation junta should be developed towards bringing the whole of their activities under the authority and control of the General Manager.*' This strengthened Garraway's position considerably, particularly giving him unequivocal control of Deviation activities, and was probably a reflection on the impact the Railway's growth was having on the Directors' spare time!

John Ransom named the Alco *Mountaineer* as a precursor to the Society's AGM on 26th April. Its cab was finished off over the following weeks.

On 27th April Garraway reported that he had arranged with Ffestiniog UDC for *Princess* to be displayed outside the Queen's Hotel. He thought it would gain publicity for the FR, especially in connection with Prince Charles' visit.

The FR's letter service was reactivated on 28th April 1969, when a set of four stamps designed by Michael Seymour was issued. The contract with the GPO had been signed by the Railway in 1891 but had not been put into effect!

After a slow start traffic picked up and by the end of May records were being broken again. The 5,138 journeys made during the week ended 25th May jumped to 21,592 journeys the following week, Whitsun. The locos continued giving trouble: the Alco's steam pipes leaked, *Blanche*'s tender kingpin broke and the *Earl of Merioneth* had an axlebox running warm. To keep the Alco in traffic it was regularly double-headed with *Moelwyn*. *Upnor Castle* was used to ferry trains between Boston Lodge and Portmadoc, and back, when locomotives needed to go into the works for emergency repairs.

At the 10th June Board meeting Garraway was complimented for overcoming difficulties in providing motive power at a time when traffic was heavier than anticipated. The appointment of Paul Dukes as Works Manager with responsibility for '*the departments of foreman joiner, mechanical joiner and locomotive crews*' was agreed at the same time.

By the time of the meeting journeys were 17% up, fare revenue 32% and sales 55%. The bank balance was '*fluctuating around a nil balance*'. £3,000 due to Stephenson & Sons for printing would be paid shortly from receipts. The improved figures, it was noted, had been assisted by the reservation of 1st class seats in the saloons and keeping two evening trains at the old fares, the latter resulting in heavy evening bookings and a better spread of traffic during the day.

With the red carriage livery having been favourably received it was agreed that all carriages should be so painted in future.

Princess was moved to Blaenau Ffestiniog on 18th June, attracting much attention from the press. Immediately afterwards, on 22nd June, Garraway appeared on the BBC Home Service 'Down Your Way' programme being broadcast from the town.

Investiture day, 1st July, was poor for both weather and traffic. The 14.45 was cancelled, on the basis that much of the population would be watching television, and the 14.00 left, with a reasonable load, at 14.25. Alan Pegler, Bill Broadbent and Lord Garnock met Prince Charles in Blaenau Ffestiniog the next day and were able to present him with 'Centenary of Steam' medals for himself and the Duke of Edinburgh, the Earl of Merioneth.

Over 200 delegates of the National Union of Railwaymen, including General Secretary Sydney Greene, conferencing in Llandudno, visited the Railway on 6th July. Paul Dukes and Ron Lester, NUR members, joined in welcoming the party.

The continued heavy use of *Earl of Merioneth* put pressure on its weakest component, the boiler.

Attending to the 30th July 1969 derailment at Penrhyn. The driver started to move into section in error then, realising his mistake, set back over the trap points, derailing the carriage bogie. Mountaineer *approaches the station with a down train.*

A.P. Burnham, FR Archives

Firebox steam leaks were traced to the ferrules under the crown stays collapsing, the same fault experienced with *Merddin Emrys* in 1962. When the problem was identified, in early July, it was hoped to keep the loco in traffic whilst attention was devoted to resolving the Alco's problems but it was soon out of service. On some days in July the timetable was modified to provide a three-train service so that *Blanche* and *Mountaineer* had lighter loads. On 9th July *Blanche* failed at Portmadoc when a regulator pin fell out in the dome; trains were worked by *Mountaineer* and *Upnor Castle*, the latter failing with an overheated axlebox in the afternoon. *Moelwyn* was put out with two carriages at 14.45, whilst *Blanche*, repaired and making steam, was sent to rescue *Upnor Castle*. Some complaints were made about the use of diesel power.

It was *Mountaineer*'s turn to fail on 23rd July, when its valve spindle collar broke at Minffordd. The day's traffic then depended on *Blanche* (nine coaches) and *Moelwyn* (three). *Earl of Merioneth* remained out of service until 6th August, having its firebox stays replaced. *Linda* was being reassembled after its winter boiler overhaul, *Merddin Emrys* was still awaiting its new boiler and *Upnor Castle* was in and out of shops having its axleboxes attended to. With the reduced haulage capacity the opportunity was taken to spray paint the four-wheelers, the last green and ivory stock, reducing the carriage liveries to two.

Not content with these locomotive problems, on 30th July one pair of carriage wheels was derailed at Penrhyn when the driver of the 14.15 set back and derailed a carriage bogie. Two trains were cancelled and some passengers received refunds. It was 16.20 before services were resumed.

Despite these difficulties the week ending 3rd August was, at 23,036 journeys, the second busiest in the Railway's history. The week had seen 11,864 bookings which generated £4,182 6s 7d (£4,182.33) traffic revenue and £1,949 16s 9d (£1,949.84) in sales. The following week was nearly as busy with sales topping £2,000 for the first time. Despite this success the number of journeys was only 1,200 up on the previous year. However, the locomotive position stabilised and the holidaymakers arrived in great numbers, with a record 25,603 journeys being made during the week ended 31st August. No. 16 had entered traffic on temporary bogies on 30th August.

Opposite: Earl of Merioneth *approaches Garnedd tunnel with nine cars in August 1969.*

D.H. Wilson

Garraway conducted locomotive fuel consumption trials over three days during the month and found that *Earl of Merioneth* with a load of seven coaches used 8cwt; *Blanche* with four or five used 6cwt and *Mountaineer* with five used 9cwt. The results confirmed his suspicions that increased consumption on heavy loads had little benefit. Water consumption was higher, too, although he gave no details.

By 17th September the total of 284,808 journeys was 18,932 up on 1968. Traffic (£53,007) and sales (£25,387) receipts had increased by 17% and 24% respectively. Cash on deposit was £25,000, similar to 1968. Reduced fares on the evening trains had doubled the loadings – it was agreed to reduce the fare on the first morning train during the 1970 summer season at Garraway's discretion, otherwise fares would remain unchanged. Any donor of £100 to the Company would be issued with one of the unissued £10 preference shares.

During the second half of September Garraway experimented with the timetable, running an extra train in addition to the advertised 11.00 and 14.30. Between 22nd and 26th September the trains ran at 11.00, 13.00 and 15.00 and passengers were interviewed on their experience. Apart from spreading the load the timetable gave another opportunity for a return trip from Tan-y-bwlch. Passengers surveyed were generally satisfied with the revised service; it was calculated to have raised an additional sum of £125 16s 0d (£125.80) in revenue from people who turned up after the 11.00 had left and who would not have waited for the 14.30.

After the busy summer the autumn had continued to be busy and on 11th October the running total of passenger journeys topped 300,000. Garraway observed that the heavy traffic had had its effect on the locomotives, citing the most recent casualty, Blanche, where two frame cracks had been discovered, fortunately soon repaired by welding. Hunslet delivered the Fairlie boilers at around the same time.

A party from Stoke Heath borstal worked on the steelwork of the new Tan-y-bwlch footbridge at the end of October. The track had been realigned to make way for it earlier in the year; the decking was in place by 1st November.

The budget for 1970 was discussed by the Board on 11th November. Assuming revenue was the same as in 1969 it would accommodate proposed expenditure, apart from £5,000 of 'special items', which would have to be paid for from increased income. The 'special items' arose from the CEGB's compulsory purchase, '*final settlement from whom might reasonably be hoped for in 1970*', noted the minutes. A donation from the Society was not allowed for in the budget but £5,000 was expected.

The Railway was expected to have a cash surplus of over £20,000 during the summer and autumn and a shortage of the same amount for a brief period in the spring. The overdraft had arisen because of the excess of expenditure involved in the '*CEGB problem*'. An improvement in liquid reserves was to be looked for in the next year or two. Routly had seen the bank manager and hoped that he could secure overdraft facilities up to £20,000.

Bill Broadbent proposed that the Penrhyn debt be settled by an immediate payment of £1,537 10s (£1,537.50) followed by eight monthly payments of £200; at the time of the meeting Penrhyn had not indicated if this was acceptable.

In acknowledgement of the efforts made by staff Garraway received a salary increase of £250 plus a bonus of £230. The remaining staff were to receive a bonus of £1,150 divided at Garraway's discretion, these figures being an increase of 15% on 1968 in recognition of the 15% increase in turnover. Alan Heywood had become Traffic and Commercial Manager; his appointment to this post at a salary of £1,400 was confirmed.

At the end of the year turnover had topped £100,000 for the first time, 60% from traffic, an increase of 19%; sales revenue, £30,719, was increased by 28%. Garraway calculated that the year's 173,942 bookings produced 319,327 passenger journeys, representing 2,584,000 passenger journey miles; passenger train miles were 21,397. *Blanche* had run 9,166 miles and *Earl of Merioneth* 7,630 miles, at the expense of considerable wear to axleboxes.

During the winter effort went into completing *Linda*'s overhaul and making *Mountaineer* reliable. In addition to its repaired boiler, now superheated

The fragility of the FR's infrastructure was brought to light during 1969, when the slate slab roof of the underbridge at Capel Nazareth, Penrhyn, was found to be deteriorating, as seen in December after the track and ballast had been removed.

A.G.W. Garraway, FR Archives

The repair was carried out as combined operation with the local authority, which wished to widen the road. The railway repaired the downhill abutment and supplied two two-ton and two four-ton reinforced concrete beams and the Council relocated the uphill abutment, the completed work seen in February 1970.

A.G.W. Garraway, FR Archives

Minffordd, 8th October 1969; Merddin Emrys' *new boiler freshly delivered from Leeds.*

Norman Gurley, FR Archives

and with a new firebox, *Linda* received a leading pony truck; the Hunslets had long overhangs that made them unstable at FR speeds. There does not appear to have been any prior public discussion on this and its implementation might have been an afterthought; Garraway first mentioned it on 8th December, when the locomotive's overhaul was nearly completed. The wheelset came from *Moel Tryfan*'s trailing bogie. *Mountaineer* received a new smokebox and its rear pony wheels were re-gauged. In the new year work commenced on adapting *Merddin Emrys* to take one of the new Hunslet boilers; the second boiler was stored until *Earl of Merioneth*'s boiler became life-expired. *Merddin Emrys*' bogies had been sent to Hunslet for new cylinders to be fitted; one was returned on 31st March, the other in May.

In the carriage shops observation car No. 101 was completed and Nos. 103–106 received the red livery. No. 104 needed to have several panels replaced due to rot; the first of the new cars, it had been found to have several design weaknesses that were corrected in later vehicles. Whilst it was in work, No. 104's bogies were borrowed by No. 106, that vehicle having lost its own to No. 101.

A permanent way innovation had commenced on 12th January 1970, with the delivery of jarrah sleepers obtained from Australia. Used instead of ex-British Railways' material, becoming more difficult to obtain and of variable quality, the new sleepers were installed first at Rhiw Plas.

Further up the line the Capel Nazareth underbridge, in Penrhyn, was renewed in a joint operation with the local authority to improve vehicular access. The Council rebuilt one of the abutments whilst, on 23rd January 1970, the Railway took care of the reinforced concrete beams that formed the new span.

The Board wished to increase the number of occasions when directors visited the Railway; it was therefore agreed to rent a cottage at Portmeirion at £325 per annum, plus charges, directors using the facility to contribute £1 10s 0d (£1.50) per day.

Remote areas of the Railway were targeted by vandals and thieves in February. Firstly, damage was sustained at Dduallt, and then 215 yards of overhead wire was stolen from Hafod-y-llyn. Following the second incident an interrupt alarm was installed and connected to Harbour station. On 3rd March Garraway was woken by the alarm at 00.55 and phoned the police. The culprits were caught on site and charged,

Members of the Society's North Staffordshire area group supplied and erected a timber fence designed to separate cars and pedestrians from the railway at Tan-y-bwlch. Construction was under way on 14th February 1970, although the wisdom of applying paint under cold conditions has to be questioned. Facing the camera, in a dark coat, is Adrian Shooter, the group's secretary; in 1971 he was elected to the society board and later became its chairman for a time; at the time of writing he is chairman of Chiltern Railways Ltd.

Norman Gurley, FR Archives

the local press reporting that the Railway's wires were protected by 'special anti-theft electrical devices'.

In March, the season started with both Hunslets in action, Garraway reporting that *Linda* was greatly improved for its additional pair of wheels and superheating. During the first two days 207 bookings, many of them members, produced £33 traffic and £45 sales revenue.

The Easter holiday produced good business, with 1,076 bookings on Easter day, 29th March, the first time more than 1,000 bookings had been achieved at this time. In addition to the Hunslets, *Earl of Merioneth* and *Mountaineer* also saw some action although still in need of some detail work. Carriage No. 101 entered service.

No. 16 was launched into service on 10th April; a small ceremony at Dduallt marked the completion of the 15-year programme to restore the surviving FR passenger rolling stock, overlooking the fact that No. 10 had never seen passenger service and was to remain out of use for another 30 years! No. 16's first-class compartment was trimmed with panelling from the former Pullman car *Eunice*.

Sales Manager Maurice Bolton and his assistant Megan Pritchard left the Railway in May, with Garraway paying tribute to their efforts in developing the Railway's retail sales. Bolton was replaced by Major Michael Ilott.

Despite Boston Lodge's best efforts the locomotives could still have off days. On 26th May *Blanche* failed with a stripped injector steam valve whilst *Linda* was still in the works having a big end attended to; it had run warm the day before. On the same day *Earl of Merioneth* failed with a seized eccentric near Tan-y-bwlch; it managed to complete its journey, via Dduallt, with only one end powered and was replaced by the Hunslets on return to Portmadoc. On 28th May *Linda* was failed twice, when its firebars collapsed due to faulty castings and the heat they were subjected to. A few days later a fracture was found in one of *Earl of Merioneth*'s expansion links; upon examination the whole motion was found to be strained, the result of the seizure. Garraway had, at its 12th May meeting, asked the Board to consider investigating the availability of suitable locomotives abroad to strengthen the fleet.

By the end of July traffic was so good that Garraway produced a special report for the directors. After a good start to the year May and early June had been disappointing, overall $2^1/_2$% up at 12th June. The situation then changed dramatically, so that by 31st July journeys were 13% up and fares/sales 14% up. Demand was such that the full summer three-train service was introduced early and a shuttle service operated between Tan-y-bwlch and Dduallt; originally Simplex *Mary Ann* and three four-wheelers, it was expanded to four four-wheelers from the beginning of August when *Moelwyn* became available on completion of an overhaul.

Upnor Castle *engaged on shunting duties at Pen Cob on 29th May 1970.*

R.E. Ruffell

Blanche *at Penrhyn Crossing, August 1964. Only one vehicle in this train had run on the FR before closure.*

Alan Bowler

The use of lower fares on the off-peak services to reduce the pressure on the popular afternoon trains was so successful that on some days there were queues forming for the 09.45 when the booking office opened at 09.00! 17.25 and 19.00 departures carried as many as 180 passengers, whilst an extra at 18.05 could carry 90. During the last week of July several records were broken; on 30th there were over 3,000 bookings, over £1,000 traffic receipts and over £1,500 total takings, all for the first time. A newly installed retail counter added to Tan-y-bwlch's turnover.

An interruption to the smooth running of the Railway occurred on 5th August, causing Garraway to report that '*One pony wheel on* Mountaineer'*s trailing truck has been causing concern for some time as it was wearing excessively compared with all the others; on Wednesday morning, on the first down train a portion of the flange broke out at Crossing Mawr, and the pony truck derailed at Tro Bagl, fortunately without derailing anything else, and only breaking one chair, apart from damaging the pony truck. . . . The train was hauled back to TyB and a shuttle service maintained between TyB and Dduallt, also between Portmadoc and Penrhyn until the line was cleared . . . . The leading pony casting and wheels have been put under the back end with a new bridle, and after trials the engine is running as an 0-6-2. The new wheels are now on their axle and are being completed as soon as possible.*'

For the rest of the peak season, ending 2nd September, traffic continued to keep the Railway busy although with lesser increases over the same period the year before. By 4th September bookings were 3,000 up, with traffic revenue 12% and sales 16% also up.

On 21st August an evening train was laid on for a visiting party of Talyllyn Railway volunteers; accompanied by FR personnel, the buffet car took £75! At Dduallt the train was run slowly onto the first embankment of the Deviation – the TR was about to start work on its Nant Gwernol extension.

Not unnaturally, the Railway's overall financial position reflected the year's operating success, the Board recording, on 8th September, that cash deposits totalled £15,000 against a forecast of £6,500. £15,000 was to be transferred to Local Authority loans. It was agreed that the Deviation budget should be increased by 50% in 1971 and that allowance should be made to pay BR Engineering £2,000 to manufacture new cylinders for *Linda* and *Blanche*.

The budget was discussed on 10th November, when it was decided to increase provision for wages from £40,000 to £43,000 and to provide for professional and legal fees at £2,000 and tax at £5,000. This would increase total expenditure to £91,400 out of projected revenue of £96,600. The Company's financial policy did not obtain universal approval. Secretary Francis Wayne had, on 26th October, circulated the Board with his observations, pointing out that if there was no revenue increase or Society donation the Company would not be able to balance its books. He was concerned about the inadequacy of the reserve needed to tide the Company over the '*six lean months*' of the winter, pointing out that the autumn's cash balances had not increased each year in line with the Railway's fixed commitments. He was also concerned about the fixed commitments generally, noting that 1971's projected wages bill accounted for nearly half of proposed expenditure; he thought fixed costs, including wages, should be limited to two-thirds, or thereabouts, of expenditure to provide a safety net in case of need.

Wayne's report was not mentioned at the meeting, which also decided to increase Garraway's salary to £2,100 with effect from 1st January 1971 and to pay him a bonus of £250 in respect of 1970.

The first step towards increasing the amount of covered accommodation for carriages was made in September, when the roof of one of the Maenofferen Slate Company's former slate sheds in Minffordd yard was raised.

On 5th October Garraway reported that *Merddin Emrys* would soon be ready for steaming and preparations were in hand for converting Linda to oil firing. *Merddin Emrys* was first steamed on 1st November and ran the public service the following weekend, on 7th November hauling eight coaches and on the next day 12. Of the latter occasion Garraway remarked that it blew off most of the way. As was usually the case with FR projects, the loco remained incomplete for some weeks. Fortunately for the locomotive's appearance plans to fit a *Moutaineer*-type cab, with sloping sides, were not put into effect.

Linda was steamed as an oil burner on 2nd November, with very disappointing results, initially identified as a lack of firebox volume. A series of modifications brought success on 29th November, when the locomotive worked the service train. By 21st December Garraway had concluded that the performance had advanced sufficiently to establish

Fireman Nigel Dant attends to Mountaineer*'s watering at Tan-y-bwlch during August 1970. The loco had a prodigious appetite for fuel and was an erratic steamer at this time. The bell originated from the England loco of the same name.*

Alan Bowler

that the system was practical, although further development would be necessary before it could be extended to the rest of the fleet.

The pressure for the FR to do away with coal-burning locomotives had come from the Economic Forestry Group. The Group had been insisting that the FR take action to eliminate the incidence of lineside fires affecting its property, objecting particularly to the cost of maintaining fire patrols. Garraway had informed it of the risks, and of precautions taken by the Forestry Commission in similar circumstances, before planting had started. He had pointed out that the Railway was operating in its current form '*long before*' EFG started planting trees yet was being put to considerable inconvenience, cost and possible loss of goodwill due to the introduction of oil firing, all for the Group's benefit. Ironically, one of EFG's members was Norman Evershed, who had donated land to the Railway for the spiral at Dduallt.

Garraway's remonstrations with the EFG must have struck home because it later offered to loan the Railway £1,000 to cover the cost of converting two of the locomotives in 1971; converting six locomotives was estimated at £4,000. Fires had cost the Railway about £1,000 during the year, Garraway reported, saying that he thought that there would also be savings in fuel handling. He later reported that fire patrols had cost the Railway £1,154 in 1969, £960 in 1970 and £352 in 1971.

A weekend of Santa trains on 19th/20th December brought the 1970 season to an end. One train on the Saturday and two on the Sunday were met by Santa at Tan-y-bwlch and seasonal refreshments were served. Trains and stations were decorated for the occasion. All available carriages were needed to accommodate the 421 participants; traffic revenue was £76 3s 6d (£76.17) and sales generated £17 11s 2d (£171.06). For Garraway the highlight was on Sunday, when the trains crossed at Tan-y-bwlch and passengers from both disembarked to join in 20 minutes of carol singing '*on an absolutely perfect afternoon*'.

Changes in the Board's administration occurred with Martin Barradell's resignation as Accountant in November 1970 and Francis Wayne's as Secretary

Merddin Emrys *was first steamed with its new boiler on 1st November 1970, during the Society's annual convention weekend. The tanks, bunkers and other components needed considerable modification to accommodate the larger boiler. In the right background is No. 59 van, the former Vale of Rheidol Railway/Welshpool & Llanfair Light Railway cattle van rebuilt by the Society's East Anglian area group.*

D.A.W. Taylor, FR Archives

in January 1971, the latter citing the need to travel from his home in Scotland to FR functions. Wing Commander Robin Scott, a Society member, was appointed Secretary with effect from the Board meeting held on 13th January 1971.

Changes to banking practices were discussed on this occasion, when Garraway asked that he be authorised to sign cheques up to a value of £50. This was agreed subject to the Secretary scrutinising all cheques drawn under this dispensation. Cheques with a value of more than £50 would be signed by Garraway and the Secretary, as previously. Garraway's request for wages to be paid by cheque was also accepted, with a complex system of pro formas devised to complement the audit trail. The overdraft limit had been increased to £20,000.

When the oil-burning project was discussed Broadbent sounded a note of caution, suggesting that the expected economies might not be forthcoming owing to the increased cost of fuel oil.

A national postal strike was responsible for a six-week gap in Garraway's reports; he spent the time saved in sorting out his office; the reports resumed at the end of February.

Several building projects had been put in hand during the winter. These included a Works Manager's office in the Boston Lodge pattern loft, a sales store, office and staff toilet at Harbour station, plus public toilets at Tan-y-bwlch, the latter courtesy of the North Staffordshire Group. At Tan-y-bwlch work on the footbridge had been carried out all through 1970 and the structure was now erected, although still incomplete; the Board had reservations about the design on aesthetic grounds and asked Garraway to consult with Clough Williams Ellis about it; he approved painting the bridge with dark green bitumastic paint and felt it would blend in with the landscape, he had seen only the drawings, not the structure, but did not consider that there was any practical way to camouflage it.

In January Garraway submitted a paper entitled '*Expansion through the seventies*' in which he considered the Railway's likely problems during the period. It was considered by the Board, on 9th March, in conjunction with a supplementary memorandum compiled by Fiennes called '*Expansion 1971–1980*'. The documents were based on an expectation of a 10% growth in journeys, both in total and in the peak. The forecast suggested the Railway would need capacity to deal with:

Seats, each way, per day	7,500
Trains	20/21
People per train	375
Coaches per train	9/10

To cope, the expansion needed was determined as:

	Proposed	**Existing**	**To build**
Coaches	41	18	23
Engines	6	2	3 or 4
Track	–	–	Budr loop
Boston Lodge	–	–	Extend

It was decided to make a submission, to be prepared by Broadbent, to the Wales Tourist Board, which had recently received powers to invest in tourism development, for 1972/4.

Possibly the first response to these discussions was the start of work on No. 37, the first of two semi-open toastrack bogie coaches built on Hudson underframes, a relatively cheap and easy way to increase capacity. It was started in April and was structurally complete by 18th June, when work started on its fellow, No. 38. It is not recorded if the Board discussed or budgeted for these vehicles.

Conversion of *Blanche* to oil firing had started in March. Laidlaw Drew had made a second burner to a modified design; following comparisons with that in *Linda*, two production burners would be manufactured, the original specimens then becoming available for trials in the other locomotives. *Blanche* was tested in April but high water consumption gave concern.

At the Board's 11th May meeting, Garraway reported on his wish to investigate the use of aluminium coaches and their construction, bodywork only, by contractors. Boston Lodge was unable to take on further construction as the facilities there were occupied fully servicing existing stock. He received authority to make further enquiries provided he made no financial commitment in advance of settling the 1972 budget in the autumn; he had received a quotation of £4,329 for a suitable body.

He also sought and obtained approval to equip *Blanche* with a superheater at the same time as it was re-tubed and for a new firebox the following winter; the £2,000 cost was committed to the 1972 budget.

A three-trains-per-day, two-hourly interval timetable had been introduced for off-peak services. At the

Earl of Merioneth *and* Linda *at Portmadoc on 10th September 1971. It took a while to source a black paint that could resist the higher temperatures generated by oil firing; the use of silver as an interim measure proved to be quite controversial in some quarters.*

John Scrace

end of May, Garraway produced a report comparing results over a 42-day period, excluding the Easter holiday week and regular coach parties, to justify the change.

	1970	1971
Average bookings per train	84	63
Average traffic cash per train	£34	£18
Gross sales profit per train	£7	£4
Days which failed to meet direct operating costs*	Nil	5
Days which met operating costs/ failed to contribute to overheads†	11	13
Days which contributed to overheads‡	31	24

* £20 taken as datum for 1970, £30 for 1971

† £20–£50 in 1970, £30–£60 in 1971

‡ More than £50 in 1970, more than £60 in 1971

There were some changes to the appearance of the stations around this time. Construction of Tan-y-bwlch signal box started in May, followed by the commissioning of colour light home signals at Portmadoc and Dduallt in June. Portmadoc starter was commissioned in July. There's no mention of Clough Williams Ellis's opinion of the concrete blocks used to build the signal box!

The laying of siding-quality track on the first part of the Deviation, as far as Barn cutting, called for a test train, which was run on the evening of 1st July hauled by *Linda*; the new semi-open No. 37 was included in the train, its first run. It was completed and put into traffic by 16th July.

Tan-y-bwlch footbridge was opened officially on 18th July. The John Player Company's steam yacht *Nottingham Castle* had been sailed to Portmadoc and its Captain and Chief Engineer joined other officials from the Nottingham-based company to perform the ceremony.

Linda's conversion to oil firing and the addition of superheating were soon considered vindicated when, in June, it had successfully hauled 10 coaches; in later years such loads were deemed to be too expensive, both in terms of wear and fuel consumption, and banned. *Blanche* had a trial run as an oil burner on 18th July, running to Barn cutting, and returned to service soon after. By the end of the season, though, two tubes had blown and been capped off, Garraway commenting that none of the tubes would have lasted the season had the loco remained a coal burner, citing rodding and cold air introduced during firing as reasons for increased wear.

From a traffic perspective 1971 did not produce the large increase the Railway had become used to. Although Easter and the spring bank holiday had been busier than in 1970 visitors had subsequently declined, a UK-wide phenomenon, and most weeks were only slightly above; the week ended 13th August was 4,000 journeys, 15% down, and the overall position at that stage was only 400 journeys up. There were improvements after the August bank holiday, when Garraway remarked that the week ended 10th September was the best since June. He circulated a comparative abstract of ticket sales (Appendix 13).

Garraway commented on the decline in 1st class travel, indicating a tightening of the purse strings coupled with increased fares, and saying that many

The Tan-y-bwlch footbridge had been sponsored by the John Player tobacco company; on 18th July 1971 the crew of the company's steam launch Nottingham Castle *performed an opening ceremony. Identified behind Allan Garraway are fireman, now driver, Paul Ingham, guard, later general manager, Alan Heywood and stationmaster John Harrison.*

FR Archives

On 15th March 1973 the superstructure of the 'old' Earl of Merioneth *was put into store at Minffordd, reverting to its original name of* Livingston Thompson. *The loco had run for the last time on 31st October 1971 and its superstructure, much of it original, was saved thanks to the efforts of a group of volunteers and staff.*

Norman Gurley, FR Archives

Merddin Emrys' *bogie awaits return to Boston Lodge after an axle broke on 29th August 1972.*

Norman Gurley, FR Archives

Kango hammers were introduced for packing ballast in 1965 with power supplied by a rail-mounted Austin 7 engine-powered generator. A 'portable' 2.5Kva generator was put into service in 1972, the London area group contributing £150 to its cost.

FR Archives

passengers opted to wait for the next train rather than pay extra to travel 1st class. Off-peak travel, on the other hand, had increased significantly.

A rail tour organised by the Society's East Midlands and Leicester groups visited the Railway on 5th September; amongst the 100-plus passengers travelling on the FR was the author of this work, visiting the Railway for the first time.

As soon as the peak season was ended, work started on adapting *Mountaineer* for oil firing – the rear-end suspension needed altering to accommodate the apparatus – and on manufacturing new smokeboxes for the *Earl of Merioneth*'s new boiler. *Blanche* was stripped in November. The roof of the second Maenofferen shed in Minffordd yard was raised in September and that of the Tan-y-bwlch signal box was completed by the end of October. Throughout the autumn permanent way staff was engaged on building the railway for Quarry Tours Ltd at Llechwedd slate caverns.

During the year volunteers and employees expressed concern about the consequence of installing the Hunslet boiler into *Earl of Merioneth*. Built at Boston Lodge in 1886, it retained the traditional Victorian appearance of a Festiniog double engine, a look that would be lost with the new boiler. Following an appeal by a group known as the '*active forty*' the Company agreed, at the Society's annual convention on 30th October, to the preservation of the superstructure, henceforth known by the locomotive's original name, *Livingston Thompson*. The group raised £1,000 to cover the Company's extra costs consequential to the decision; by this device the locomotive to be built around the new boiler became the 'new' *Earl of Merioneth*. The old *Earl of Merioneth* ran for the last time on 31st October.

The 1972 budget was considered by the Board on 11th November. Considerable anxiety was expressed at the increase in wages from 1968 (£18,000) to 1972 (estimated £60,000); comment was also made about the bonus increasing from £1,920 in 1970 to £2,400 in 1971. Fiennes asked for a breakdown of wages paid and the Secretary was deputed to produce updated cash flow forecasts at each meeting. They agreed to purchase land in Glan-y-mor yard, Boston Lodge, from Sir Osmond Williams for £400/450.

After many years of delay and prevarication the compensation claim against the CEGB had been heard at the Lands Tribunal earlier in November. An award in favour of the Company, for £65,000 plus interest, about £105,000 in total, was announced on 19th.

More good news on the financial front came at the 29th November Board meeting, when Bill Broadbent announced that the Wales Tourist Board would accept applications for various projects to a total of 49% of the cost, or £9,506 maximum, provided no other funds were received for the same projects from public sources. The projects the WTB was willing to support were new tourist coaches, new buildings at Tan-y-bwlch for toilets, Dduallt station and Gysgfa loop. He pointed out that as the first three projects had already been put in hand the entire £9,506 should be available for the loop.

John Routly said he had approached the Carnegie Trust for grants and Fiennes said he would contact the Department of the Environment to see if the Railway would qualify for the 85% grant for new rolling stock being paid to British Rail. By the January 1972 Board meeting the Carnegie Trust had replied that it did not make grants to railways. A negative response had been received from the government department by the March meeting.

Garraway had established a building department by taking on men formerly employed by its regular contractor, Harold Creamer. Fiennes queried the need for this but '*more than one*' director supported the move, commenting that the quality of repairs and new works had improved. After discussion budgeted expenditure for the department was allowed to stand.

Mountaineer was steamed on oil for the first time on 15th December, taking seven coaches to Tan-y-bwlch. It was then used on the Santa trains on 18th/19th. After Christmas its internal steampipes were removed for renewal. At the same time *Blanche* was receiving attention to its smokebox, frames, stretcher and buffer beam; its pony truck was in course of manufacture.

At the 11th January 1972 Board meeting the issue of staff wages and the budget was again discussed. At the previous meeting Garraway had been given an unminuted rise of £150 and had subsequently suggested that the heads of departments should also have their salaries increased. Scott said that his estimates had been generous and he thought that an increase could be found within the salaries budget, recommending £100 for Paul Dukes, £80 for Alan Heywood and £50 each for Ron Lester and Bunny Lewis; the Board accepted the proposal, to be implemented from 31st January.

Mountaineer *passing Pen Cob on 30th July 1971. The large spark arrester had been installed to reduce the loco's fire-throwing properties.*

P.H. Groom

Garraway requested approval for the construction of an aluminium-bodied coach to be known as XP72; he wished to progress construction of the coach in order to gain experience with construction and use of this type of vehicle as soon as possible. Fiennes said that the policy decision on whether or not to use aluminium coaches should be deferred until after experience had been obtained with XP72, otherwise he supported the project. The Board authorised expenditure of up to £5,000 providing a grant from the Wales Tourist Board was applied for; by the next Board meeting this figure had been revised to £6,000, including the bogies.

Les Smith was concerned about the future of Garnedd tunnel. Following discussion it was agreed that Broadbent should approach the explosives expert, and raconteur, known as 'Blaster Bates'. Some additional strengthening was installed in February. Bates had made an inspection by 7th March, when Broadbent submitted his report to the Board, but details were not recorded. It was agreed, however, to proceed with care '*so that the already delicate condition of the tunnel was undisturbed and the line throughout being available and safe for traffic.*' It was also noted that rock disposal, presumably if the tunnel roof were removed, would present some difficulties.

The permanent way gang took on an outside contract job, aligning and tamping the Llanberis Lake Railway between Cei Llydan and Penllyn over a period of several weeks. On 28th February Ilott, the Sales Manager, left the Railway for the Welshpool & Llanfair Light Railway and was replaced by David Williams.

Routly suggested to the Board on 14th March that £100,000 of the Lands Tribunal award (still not received) should be invested in a property development scheme in Canterbury. Alternatively it should be put on deposit with the London & Counties Bank. It was considered that the Company should put the compensation money to work before it was spent and investing in property development might have generated substantial profits. However, that would have been a high-risk strategy to pursue.

On the Railway, *Linda* was in the wars on 31st March, Good Friday. Whilst working an evening train for training purposes a piston rod broke through its cotter slot. Components borrowed from *Blanche* made it possible for the locomotive to be returned to service on Easter Monday. A contract to construct seven passenger cars for Quarry Tours Ltd was completed by the end of the month.

Notwithstanding the proposals for investing the CEGB compensation, on 9th May the Board authorised expenditure for: blasting tunnel north cutting (£2,600); a new lorry (£1,700); Boston Lodge erecting shop extension (£5,000) and, in 1973, a new carriage shop (£7,000). Routly, in the meantime, had found details on another property development scheme, in Leicester (20,000 square feet of offices on which the Company would hold the first mortgage), in which to invest the money; Routly and Smith were to negotiate with the Redwing and Carpgate companies.

Robin Scott presented a bank reconciliation together with a note of outstanding bills received from Garraway, away on holiday. The Board appeared quite shocked to discover that the Company owed nearly £36,000, of which the bank was due some £20,000. More information was requested from Garraway and his weekly reports were to include cumulative and comparative figures. There is no indication of any action being taken to reduce or eliminate the level of indebtedness. Afterwards Garraway submitted a breakdown of income and expenditure to 28th April, presumably, but not stated, from 1st January, revealing that the overdraft at that date had been £18,629 and commenting that it had peaked at £21,000 during the month. Expenditure of £22,595 was on budget, he said, but there were additional items, including contract expenses, of £1,803. Income during the same period totalled £14,222.

Some significant changes to the Board's structure were agreed at this meeting, in consequence of Alan Pegler's adventure with ex-LNER 4-6-2 Flying Scotsman in the USA; he had written resigning as Company Chairman. David Garnock had also resigned as President so Pegler was unanimously elected to that figurehead position. Routly, on Gerry Fiennes' nomination, then became Company Chairman, combining that function with that of Chairman of the Board. Les Smith was then elected to be deputy Chairman of both the Company and the Board.

Also on 9th May an East German Orenstein & Koppel 0-8-0 owned by John Snell was delivered to the Railway in expectation, never fulfilled whilst it

New bogie carriage No. 116 was delivered during 1972, manufactured by commercial body builder Edmund Crow in Cleator Moor, Cumbria, a company that had built carriage bodies for the 15in. gauge Ravenglass & Eskdale Railway. On arrival at Boston Lodge some deficiencies were found in its manufacture, including lack of provision for attaching it to its bogies. 100 years after the first bogie carriage it was the first FR carriage to have inward opening doors.

FR Archives

The photographer gets a wave as Mountaineer *arrives at Tan-y-bwlch in June 1974. In the siding is wagon No. 63, a bogie Hudson piped for vacuum brakes to allow it to be run in passenger trains.*

Alan Bowler

stayed on the FR, that it would be repaired and put into working order.

The route having been agreed with the CEGB, the second LRO needed to complete the Deviation was discussed by the Board on 19th May and the application made on 2nd June. Its passage through the Order processing department did not tax the Board at all, for it was not mentioned again until 1975.

In pursuit of the Board's demand for more financial information, Garraway produced a year-to-date analysis on 2nd June (Appendix 12). He commented that the pattern of expenditure was similar to that of 1971, when it had been £7,000 per month for five months followed by £17,000 in June, when outstanding bills were settled. There was £15,156.61 in the bank, excluding the No. 2 account; this was the account used to pay Garraway's salary – he couldn't sign the cheques drawn on it. The receipt from Kenneth Brown, Baker, Baker, often abbreviated to KB3, the Company's solicitors, implies a payment on account from the CEGB.

Blanche's boiler was returned during June; unfortunately it was found that the superheater header had a different flange from that on the old steam pipe so some time, '*considerable humbug*' Garraway later called it, was spent on finding a solution. Tanks were being made for *Earl of Merioneth*.

When the Board met on 4th July decisions on the use of CEGB funds were deferred until the money was received.

In advance of the meeting Garraway had submitted a report on Harbour station, proposing an extension located between the existing building and the goods shed. The Board accepted the proposal and agreed to appoint Society member Eddie Jones as architect; he

Opposite: Merddin Emrys *near Garnedd on 26th July 1973; the loco had been converted to oil firing the previous year. The photograph shows one of the many 'breastwalls' that had been built to reinforce the railway's structure during the later part of the 19th century.*

P.H. Groom

was an architect employed by Lloyds Bank. Fiennes asked if painting could be eliminated or the need for it reduced in order to save a recurring expense, presumably explaining the plastic cladding on the structure erected. The extension would give room for an enlarged shop and a cafeteria seating 40 on the ground floor and additional office space on the first floor.

The proposed Gysgfa loop could not be proceeded with, Garraway told the Board, until the Economic Forestry Group agreed the layout. Francis Wayne, the former secretary, was to be asked to try and induce the group to deal with the matter.

During the last week of July, the aluminium-clad coach body arrived on the Company's lorry from the Cumbrian premises of Edmund Crow Ltd. Having seats for 32 third-class passengers in an open saloon and for four first-class passengers in a compartment with a side corridor its layout was very different from previous passenger vehicles. Like the 'barns' it had corridor connections, but unlike them it had inward opening doors giving access to vestibules at each end. Numbered 116 in recognition of the centenary of the first bogie carriages, Nos. 15 and 16, it arrived unpainted and needed some modification to mount it on bogies.

A new type of traffic record was established on 21st July, when for the first time the running total of the year's passenger journeys was lower than the previous year's. This was attributable to several weeks of poor weather; by 4th August, however, the weather had improved and a record 28,254 journeys made in the week, beating a record, 28,232 journeys, that had stood for two years. The new record, though, only lasted until the week ending 18th August, when 29,029 journeys were made; traffic revenue was £6,512 and sales income £3,361.

The year's locomotive mishaps occurred at Portmadoc. On 29th August *Merddin Emrys* derailed in the carriage sidings when an axle broke; as it blocked the run-round loop the service was maintained by use of a shunting loco. It took most of the day to restore *Merddin Emrys* to a state of equilibrium by replacing the defective bogie with one from *Earl of Merioneth*. Two weeks later, 11th September, *Mountaineer* was the centre of attention when it overshot the headshunt and derailed.

The bulk of the CEGB compensation, some £76,000, was received in mid-September and was put on deposit immediately after the Board meeting held on 14th September. Routly was to pursue the Wales Tourist Board and Garraway the Department of Trade & Industry for grants that might be available to the Company.

Whilst routine maintenance was being carried out at Boston Lodge in September the origins of the Fairlie wheelsets were investigated; *Merddin Emrys*' were from *James Spooner*, *Earl of Merioneth*'s from *Merddin Emrys* and the spare set from *Livingston Thompson*; the latter had cast iron centres and were in poor condition, being suspected of being loose on their axles. The best wheels, said Garraway, had belonged to Taliesin and were probably made of steel.

No. 116 entered service during the week ended the 20th October. A press release dated 27th October said that '*design details of this coach can now be studied through passenger reaction in service before a further batch of vehicles is built ready for the extension of services to Blaenau Ffestiniog planned for 1978.*' No. 16 was varnished at this time, partly in commemoration of its own centenary and partly in recognition of No. 116's launch.

Blanche was completed in October, returning to service by 3rd November. Like *Linda* it now had a new firebox, a superheater and a leading pony truck; it also had piston valve cylinders. In use these were found to be poorly made: improper weld preparation and lack of stress relieving, Garraway said, and the set obtained for *Linda* was never installed. The boiler had been repaired and modified by the Midland Rolling & Haulage Company in Birmingham.

By the time the Board met on 17th November the Company had £116,710 on deposit and the 1973 budget was under scrutiny. Of particular concern was the trend for the declining margin between revenue and wages; the Board agreed that quality of staff was paramount; the target should be to have fewer, yet well-paid, permanent staff and many more volunteers. Other costs commented upon were Deviation expenses, rates, postage and telephone; Routly asked for calls to be logged for a quarter; when the Board next met Garraway reported that telephone expenditure had been less in 1972 than in 1971.

From 1973 Garraway's reports are much less detailed than previously, with almost no information about personnel matters and less information given about any incidents that occurred. Whilst this was perhaps an indication that administration was taking up more of his time, he was still to be seen at *Linda*'s controls when it was rostered.

Contract work carried out during the winter included building six more carriages for Quarry Tours and providing facilities for a British Railways machinist, Roger Goss, previously an FR employee, to reprofile the wheels of Vale of Rheidol Railway 2-6-2T No. 8.

Routly had good news on Department of Trade & Industry grants at the 6th February 1973 Board meeting. Under the Regional Development Scheme a 20% grant was available for building work and new equipment and projected work at Boston Lodge would qualify. He gave this projection:

	Cost	Grant
Erection of new buildings at Boston Lodge	£22,200	£4,500
Equipment for Glan-y-mor carriage workshop	£7,000	£1,400
Smalley excavator (for Deviation)	£6,000	£1,200
Total	£35,200	£7,100

Furthermore if employment was increased by 50%: six at Boston Lodge and four on permanent way, postulated Routly – presumably it had to be employment that produced a manufacturing output – 'selective assistance' would be available, details not given, and loans of up to 50% of the total cost of new schemes could be obtained. He projected grant aided expenditure as above £35,200; crane (grant aided) £2,000 and coaches £100,000, making a total of £137,200.

This would qualify for a net loan of £61,500, after deducting the projected £7,100 grant, interest free for three years, thereafter attracting interest at 7% for five or eight years. Garraway was to process the paperwork.

Traffic in 1973 got off to a slow start, with an unsought record for low bookings of only 13 on 4th April; the week's bookings total of 783 compared poorly with the previous week's 864. Whilst traffic by mid-May was 16% up on 1972, the closure of a Council-operated car park on the site of the present Ganolfan without provision of a replacement was identified as a contributory factor to a net loss by the spring bank holiday.

Mountaineer was back in service, along with *Linda* and *Blanche*, before Easter; Good Friday was on 20th April. *Merddin Emrys* was turned out for a test run on 24th April and immediately afterwards put on the 15.15 service train with 12 cars. The expense and effort of reboilering and converting to oil firing were fully vindicated although at the cost of the loss of even more of its 'as built' elegance. The Portmadoc coaling stage had been removed in March.

The Board's 5th April meeting considered a report on proposals made by the Joint Publicity Committee; ideas put forward included a competition for the area group publicity officer gaining the most publicity for the Railway, advance sale of 'first day tickets' for the Blaenau Ffestiniog reopening and the carriage of slate on the first down train to generate a publicity opportunity of paying a toll to the Tremadoc Estate.

The Board agreed to commission a book on the Railway to be jointly published by Michael Joseph, the Company advancing up to £1,000 towards production costs. Derek Tangye, author of the Minack Chronicles, was reported as unlikely to take on the commission but other Michael Joseph authors were to be considered.

Garraway reported that he had submitted an application to the Wales Tourist Board for a grant for the Harbour station extension. The grant for Gysgfa loop, now relocated to Rhiw Goch, was thought to have been lost but had become available again; authority to proceed was given once details on cost and timing had been resolved.

To raise awareness of the Railway's ambitions a train was to be run for members of the newly created Gwynedd County Council; the members would be involved in processing the Railway's grant applications to government departments. The train was to terminate on the spiral whilst lunch was served. A budget of £1,000 was approved and the date chosen was 7th July.

A train of skips had derailed at Tan-y-bwlch on 30th March; the Board instructed Garraway '*as to the steps required to prevent a recurrence*'.

Grants were discussed again at the Board's 8th June meeting, following a visit Routly and Garraway had made to the Regional Grants and the Selective Assistance offices of the Department of Trade & Industry and the Wales Tourist Board in Cardiff. The first offered modest grants for Boston Lodge, the second discretionary grants of £1,000 for each additional post created and the third, subject to confirmation, £150,000 payable over three years.

The Company's requirement was summarised as £550,000 to reach Blaenau Ffestiniog, sourced from: £100,000 – CEGB compensation; £200,000 – volunteer effort; £100,000 – operating profit. The shortfall of

Erecting the frame for the erecting shop extension in 1973. The cranes had only been able to access the site by a new road that had just been built around the old loco shed.

Geoff Hall, FR Archives

£150,000 could therefore be met by the WTB with the DTI grants acting as a capital reserve! Fiennes, not present at this meeting, was to dispute this analysis, observing that the volunteer effort did not represent cash flow and that the profit had not been associated with Deviation expenditure.

A delivery of new 60lb rail was received from British Steel at Workington in June; it was unloaded by the Jones mobile road crane which the Company had just acquired. The drought that year had the Railway putting effort into improving locomotive water supplies at Portmadoc, Minffordd and Dduallt. At Boston Lodge, in addition to routine maintenance and running repairs on locomotives and rolling stock, four 75lb turnouts were prepared for Rhiw Goch loop.

The councillors' visit to the Deviation on 7th July was considered a success. It cost £813.58 of the budgeted £1,000 so at the 13th September Board meeting Garnock was authorised to pay an additional £100 to Holliday & Edwards, the public relations firm involved.

At that meeting, Scott reported that the return on the CEGB compensation deposited with the Anglian Building Society was 0.9% less, after tax, than could be obtained by using a National Westminster Bank deposit account. He was authorised to transfer the money to get a better rate.

Staff conditions, wages and pension scheme were also discussed. The staff was seeking a 25% increase to give parity with British Rail's basic rates. Routly was of the opinion that 25% need not be paid and Fiennes pointed out that any substantial increase would be constrained by the government's incomes policy. Bonuses were agreed upon, payable on 30th September, and it was Garnock's opinion that increases in wages and the cost of raw materials should be identified in the 1974 budget. Garraway was the only employee with a Company pension; the Board had been investigating a scheme for other employees for several months, Routly and Smith were to finalise details of an Equity & Law Life scheme and have it brought into existence as soon as possible.

A more wide-ranging discussion on pay took place at the next meeting, on 8th November, concluding with Garraway being asked to produce a breakdown of wages by department. He had recommended a 40-hour working week; implementing the government's pay policy on that basis would give a 15% increase.

Routly reported that the Wales Tourist Board had agreed a £50,000 grant for 1974 and anticipated similar amounts for the following five years; he requested production of a quarterly report of capital spending. Fiennes sought approval for capital expenditure on Deviation salaries and wages, Deviation materials, tunnel south cutting blasting, Tanygrisiau station blasting and the pressure pipe bridges to be started on or progressed as much as possible. Smith requested a further £25,000 for the Cwmorthin bridge.

The meeting closed with the acceptance of Fiennes'

Boston Lodge from above in June 1974. The incomplete carriage workshop on the left was partially funded with CEGB compensation. The oil tank was moved to Harbour station after the water tank there was replaced with the present structure.

Alan Bowler

resignation, submitted some time before, and his replacement by Air Vice-Marshal Sir Ben Ball.

Building work was got under way on two fronts during the year at Boston Lodge: Glan-y-mor carriage shed and the new erecting shop were started in August. The Harbour station extension was started in December, when the erecting shop was considered complete; the work almost immediately came to a standstill due to a delay in obtaining steel supplies. In the works routine maintenance was the priority whilst No. 20's body received attention from the joiners. On the track the turnouts for Rhiw Goch loop were installed in November. In December old rail was recovered from the Stesion Fain at Blaenau Ffestiniog and sidings laid at Glan-y-pwll in preparation for restoration works to start. At the latter site the old loco shed received attention to make it more secure.

The year-end passenger journeys reached 408,000, an increase of 3½%; traffic revenue was 21% up and shops sales 17%. The Santa trains did well but post-Christmas traffic was poor. Events in the Middle East, with the consequent oil embargo that led to increased prices, meant that the value of the CEGB compensation reduced considerably.

When the Board met for the first time in 1974,

on 14th February, the capital budget had reached £88,050. Items included: 5,000 jarrah sleepers (two miles) – £11,250; 100 tonnes (one mile) 60lb rail – £7,500; Harbour station improvements – £18,300; Atcost buildings at Boston Lodge – £5,000; and the power station pressure pipes bridge and Blaenau Ffestiniog rehabilitation work – £37,000. The rail had been paid for and another mile (not paid for) had been ordered.

Routly reported that whilst he expected a £50,000 grant from the Wales Tourist Board during the year that body had asked the Railway to submit five stand-alone applications that would be each worth that sum, which he did not think feasible and had refused. He also expected to receive grants for the improvements at Harbour station, Boston Lodge and Rhiw Goch.

Garraway recommended that the Board consider the question of obtaining a new boiler for *Mountaineer*; Hunslet had quoted £9,000 but the FR would have to buy the flanging blocks, £3,000, as Hunslet no longer had the necessary equipment.

Smith was hoping to conclude a sale of the WHR-related land, the slaughterhouse field, in Portmadoc. He also reported that the CEGB was likely to agree to the sale, to the Company, of land between Afon Cwmorthin and the original Tanygrisiau station site. Garnock was authorised to sign a production contract with Michael Joseph Ltd for the new book; after 3,500 copies had been sold the Company would be reimbursed its £1,000 advance.

On the subject of the new catering facility at Portmadoc, Broadbent thought it should be self-service whilst Garnock thought its management should be contracted out. Garraway, however, argued for in-house management with former volunteer Ian Rudd as Manager.

Finally, the Board agreed to implement a staff pension scheme backdated from 1st December 1973. The Company would contribute $7\frac{1}{4}$% of payroll, weekly staff $1\frac{1}{2}$% of pay and salaried staff $2\frac{1}{2}$%; a further $\frac{1}{2}$% Company contribution would add benefits back to 1969; the cost to the Company would be £629 per month.

A public relations exercise was put in hand to prepare residents of Tanygrisiau, Glan-y-pwll and Blaenau Ffestiniog for the Railway's return. In March Garraway organised a public meeting followed by a trip on the train, attended by over 70 people. With Routly, Garraway also met the Chief Executive of the new Gwynedd County Council.

During the first months of the year work on the Harbour station extension continued and a larger locomotive water tank was installed; the latter was followed by installation of an oil tank wagon stabling siding. At Boston Lodge *Linda* and *Mountaineer* received light overhauls and *Blanche* new crankpins. No. 14's bottom-end bogie received attention, No. 104's bodywork was strengthened, No. 19 was varnished and No. 20's overhaul was completed. There were some delays to on going work and the supply of

A BR permanent way gang severing the connection to Minffordd yard during 1974.

Geoff Hall, FR Archives

Blanche *hauling an evening train towards Rhiw Plas on 28th July 1974. The train is made up of post-revival stock, in unusual formation, two corridor sets coupled together. No. 116 is next to the loco, followed by buffet car No. 103, third is one of 104-106 and fourth is observation car No. 100 or 101; that is followed by more corridor stock.*

John Alexander

materials caused by the government's imposition of a three-day working week.

When the Board met on 3rd April the engineering report mentioned, in passing, the recent delivery of bogies obtained from Poland; neither Garraway nor the Board had previously commented on the decision to obtain equipment from behind the Iron Curtain. Two of the bogies were intended for a second tourist car to be built during the year.

Following a discussion on costs the Board agreed to order a boiler for *Mountaineer*. The rebuilding of *Prince* and the possibility of installing superheating was considered, leading to a decision that Broadbent and Garraway should conduct a review of locomotives and rolling stock. Broadbent's request for details of the proposed sale of *Palmerston* to the Group Five Engine Association revealed that a price of £350 had been established; the Association was led by former Boston Lodge employee Alan Headech. On 6th June the sale was agreed for £450, provided the group agreed that the locomotive would not be run in North Wales; doubts about the group's motives for taking on the locomotive – it might be used in competition with the FR – were behind this proviso.

The Wales Tourist Board had been asked to contribute £1,200 towards Rhiw Goch loop and £2,000 towards Harbour station improvements.

By the end of May, *Linda* had been equipped with improved filters to facilitate the use of waste oil; the realisation that the locomotives could burn recycled oil that could be obtained either cheaply or freely had a big impact, with oil being sourced from many parts of England and Wales. The initiative arose from the increased oil prices following the Six Day War, the latter also resulting in a mid-season fares increase. Some consideration was given to building a road/rail vehicle for oil transportation. Modern legislation and health and safety implications brought an end to the scheme after more than 20 years' although there was an increasing perception that the effort put into processing the second-hand oil cost more than it was worth.

On 6th June Hugh Eaves, the Board's financial adviser, reported that capital expenditure was not meeting budget targets, owing to material shortages; the Harbour station extension would require capital expenditure '*in the next few months*'. He also reported that stocks for resale had risen to £20,000; at December 1972 and December 1973 the figures had been £8,000 and £13,500 respectively.

The locomotive programme was agreed: *Earl of Merioneth* to be completed for 1975 peak season and the new boiler to be obtained by end 1975; *Mountaineer* to be re-boilered 1975/6 and the Peckett to be overhauled 1976/7.

Prince was to represent the Company at the Stockton & Darlington Railway 150th anniversary celebrations proposed for 1975. Superheating the boiler would cost £1,500 although, according to the minutes, that was physically impossible.

Some employees had joined the National Union of Railwaymen, requiring that body to represent them in dealings with the Company. The minutes recorded that an agreement made between the Company and the union in 1920 was to be scrutinised to establish if it had any bearing on the current situation!

Sir Ben Ball was put forward as the Company's nominee to the Society Board in replacement for Fiennes.

Building work carried out during the year included a substation at Boston Lodge, reflooring Portmadoc goods shed to form a museum and constructing Rhiw Goch signal box. The Harbour station extension was continued throughout the year, with the roof completed in November.

At Boston Lodge work was started on *Earl of Merioneth*'s fuel tanks and stripping *Prince*'s firebox, including removal of the foundation ring. A Hunslet mines loco, purchased for £50 in 1969, was stripped and cleaned for evaluation. Under the heading of 'Carriage & Wagon' Garraway recorded, on 6th September, that work on the ex-standard gauge Matisa tamper had restarted.

On 14th August 1974 the loco and first carriage of the 09.40 had derailed on the top-end trap points at Minffordd, due to a signalman's error. In the light of this incident and '*other irregularities that had occurred*' Routly asked the Board, on 12th September, to consider the procedures to be adopted so that its responsibilities were not only taken seriously but were seen to be so. Broadbent undertook to make recommendations for the next meeting whilst Garraway reported on the incidents that had occurred during the previous two years and described the procedures already in place for dealing with them. The Board considered he had handled these matters properly but felt that a standard procedure should be laid down by the Board. New forms for reporting accidents/incidents were approved when the Board next met.

Other matters dealt with on 12th September included a long debate on the subject of grant income; the Wales Tourist Board's grants committee had intimated that it was prepared to consider applications in respect of Dduallt – tunnel north; tunnel north – Tanygrisiau; Tanygrisiau station and one train set. Routly also hoped to secure other funding from the County Council.

£3,500 would be paid to Aneurin Davies for his land, including also compensation for peat dumped on his property, needed for the Deviation. A new tourist car was to be built for 1975; it was not explained that it would be used to operate a shuttle between Dduallt and Gelliwiog and would be much more substantial than previous tourist cars.

Alan Pegler, returned after his US adventure with *Flying Scotsman*, attended the 11th November Board meeting in his role as Company President.

The Gelliwiog shuttle to be operated in 1975 was to have standard fares applied, 25p for adults, including Society members, and 13p for children. Broadbent reported that *Prince* would not be ready in time to attend the Stockton & Darlington Railway event; *Princess* attended instead. During a discussion on monitoring wage levels Broadbent stressed the necessity for them to keep pace with inflation and considered a budgeted annual increase of 20% to be reasonable.

Later in the month Welsh TV broadcaster HTV transmitted a programme about the Railway. In viewing terms it was placed 3rd equal with 'Miss World'!

The year ended on a down note, when Assistant Works Manager Bob Harris fell from *Blanche*'s tender whilst taking water at Tan-y-bwlch on 21st December. He sustained a broken leg and cheekbone.

Eaves, the Company's financial adviser since 1973, was appointed Treasurer at the 2nd January 1975 Board meeting. Secretary Scott had intimated his wish to retire and a successor, to be known as the Clerk, as defined in the 1832 Act, was to be sought.

The underframe of the new tourist car, No. 30, was completed by mid-February and other work in hand at Boston Lodge included overhauling the Hunslets and one of *Merddin Emrys*' bogies, plus making the mines loco fit for passenger service. A total of 144 loco and carriage axles were electronically tested, the first time this technology was used on the FR.

As the grants sought for various projects had not actually been awarded Eaves requested, on 4th February, that the 1975 budget be redrafted to bring the year's plans within the anticipated available resources. Garraway gave details of the measures required to comply with this request and the Board agreed that a revised budget should be compiled. On that basis, Eaves reported that both the overdraft and surplus would peak at around £50,000; Routly

Above: *Funded with the CEGB compensation was the two-storey extension to Harbour station, seen here under construction.*

Alan Bowler

Arrangements being made to rerail Upnor Castle *after it derailed on the trap points at Minffordd on 14th August 1974.*

A.G.W. Garraway, FR Archives

Linda *arrives at Tan-y-bwlch, June 1974. Next to the loco are the two semi-opens built on Hudson underframes in 1971.*

Alan Bowler

would approach the bank; he secured an overdraft of £35,000 and a further £50,000, dependent on grants being obtained, for its share of the Deviation expenditure between Dduallt and the north end of the tunnel.

The Dolrhedyn bridge was discussed; Smith was to pressure Gwynedd County Council to include a diversion in its 1975/6 capital works programme. The original bridge had been removed, with Railway consent, whilst the Tanygrisiau power station was being built; the local authority, abolished in 1974, had agreed to replace it when required by the FR. In the meantime usage had increased and a bridge at the previous level would close the road, and Dolrhedyn, to motor vehicles; the Railway was hoping that Gwynedd CC would adopt part of the CEGB's private road to the Stwlan dam to provide a new access to the village and facilitate the reinstatement of its bridge. In April it was established that the Council had made provision for the works to be carried out.

As Garraway was to move out of his railway flat, the Board when it met on 7th April agreed to increase his salary by £500 and to pay for his telephone.

Pegler's association with the Company was reviewed. He had been paid £1,000 per annum for a consultancy for three years, which arrangement was due to expire. It was agreed to pay him £500 per annum for a further three years, at which point the payments would cease. The original agreement was not recorded in the minutes.

Dealing with financial matters, the Wales Tourist Board had agreed to fund 49% of the Dduallt - tunnel expenditure forecast at £100,000; a retrospective claim for £11,000 had been submitted. Eaves was to try and recover for the Company the tax paid on the interest generated by its deposit with the Anglia Building Society and that deducted at source by the CEGB from the compensation interest.

Major Peter Olver inspected the Rhiw Goch passing loop and the Dduallt - Gelliwiog section of the Deviation on 13th May. An extra platform was built at Dduallt for the shuttle.

John Pratt, writing under the pseudonym John Winton, published his book about the Railway, '*The Little Wonder*', on 14th May, when a special train was operated to launch it. The special crossed a service train at Rhiw Goch, a precursor of regular crossings there that started on 17th May. The new café was used for the first time on the same day.

The Gelliwiog shuttle, formed of the mines loco and the new tourist car, No. 30, commenced operation on 27th May following a test run the day before. There being no loops the train ran in 'push-pull' mode although the driver remained on the loco whilst the guard, stationed in a 'driving' compartment at the downhill end of the coach had access to a brake handle and a warning device. Both locomotive and carriage were incomplete, the latter having no doors and windows and basic temporary seating. The name *Moel Hebog* was applied to the locomotive on Paul Dukes' suggestion, chosen for its similarity to *Moelwyn*. The carriage was the FR's first attempt at steel body construction.

During the week ended 30th May, the bank holiday week, the new shop took £2,400 and the café £670, an increase of 45% over the previous year. The shop was operated in two parts as the ladies' toilet still required relocation. The timetable had been tightened up, with trains turning round in two hours instead of two and a half, thus the crews needed to be on their toes to keep time; the improved spread of departures lead to better utilisation in Garraway's opinion. He also reported that the shuttle had operated full on two days; 2,212 journeys had been made during the week, but it would need hard selling to exploit fully its potential.

Mark Wright was appointed Company Clerk with effect from the 12th June Board meeting. The appointment was discussed whilst Routly absented himself from the meeting; he was Wright's father-in-law. The wages budget was to be increased by 10% from 1st July; its allocation to individuals was to be at the discretion of the heads of departments. A fare increase was to be introduced from 14th June.

The National Railway Museum was to be offered the Tasmanian Garratt on loan provided the museum paid for its transport and acknowledged the FR when it was put on display; the NRM had accepted the terms by September.

Whilst letters of thanks were to be sent to the Harbour station architect and the Company's building gang, Routly was concerned about escalating costs and asked Smith to investigate the possibility of applying lower standards to the outstanding works.

Boston Lodge personnel had produced a boiler design that could be utilised on the Alco and the Hunslets; Broadbent reported that it had been submitted to the insurers. Part of the £2,000 deposit paid on ordering a new Alco boiler might be recovered

A very incomplete No. 110 at Dduallt on a test run in 1975; the locos are Upnor Castle *and* Moel Hebog. *The latter and No. 110 entered service shuttling between Dduallt and Gelliwiog, near the new tunnel, on 26th May. The carriage had a driving compartment at the leading end with brake and horn controls for the guard to use on the downhill journey. The first Boston Lodge-built steel-bodied carriage developed around the metal folding skills of Warren Shephard, it was progressively completed during the summer.*

FR Archives

when the insolvent manufacturer was wound up, Broadbent said.

The future of the Railway's headquarters was considered. The lease for the land occupied by Harbour station, £75 per annum, was due to expire in 21 years, when the rent was expected to be increased considerably due to inflation and improvements; a decision was taken to open negotiations with the Tremadoc Estate to purchase the freehold, including the car park land, for about £3,000. The site occupied by the Guide hut, in the car park, might be obtained if that group accepted an offer of some of the slaughterhouse field land; part of the stone building alongside the goods shed was also on offer for £1,500 – a counter offer of £1,000 had been made. Garnock was to approach the Halifax Building Society for funds to finance the acquisition(s).

The arrangement for the Company's use of Glanmeirion at Portmeirion had been terminated in favour of a cottage at Bron Turnor; the changeover was not recorded but '*the rent for the cottage at Minffordd has been arranged for a further year for £700*'.

A visit by HRH Princess Margaret and children had been arranged for 25th July; Ball's report on protocol proved useful, it was recorded. The Lord Lieutenant had reconnoitred the line, in fog, and agreed a schedule. A special train would carry the party from Minffordd to Gelliwiog and back to Dduallt; from Dduallt to Tan-y-bwlch it would travel in a coach attached to the service train. '*Directors and wives will be presented at Minffordd together with the General Manager and his wife, certain staff and the train crew; others will be presented at Dduallt. The royal party may request some directors or officers to travel with them on the train. The matter awaits clarification.*'

The Welsh Office's decision on the Wales Tourist Board's recommendation to award the FR a £200,000 grant in 1976 was awaited, said Routly. If it was refused the Railway would ask for the money in 1977, having already arranged for a bridging loan, or for 50% grant and 50% loan, interest free for several years. If the Welsh Office refused the WTB would approach the European Economic Community.

Although the increased use of waste oil had reduced the cost of locomotive fuel some small capital expenditure was required to improve supply, handling and storage facilities. Once the 'system' was established '*we should see a really worthwhile overall saving*', said Garraway on 13th June. By November 32% of consumption was sump oil.

The Festiniog Railway (Light Railway) (Amendment) Order 1975 was made on 17th June, giving approval to '*a railway (No. 4) 2,735 metres in length including a tunnel commencing by a junction with the railway (No. 3) at a reference point 677428 and terminating by a junction with the principal railway at reference point 683449.*' Part of the 1968 railway, to Brookes Quarry, was formally abandoned. Article 9 contained 20 clauses for the protection of the CEGB, including the requirements to use an approved civil engineering contractor to construct the section behind the power station and to take no longer than nine months to do so.

While revenue was increased, owing to fare

increases and shop improvements, passenger traffic was poor, Garraway submitting this table to the Board for the week ended 18th July:

	1975		1974	
	Week	Year to date	Week	Year to date
Journeys	16,104	89,701	9,155	91,031
Shuttle	1,263	3,826		
Fares	£7,623	£70,608	£5,679	£52,174
Shuttle	£275	£837		
Sales	£3,725	£38,649	£2,926	£29,743

The overdraft stood at £17,273.44.

The week was not a good one for the steam locomotives. *Mountaineer* had a leaking steampipe joint fixed, only for its 'J' pipe casting to fail. *Linda* failed with a broken pony truck equaliser beam and *Merddin Emrys* with a loose wheel. By the end of the month one of *Linda*'s superheater elements had failed, both were replaced, and *Mountaineer*'s firebox wrapper had developed a crack; it too was repaired.

Whilst playing host to Princess Margaret on 25th July the Board started a meeting on the train that was concluded at Harbour station!

Smith was concerned that the Board's policy of concentrating Harbour station expenditure on revenue-earning activities was not being followed, particularly with regard to moving the ladies out of the shop area. The Board agreed that there should be no unbudgeted expenditure on the building and, despite a long report on the matter submitted by Paul Dukes, priority should be given to moving the ladies rather than completing the offices. The scaffolding had been removed at the end of June.

It was agreed that Garraway should consult with the Directors holding functional responsibilities when compiling the 1976 budget; the policy should be to give cash priority to the Deviation whilst maintaining safe operation of the existing line.

Hot weather – '*phenomenal*', said Garraway – kept people off the trains in early August, leading to the worst August week for several years. 29th July had been a record day when 3,375 passengers had been carried; the Railway had coped so well that no one had realised the day's significance until the paperwork was completed! The £18,092.59 overdraft of 25th July had been converted to a credit balance of £9,651.57 by 8th August.

It was at this time that eight steel carriage underframes were acquired from the Isle of Man Railway Company for future use.

The royal visit was briefly mentioned when the

The Harbour station extension, providing a larger shop, sit-down catering and offices, was brought into use in 1975. Evidence of previous expansion is shown by the dormers in the single-storey section; that on the left was then, and is still, the control office.

FR Archives

Board met on 11th September. Routly bemoaned what he called the '*sad inadequacy*' of the Court Circular and had complained about it!

In Blaenau, the Company was planning to terminate the line opposite the BR station, a location given the soubriquet 'seven acre site' for obvious reasons. The local authority, however, wanted the Railway extended to the former GWR site in the town centre. The Board agreed to seek the Council's support for the grant application to the Welsh Office.

Broadbent submitted a comprehensive engineering report. *Mountaineer*'s boiler was expected to fail its test in November; in that case planned maintenance should be deferred and the hours transferred to *Prince*, with the latter taking the former's place in the roster in 1976. The carriage fleet was in good order although No. 30 still required considerable work. Concern was expressed at the amount of time being allocated to scheduled work, three years for *Earl of Merioneth* being cited, and greater efficiency called for; the minutes don't make clear who was concerned. Eleven people were employed at Boston Lodge and he thought that ideally they should concentrate on maintenance, with others recruited for new works. Fred Howes had suggested that half a mile of track should be relaid each year for the next ten years. S&T at Minffordd and Tan-y-bwlch must be improved to meet Railway Inspectorate requirements. Routly said that the expected Wales Tourist Board grant for *Earl of Merioneth* should be taken into consideration when forecasting cash flow.

When discussing the accounts it was agreed that expenditure on Rhiw Goch loop should be treated as restoration whilst *Mountaineer*'s boiler was a current item.

Later in the month occupation of the new offices at Harbour station commenced and work started on locating the ladies' toilet in the old beer store.

The age of the Railway's infrastructure was brought to prominence with the discovery of subsidence in the embankment above Penrhyn crossing. It was filled in and some reinforcement added. In October a 'dubious' wall at Bryn Mawr needed attention and then on 19th November a rock fall from beneath the line at Penlan, Tanygrisiau, occurred, weakening the formation. This caused both administrative (the owner was not immediately identifiable) and practical problems before it could be resolved, as the surrounding rock was severely flawed.

At Boston Lodge a mechanical overhaul was started on *Linda*. In the carriage shops work continued on No. 30 and modification of one of the Manx underframes for No. 31 was started. What started as a repaint job on No. 15 in mid-October had become a heavy body overhaul by the end of November!

NUR recognition was expected to be discussed during a proposed joint meeting of the Society and Company Boards, and on 30th September Routly produced a briefing note entitled '*FR industrial relations*':

> '. . . . *what seems to be emerging are the conclusions that . . . . Recognition of the NUR appears inevitable. . . . It is conceivable that the volunteer element could be diminished and even destroyed if union intervention were to go too far and therefore the future of the Society could eventually be at stake. . . . In the joint interests of the Society and Company and the future of the railway and of its employees legitimate union activity should be contained within reasonable limits.*'

He continues by explaining certain basic facts about the FR to illustrate that it was totally different in its structure and working practices to that of British Railways:

> '. . . . *The total value of the voluntary contributions in labour alone (without counting cash) well exceeds the Company's operating profit. . . . the Directors of the Society and Company provide their services voluntarily as do their treasurers, clerk, secretaries and registrar.*'

He proposed that if the Company and the Society agreed to recognise the NUR as the trade union to represent its members then conditions should apply:

> '*a. NUR will not seek to change the role of the Society or restrict voluntary work by its members or by independent volunteers or by civil engineering groups (hereinafter referred to as volunteers) at any time or on any duties*

Right: Prince *heads the 2.45pm from Porthmadog at Tyler's Curve in August 1964.*

Brian Jones

approved by the Company.

b. NUR will not seek to establish demarcation, because flexibility of labour functions in such a seasonal business is essential to viability.

c. As volunteers provide a substantial part of the labour required and work alongside paid employees all consultation regarding Health and Safety at Work and conditions of employment will include representatives of volunteers.

d. NUR will recognise the great differences between the Festiniog Railway and BR and will not seek to establish parity with BR. . . . '

The Board meeting on 13th November started with the news that the Manpower Services Commission had agreed to fund the employment of 12 men for 12 months on the Deviation at a value to the FR of some £27,250; this was the first of the job-creation schemes. The CEGB had indicated that it would probably agree to a temporary terminus at Buarth Melyn, in response to pressure from the Wales Tourist Board anxious to see a visible return for its investment in the FR.

On the budget, it was revealed that the overdraft was expected to reach £96,000 although approval was sought for only £90,000 in anticipation of adjustments. Eaves pointed out that the budget was based on a 10% increase in wages; the Board agreed that if settlement was reached for a larger increase staff numbers would have to be reduced. Garnock voiced concern about redundancies although all agreed that loyalty to the Company must transcend loyalty to individuals; the 10% increase was implemented from 1st January 1976, on the basis that there would be no other increases during that year.

Broadbent had secured a reduction in the Boston Lodge budget to a level representing the minimum necessary to maintain traffic needs. A new boiler would be obtained for *Mountaineer* despite the current vessel having passed its examination. Carriage No. 30 would be complete and No. 31 built for the 1976 peak season, whilst No. 32 would be ready for 1977. Smith was concerned about the state of the locomotive running shed, known as the long shed.

Routly said there was an urgent need to estimate the outstanding costs involved in returning to Blaenau Ffestiniog in order to assist grant applications; in January Garraway was asked to update such estimates as existed with a view to producing accurate costings of restoring the Railway to Blaenau Ffestiniog, firstly on a shoe-string budget and, secondly, to the standards and with the facilities envisaged in the medium term.

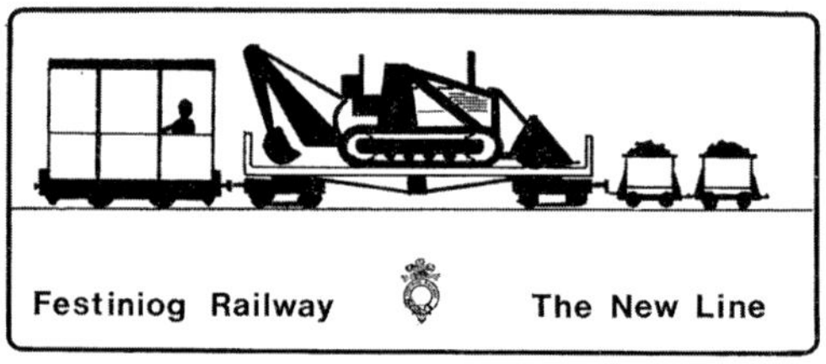

Passengers travelling to Dduallt are invited to view the new works involved in our future extension of services to Blaenau Ffestiniog.

Please alight at Dduallt for the special push-pull train which operates as required on the new railway.

Fares payable on the special train:

Adult — 30p

Child — 15p

FESTINIOG RAILWAY

Winter Timetable 1974-75

23rd September, 1974 to 23rd March, 1975

(DAILY SERVICES recommence 26th March)

	DAILY Mon., 23 Sept. to Thurs., 31 Oct. (except Fridays, 11, 18, 25 Oct.)	EVERY SAT. & SUN., 2 Nov. to 15 Dec.	SAT. & SUN. 21–22 Dec. SO	BOXING DAY 26 Dec.	DAILY 27 Dec. to 1 Jan. Also Sat.-Sun., 4–5 Jan.	EVERY SAT. & SUN., 15 Feb. to 23 Mar.
PORTHMADOG	1115 1315 1515	1415	1330 1415 1915	1315 1515	1415	1415
BOSTON LODGE	RQ RQ RQ	RQ		RQ RQ	RQ	RQ
MINFFORDD	1126 1326 1526	1426	CHRISTMAS	1326 1526	1426	1426
PENRHYN	1132 1332 1532	1432	EXCURSIONS	1332 1532	1432	1432
TAN-Y-BWLCH *arr.*	1150 1350 1550	1450	Details	1350 1550	1450	1450
dep.	1155 1355 1555	1455	see below	1355 1555	1455	1455
DDUALLT	1205 1405 1605	1505		1405 1605	1505	1505
DDUALLT	1218 1418 1618	1518		1418 1618	1518	1518
TAN-Y-BWLCH *arr.*	1228 1428 1628	1528		1428 1628	1528	1528
dep.	1230 1430 1630	1530		1430 1630	1530	1530
PENRHYN	1249 1449 1649	1549		1449 1649	1549	1549
MINFFORDD	1255 1455 1655	1555		1455 1655	1555	1555
BOSTON LODGE	RQ RQ RQ	RQ	SO	RQ RQ	RQ	RQ
PORTHMADOG	1305 1505 1705	1605	1615 1645 2105	1505 1705	1605	1605

RQ – Calls on request.   SO – Saturday Only — Off peak fares apply (3rd Class 70p, 1st Class £1·10)

Although every possible effort will be made to ensure running as timetable, the Festiniog Railway will not guarantee advertised connections in the event of breakdown or other obstruction of services.

SATURDAY AND SUNDAY, 21/22 DECEMBER

Special Father Christmas Excursions will operate as follows:

Porthmadog depart 1330 and 1415 (arrive back 1615 and 1645, respectively). Father Christmas will meet the trains at Tan-y-Bwlch with presents for the children.

Fares: 3rd Class. Adult Return £1·10. Children (under 14) 55p. FR Society Members 50p. 1st class 40p supplement in all cases. Seasonal snacks from buffet car optional extra. Advance booking advised on these trains.

PRINCIPAL FARES ON ALL TRAINS EXCEPT EXCURSIONS

Porthmadog to Dduallt: 3rd Class return 90p. 1st Class return £1·20. Children under 14 half fare. Buffet and observation cars on all trains.

PLEASE NOTE. Whilst the Company continues to use steam traction on the majority of its trains, it reserves the right to use diesel locomotives where necessary during the winter service.

SPECIAL PARTIES AND PRIVATE CHARTER TRAINS BY ARRANGEMENT

Festiniog Railway Company, Porthmadog, Gwynedd. Tel. Porthmadog 2384

One of the Great Little Trains of Wales

T. Stephenson & Sons Ltd., Printers, Prescot, Merseyside

The Facts of the Matter 1972 . . . . .

'High in the mountains of Snowdonia volunteers are busily engaged on a major construction project. The narrow gauge Festiniog Railway is being extended once more to Blaenau Ffestiniog.

Two and a half miles of earthworks are having to be built to deviate the line round Llyn Ystradau, a lake constructed by the electricity authority during the period the line was closed.

So far 25,000 tons of rock have been excavated to form the new cuttings and embankments, but there remain a further 45,000 to shift.'

'This is the largest scheme of its kind ever undertaken in Britain, and we need your help to complete it.'

'How you can help . . . .'

- *'A willingness to lend a hand is more important than strength.*
- *Each weekend has its own organiser who makes all the prior arrrangements necessary for the smooth running of a successful working party.*
- *Travel by car is arranged and a charge of 55p per day is made for accommodation and food.*
- *Volunteers live close to the work in their own accommodation which is equipped with bunks and all the basic necessities.'*

Extracts from a brochure produced in 1972 to recruit volunteers for the Deviation Project.

Programme for 1972 * Bank Holidays

	Jan	Feb	Mar	Apr	May	Jun
Northern	1-2	–	–	–	–	–
London B	8-9	5-6	4-5	1-3*	–	–
Western	15-16	12-13	11-12	8-9	6-7	3-4
London A	22-23	19-20	18-19	15-16	13-14	10-11
Northern	29-30	26-27	25-26	22-23	20-21	17-18
London B	–	–	–	29-30	27-29*	24-25

	Jul	Aug	Sep	Oct	Nov	Dec
Western	1-2	–	–	–	–	–
London A	8-9	–	2-3	30-1	–	–
Northern	15-16	12-13	9-10	7-8	4-5	2-3
London B	15-16	12-13	16-17	14-15	11-12	9-10
Western	29-30	26-28*	23-24	20-21	18-19	16-17
London A	29-30	26-28*	30-1	28-29	25-26	30-31

Weekend Organisers

Alan Petrie (London A)	37 Teignmouth Road, London, N.W.2.	01-452 5385
Chris Noel (London B)	2 Ilchester Mansions, Abingdon Road, London, W.8.	01-937 2674
David Yates (Northern)	39 Warburton Lane, Partington, Cheshire.	061-775 4104
Sheila Ross (Western)	1 Sion Hill, Clifton, Bristol BS8 4DQ.	0272 32643
Roger Moore (Western)	19, Chepstow Villas, London, W.11.	01-727 8922

Weekday Parties

Peter Jamieson	24, Falkland Road, London, N.W.5.	01-267 1733

Issued by the Festioniog Railway Company, Civil Engineering Department (New Works), Llyn Ystradau Deviation Project. 1972.

Chapter 9

On to Tanygrisiau – the Deviation Years

1976~1978

By 1976 the operating railway could have been regarded as 'restored'; the locomotive and carriage fleets had been expanded and were arguably adequate for the Company's needs; there was new construction under way under both headings. Both Harbour and Tan-y-bwlch stations had received attention to improve their capability to deal with increasing passenger numbers. The Deviation was substantially complete as far as the tunnel, the tunnel itself had been started and the CEGB was proving to be much more amenable to the Company's suggestions. Whilst the Company's finances were not as closely controlled as might have been appropriate it was learning to profit from any grants which might be used to its advantage. It had become clear that there were problems with employee morale and the Board sought to find a way to strengthen the Railway's day-to-day management.

When the Board met on 21st January 1976 all current activities were reviewed in detail. Highlights included Les Smith's report that the County Council also wished the Railway to terminate at the GW site in Blaenau Ffestiniog; this was perhaps as well as the district valuer was being intransigent over the value of the seven-acre site.

The issue of the Penlan rock fall was raised and Richard Whittle's report was submitted. The latter, an engineering geologist working as a consultant on the tunnel on a voluntary basis, found evidence of historic movement on the site and suspected that previous failures were the reason for buttresses being built in the locality in the past. The condition of the rock was poor, he said, and it would be difficult to get a good foundation for grouting and pinning with rock bolts, the usual technique for such circumstances. He had considered building but rejected an avoiding line in a tunnel before recommending that the railway formation be widened by trimming back the rock face, this having the benefit of reducing the load on the toe of the embankment. He suggested that his report be used as a foundation for further investigation.

A mortgage deed had been executed and would be deposited with the bank, securing the overdraft against the Company's freehold property. Hugh Eaves was concerned about the shortage of clerical staff at Portmadoc; the clerk, Ken Howes (Fred Howes' father) was on the sick. Both the Wales Tourist Board and the Manpower Services Commission were paying their grant aid promptly; the former was to be asked to consider making a top-up payment for the Harbour station work due to the inflation that had occurred whilst the project was in progress. Except for consumables a bar was placed on reordering by the sales department; stock levels were considered adequate for the time being. Eaves was congratulated for saving audit charges by keeping better accounts.

The pension status of the Company employees wives' who were employed on a part-time basis was discussed; Allan Garraway was to tell them that as the pension scheme was open only to full-time employees they could only contribute to it if their pay was paid to their husbands! The wives were to agree that their pay was not pensionable. The author was told of an unusual situation that affected married couples occupying Company property when both were employed by the Company; rent was deducted from the husband's pay or salary at source – when the wife joined the payroll rent was deducted from her pay also, increasing the Company's income from the property!

Viscount Garnock reported that 2,932 copies of John Winton's book, 'The Little Wonder', had been sold; the author was writing a film script and was seeking a backer. Whilst accepting, obviously, that the FR's story is quite fascinating the present author has difficulty in envisaging it as a feature film; needless to say there was none!

On 13th February, Allan Garraway reported that an intermediate repair of *Linda* was close to completion; the pony truck and leading coupled axleboxes had been overhauled, new drag box and chimney

Garratt 'K1' being shunted by Upnor Castle *at Harbour station in June 1976, preparatory to being loaded for transporting to the National Railway Museum. The former has been restored for use on the Welsh Highland Railway whilst the latter has been allocated for use on WHR construction duties since 1997.*

Alan Bowler

fabricated and all mechanical parts serviced. It was back in traffic by 5th March. *Mountaineer* was being reassembled, progress on *Prince* was slow, a tank for *Earl of Merioneth* had been fabricated. *Upnor Castle*'s transmission had been overhauled and the loco had been equipped for auto train working.

Following the death of his wife, Bill Hoole left Boston Lodge during February, moving first to Bron-y-Garth hospital and then to Moseley Hall hospital in Birmingham; the dates were not recorded, either by Garraway or the Society's magazine.

At Harbour station the new shop counter had been completed, following completion of the new ladies' toilets in January, and telephones installed in the new offices. Exterior painting was completed by 5th March.

The shuttle coach, No. 30, had become No. 110 by this date and Nos. 31 and 32 had been renumbered Nos. 117 and 118.

When it met on 10th March, the Board agreed to encourage efforts of both Company officers and outsiders to enable the Railway to terminate in the centre of Blaenau Ffestiniog, providing the Company incurred no additional expense to terminating at Stesion Fein. In the meantime the local authority was removing the Glan-y-don slate tip from Rhiwbryfdir and tipping it on the seven-acre site, a bog; the Company granted a two-year easement over its land at Glan-y-pwll and Stesion Fein for £12,500 although it had hoped for £15,000. This must have been the reason, incidentally, that Smith and the district valuer failed to agree on a price for the seven-acre site; Smith was bidding low on an unimproved basis, whilst the valuer wanted to see the value of the tipping reflected in the price.

The new café was to be named 'Little Wonder' on the recommendation of the publicity committee, following a competition amongst Society members.

On 26th March Garraway reported that the building was substantially complete and that the enquiry office (the old tea bar), had been refurbished to Wales Tourist Board standards, at its expense, as a tourist information counter. The building gang moved on to the Boston Lodge amenities block.

Garraway had submitted a report after the Board meeting on 18th March. Amongst other matters that he was concerned about was that of the Company's financial position, which had not been discussed on that occasion. He said:

> *'Cash Sources ~ It grieves me to pay the bank's high rate of interest on our loans, when there are many people who would be quite prepared to lend money to us at lower rates of interest. The TR is currently in a similar position to ourselves, and their current magazine appeals for sums of £100 or more at up to 9% pa interest, pointing out that for people in the higher tax brackets, the loss of income through lower interest rates is negligible. Money loaned at low interest rates can be equivalent to a large donation in worth to the Company, and is worth more to the recipient than to the donor.*
>
> *Over the next few years we are going to need to borrow a lot of money. The present arrangement with the bank is only a temporary palliative and I cannot see how we are going to complete to Blaenau Ffestiniog without borrowing very much more. We have several times talked about making more use of the Trust to enhance subscription income, and the recent Company AGM mentioned the matter of selling shares. Obviously these are all matters outside my jurisdiction, but I feel someone should be activating matters just as hard as we are trying to save every penny of expenditure and get more revenue.*
>
> *However it may seem that I criticise the way we are doing some things, I still believe in the FR and have already shown that I am prepared to back my beliefs with cash; open the door and I will lead the way to more.'*

He also reported that the stone building in the

A portrait of Moelwyn *whilst shunting at Porthmadog in June 1976. The Britannia Foundry buildings were demolished to make way for an Inland Revenue office block.*

Alan Bowler

The Stesion Fein site in use for the clearance of the Glan-y-don tip, 1976. The footbridge was rebuilt before the FR was reopened.

Geoff Hall, FR Archives

car park had been sold by the Tremadoc Estate, without the knowledge of the Estate's solicitor! The Railway had been hoping to acquire the property. The Company was offered its own freehold in July and offered £5,000 for it.

Eaves submitted unaudited accounts for 1975 to the Board on 11th May; they showed that there had been strict adherence to the budget and trading profit had increased due to fare increases. Capital projects had accounted for 24% of staff costs. The Society had loaned £9,000 to the Company; £7,000 from a legacy. Eaves also commented on the current year-to-date position, which was on budget although the overdraft was below forecast, both because £25,000 of cheques had not been sent out and grants had been received more quickly than anticipated.

John Routly reported that the National Westminster Bank had offered a grant of £7,000 or a 12-month interest-free loan of £50,000 for the Deviation. He hoped to secure 100% of the cash required in grants but he might have to concede the Company paying something, say £20,000, to the McAlpine company. Eaves said that in his opinion the Company could afford £25,000 from profits for two years if there were no other capital projects; wage increases were limited to 5%; increases in materials costs were limited to 10%; fares were increased by 4% and track laying continued at the present rate of half a mile per annum. The Department of Trade & Industry had paid £3,500 towards work carried out at Boston Lodge.

It was thought unlikely that Blaenau Ffestiniog could be reached in time for the 1978 season, in which case Tanygrisiau might have to serve as a temporary terminus. The Board proceeded on the basis of opening through the tunnel to Buarth Melyn in 1977. The local authorities had requested an indefinite adjournment on proceeding with the Dolrhedyn bridge which had been emphatically refused; Routly had spoken to the County Council's Chief Executive.

The Queen's Jubilee tour in 1977 raised the possibility of a royal visit, Routly informed his colleagues, suggesting that the tunnel might be named after the event. The rest of the Board welcomed the idea of a visit but preferred the appellation 'Moelwyn' for the tunnel.

Names to be affixed to the buffet cars were reported to the Board by Garnock; they were: No. 14 *'Charles Spooner'*, No. 12 *'William Madock'* and No. 103 *'Samuel Holland'*.

The ability of the locomotive fleet to throw up the unexpected continued on 25th May when *Blanche* returned to Porthmadog with warm driving axleboxes; when no immediate cause could be found the wheels were removed, revealing a broken axle – examination showed that it had obviously run for some time in that condition: the advantage of outside frames, remarked Garraway. It was back in service by the end of June.

On the carriage fleet the Lynton & Barnstaple bogies had required heavy maintenance and were close to needing new wheels; they had covered 108,400 miles in FR service, reported Garraway, and *'did not owe the Railway anything'*. On 3rd June No. 116 derailed in Tan-y-bwlch loop causing delays and reductions to the service; the cause was identified as subsidence following drain laying under the track and lack of attention to the track because it was due to be relaid.

After some 10 years out of sight at Boston Lodge the Tasmanian Garratt K1 was loaded for transport to the National Railway Museum on 25th June.

Routly informed the Board on 28th July that subject to confirmation the Wales Tourist Board had offered a £50,000 grant for the power station bridges and £10,000 for the Tanygrisiau – Blaenau Ffestiniog restoration. The Welsh Development Agency had agreed to pay for site preparation between the LNWR and GWR stations. The Board accepted with enthusiasm Garraway's suggestion that there should be a joint BR/FR station on the GWR site.

Eaves reported that the cash position was £2,000 to £3,000 better than expected, even without taking into account the Glan-y-pwll easement money, which had already been paid. The current account was expected to be in the black by 17th August, although he thought total receipts were unlikely to exceed the budget and cautioned that there was no capacity for increased expenditure. Routly had approved the expenditure of £16,000 on rail.

Bill Broadbent had met some employees who wished to be represented by the NUR. The Board expressed its fears that recognition of the union, and the prospective legislation that might be imposed on it, might damage individualism and the FR spirit. It was agreed that the NUR should be approached, saying that the Society must be consulted about any agreement. Broadbent duly wrote to the union's local officer putting this view on 12th August, only to be told that the matter was nothing to do with the Society.

When the Board next met on 8th September Garraway's report led on to the subject. Broadbent covered the Society Board's views, *inter alia*, that union recognition was inevitable, that better communication was vital and that the activities of the NUR needed to be contained. Fears that the union could or would oust volunteers were expressed again; it was confirmed that any agreement should refer to the record of 22 years' of Society and Company cooperation; the extant legal agreement between the two bodies; acknowledge the contribution of volunteers and deviationists and require the NUR not to seek to oust the volunteers, respecting their wish to work; recognise the special nature of the FR's business and not seek to impose demarcation; agree to the Society being consulted on health and safety matters; not seek parity with BR and accept the retention of existing negotiating procedures for non-union staff. Regrettably the minutes fail to record the origin of the remark that the problem with the NUR was that it was not used to dealing with profit -making organisations! It was agreed that the Board would meet the staff on 18th September.

A discussion on the 1977 budget revealed the cash flow assumed a surplus of £37,000, of which £25,000 would be allocated to the power station section of the Deviation. Income of £245,000 from traffic would contribute to total income of £452,000, therefore expenditure should not exceed £415,000. The easement money, treated as a windfall, was allocated to the tunnel budget. Ben Ball pointed out that the £6,000 cost of the Afon Cwmorthin bridge had not been budgeted for.

Les Smith had offered the Tremadoc estate £12,000 for the Harbour station freehold and £85,000 for 'the lot', probably the Cob, including the revenue-earning tollgate. The Estate's agent countered with £20,000 for the station site; the Board agreed to go up to £15,000 and to seek a first-refusal option. £13,000 was offered and agreement was reached for £15,000 the following January.

It was around this time that a particularly fraught meeting took place between Routly and the staff. The former was obviously determined that the restoration to Blaenau Ffestiniog would be completed, whilst the latter were concerned about the effects on their employment. The meeting came to an end when Routly, conscious that many staff had previously been volunteers, said: '*You are the only group of employees I know whose jobs are underwritten by volunteers. But for them you would not have jobs at all – and also you are doing work you really want to do – and in any case it's jolly good fun.*'

The last three words really made an impact, although perhaps not in the way that Routly might have expected, and before too long reminders of them, in the form of the initials 'JGF', had spread throughout the Railway: on wagons, locomotives, on the podium when the line to Tanygrisiau station was opened; someone noticed that the three words had 12 letters, so the clock in the Boston Lodge erecting shop even had its numerals replaced by '*jolly good fun*'.

Out on the line the autumn wasn't without incident. On 3rd October Tan-y-bwlch café was broken into and cigarettes and the £15 float were stolen, the latter from a locked drawer. On 22nd November half a mile of the telephone overhead was cut down and removed; Garraway did not record the location and there was no comment about the alarm system that had been so effective in 1970.

A mixed train of skips and other vehicles was derailed at Tan-y-bwlch on 14th November, due to the use of an improper coupling. Finally, on 25th November the Jones road crane overbalanced in Minffordd yard, damaging the cab and parts of the structure.

Good progress was reported on the negotiations with the NUR at the 10th November board meeting. The union had accepted the Railway's position subject to discussion on one point. The union's officer joined the Society!

A projected fare increase of 15% plus 20% for the extra distance to Llyn Ystradau contributed to an assumption that revenue would increase by 25% in 1977. Routly suggested that the budget should be reviewed after six months. Broadbent was concerned about the tunnel costs but Ball thought that estimates would be met when the sale of surplus machinery was accounted for. Costs of the power station bridges would be monitored monthly.

Figures collated at the end of the year showed a reduction in traffic over 1975, down to 372,310 journeys from 397,506 and bookings down to 202,623 from 219,110. The revenue was £190,298 (£176,229) from traffic and £115,129 (£95,024) from sales. Subject to audit the year's profit was £40,000.

When the Board discussed the Company's finances on 5th January 1977 a projected peak overdraft of £145,000 was reported, attributed to the anticipated completion of the power station bridges during the year; a Wales Tourist Board grant was not being paid until 1978, and there was £15,000 needed to buy the Harbour station freehold. The bridges were budgeted at £247,000 and the contract would include the Penlan works too. The current cash flow was £30,000 better than expected.

Progress with the Deviation was indicated by the news from Garraway's report that the first service stock, *Moel Hebog* with wagons loaded with rail, traversed the tunnel bound for Llyn Ystradau on 2nd February. There was still a great deal of work to be carried out before the line could be opened, particularly lining the tunnel with concrete, an unplanned requirement needed to seal fractured rock in the bore. By 1st April Garraway was predicting completion about 26th May, inspection 28th, deviationists' special 29th and public services during the following week!

An agreement had been reached with the NUR over staff representation by the time of the 4th March board meeting. Grievance and disciplinary procedures had also been agreed. A grading exercise had been carried out; a comparison with other minor railways had shown that the FR paid poorly and an increase was to be considered in connection with it.

Eaves reported that budget estimates had been broadly met at the year-end; the cash flow had been £12,000 better than forecast in February. Gross margin on sales had been 28% on a turnover of £120,000; year-end stock levels had been £34,000 and pricing policy, especially on catering, needed reviewing. The tunnel had cost £67,000 to date, with up to £15,000 more to spend. £30,000 of an estimated £40,000 had been spent on the power station bridges and work was ahead of schedule. Late opening to Llyn Ystradau would cost £5,000 in lost revenue. The Wales Tourist Board had paid £7,350 for the inflationary element of the Harbour station works.

Publication of the Porthmadog – Ffestiniog structure plan was the subject of a special report by Garraway on 9th May. The plan said it was most important that the great economic benefits the Railway had brought to Porthmadog were realised in Blaenau Ffestiniog when the FR was restored there.

A major change in the Company's structure was agreed at the 16th May board meeting, attended by Routly, Smith and Broadbent, at which the latter was appointed, via an independent company, Chief Executive for six months. His function was to review the Company's structure and to increase the Company's business with a bonus payable on results against predetermined targets. Garraway was to report to Broadbent under this scenario. No explanation was given for the move but on 18th April 1978, after the Company had advertised for a Chief Executive, Smith informed the Society Board that the Company Board had *'realised that the task of running the Railway overall had become too much for one man'*. Broadbent continued as Society Chairman throughout the period of his appointment as a Company office holder, a situation that caused some disquiet amongst the membership that was manifest at the AGM on 22nd April 1978.

The routine of normal train operations was interrupted twice during the spring. On 27th May a fire that started on the Plas Tan-y-bwlch estate spread up the hillside and crossed the Railway, isolating a down train at Tan-y-bwlch for a while. Afternoon trains from Porthmadog were terminated at Rhiw Goch and a firefighting train was sent up the line. It was 18.15 before the down train arrived at Porthmadog, which it had left at 12.45!

Two days later *Blanche*'s tender derailed at Crossing Bothy when working the return leg of the evening train; it had derailed at Harbour station during the day but no fault was detected. On the second occasion it had just turned dark and the passengers were rescued by *Mary Ann*, which happened to have been stabled at Tan-y-bwlch. It was 03.30 before the train was returned to Porthmadog. Garraway attributed the derailment to a bearing brass becoming dislocated.

The 29th May also happened to be the day that Major Peter Olver inspected the line to Llyn Ystradau. A special train consisting of four carriages and bogie wagon No. 63, with a loading gauge template affixed, hauled by *Mountaineer* was operated. The opportunity was taken to give the deviationists their ride during the day.

The first carriage built on an ex-Isle of Man Railways underframe, No. 117, entered service by 3rd June; as always it was in need of some internal finishing. No. 26 had been painted aluminium and blue to mark the Queen's silver jubilee, at Broadbent's instigation. Explanatory boards were fitted and postboxes, for use by the Railway's letter service, mounted on the running boards – the latter did not last long; the public thought it could post ordinary mail in them and they fouled the loading gauge on some of the curves.

On 12th June the Railway handled its largest-ever single party, when the Leicester Chronicle newspaper took 997 passengers to the line on two trains, one to Blaenau Ffestiniog, the other to Minffordd. A fleet of buses made the link between Tan-y-bwlch and Blaenau Ffestiniog and participants had a single journey on the FR before returning home by the opposing route.

A special train was run on 15th June to Llyn Ystradau in connection with filming for the BBC's 'Go with Noakes' TV programme, a spin-off from 'Blue Peter', the popular children's magazine show. The presenter, John Noakes, had made several visits to the Deviation and the film of this journey, made before the tunnel was technically complete, formed the programme's climax.

The line was formally opened on 25th June and to the public with effect from the 15.15 departure from Porthmadog on 8th July. The day before, *Mountaineer*, still in use despite pessimism about the state of its boiler the previous year, had derailed on the top points at Dduallt, the last time it was scheduled to run-round there. Following the opening Bunny Lewis left the Company and was replaced by Dave Payne.

Apart from one week in October 1976 the current account had been in the black for around 18 months. This position had been helped by a loan scheme, whereby the Society's area groups and other supporters had loaned money to the Company at either low or zero rates of interest. In May and June the loan account reached £170,000.

When he reported to the Board on 14th July, Eaves commented that wages were high (and rising) as a percentage of traffic receipts, that the percentage of the labour force engaged on new works had risen and around 15% of maintenance was deferred, much being pre-1954 arrears. He also stressed the need for additional long-term capital and went on to discuss the prospectus for a proposed share issue.

Broadbent's proposal for a four-band pay increase for non-management staff, equating to 7%, payable from 1st August was agreed. He and Routly would determine increases for management grades.

The rent for the Company's accommodation at Bron Turnor had been increased to £785 for the winter. It was determined to retain it for September and then

With Blaenau in

Back to Blaenau . . .

The Chairman and Directors of the Festiniog Railway Company have pleasure in inviting

to join them in celebrating the completion of the Llyn Ystradau Deviation and the official opening of the line to Tanygrisiau by Mr. Dewi Rees, North-West Regional Manpower Services Director, and formerly National Director of the Job Creation Programme.

Saturday, 24th June, 1978

Programme

11.00	Assemble for coffee at Porthmadog Harbour Station.
11.30	Depart Harbour Station
12.45	Arrive Tanygrisiau: "Golden Spike" ceremony
13.30	Depart Tanygrisiau
13.35	Arrive Llyn Ystradau. Lunch on train
14.25	Depart Llyn Ystradau
14.30	Arrive Dduallt
14.50	Depart Dduallt
15.45	Arrive Porthmadog

Dewi Rees, from the Manpower Services Commission, performed the ceremony that marked the completion of the deviation at Tanygrisiau on 24th June 1978; the initials of John Routly's phrase 'jolly good fun' were insinuated onto the crest decorating the podium. The bared heads in the photograph are deceptive, for it rained heavily throughout.

FR Archives

sight . . .

Left: *The railway was extended to Llyn Ystradau on 25th June 1977, Dafydd Elis Thomas MP cutting the ribbon. To his right are Bill Broadbent and Clough Williams Ellis (in hat). John Routly is in front of the ribbon, in front of him, with white hair behind child, is Les Smith; the Society's Arthur Lambert, with dark-framed glasses, is slightly behind Smith. Michael Schumann stands centre with hands clasped, and to his right, back turned holding hard hat, is Viscount Garnock; immediately above his head is the Society's treasurer Bryan Chicken; standing arms folded against the cutting side, second from left, is company clerk Mark Wright.*

G. Livingstone Evans, FR Archives

Below: *Tanygrisiau terminus in December 1978, with* Merddin Emrys *decorated for the Santa trains.*

Ron Cox, collection Alan Bowler

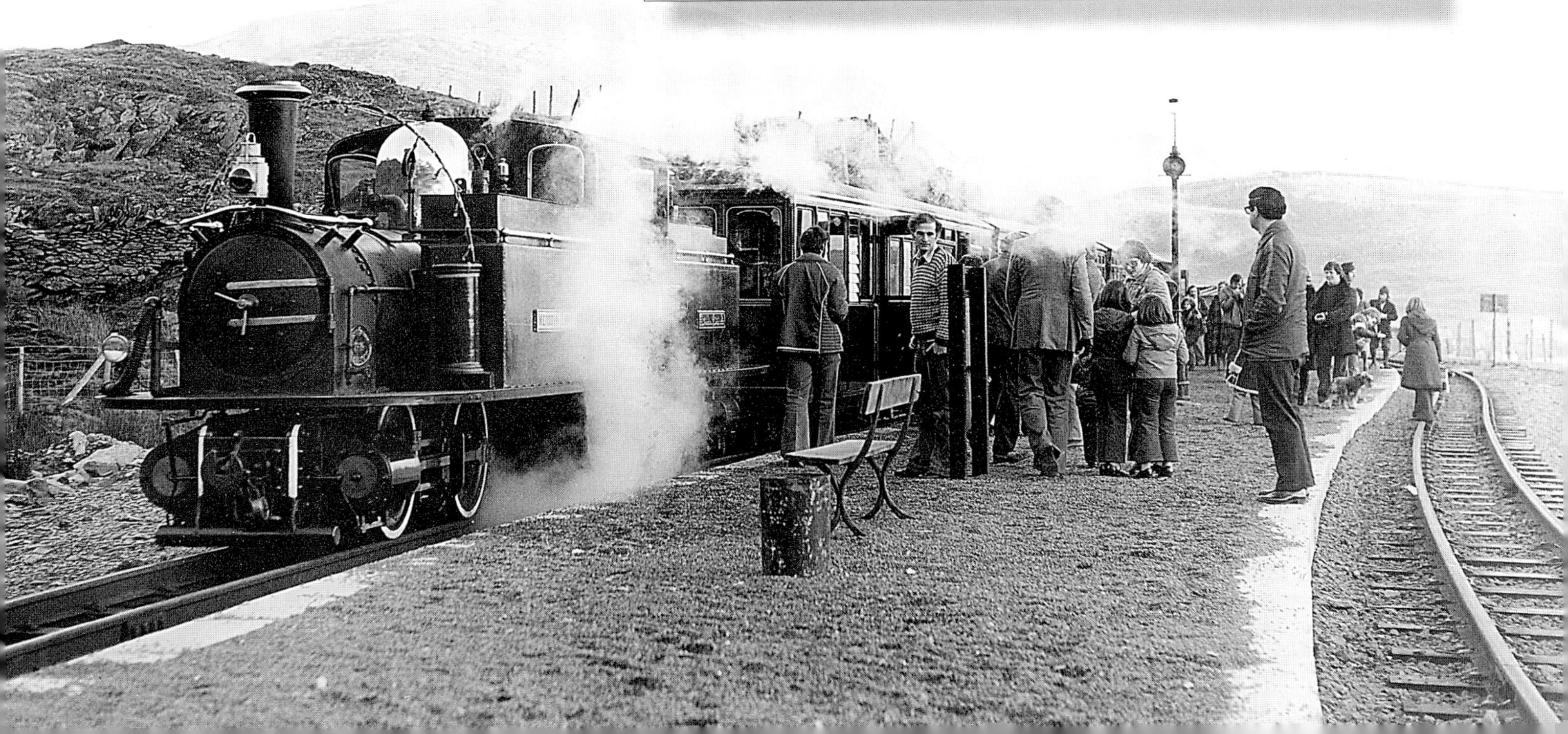

make use of one of Keith Catchpole's cottages for £10 per week.

By 19th August traffic had edged in front of 1976, 267,771 (265,946) journeys, 14,777 (12,871) bookings and revenue was considerably increased: £170,081 (£135,558) traffic, £89,725 (£80,222) sales. Garraway remarked that it was a satisfactory week, the busiest since spring bank holiday the previous year. There was £22,842 in the bank and the loan account had been reduced to £100,000.

Minffordd station house received attention from the building gang when a kitchen extension was built; this followed an intervention by the local authority, which had declared the property substandard because there was only one entrance/exit.

Despite the revenue increase Broadbent forecast, at the 2nd September board meeting, that both traffic and sales were likely to be 3% down on the budget. The use of the Railway as a fairground attraction by children holding a £2 junior society membership granting unlimited travel had been causing concern. Following consultation with the Society, members would in future be allowed three free journeys with subsequent journeys paid for at the privilege fare rate. Talyllyn Railway Preservation Society members would be allowed two free journeys, while FRS members visiting the TR would still enjoy unlimited free travel on that line.

Llyn Ystradau halt was to be closed 'temporarily' in 1978; a temporary permanent-way depot was established on the site and the station was never reopened.

Eaves reported that the projected overspend on the tunnel was likely to be £30,000–£35,000 and on the power station bridges, about £20,000. With the 3% reduction on income expected by Broadbent he called for a new financial strategy. This meeting was, incidentally, held at the Great Northern Hotel, King's Cross, a change from the East India & Sports Club, the usual venue since Francis Wayne retired.

British Rail was the client for contract work carried out during the autumn; following the 1976 drought it had decided to convert the Vale of Rheidol Railway, its last steam operation, to oil firing using the FR design and Boston Lodge manufactured the components.

By the end of the month No. 26 was losing its silver jubilee livery in favour of the standard carriage livery. It was returned to traffic by 14th October.

When the Board met on 4th November it was joined by new member R.H.N. 'Dick' Hardy, a career railwayman and replacement for Ben Ball who had died suddenly on 24th January.

The main item discussed was the Company's organisation. Routly and Broadbent had met Garraway, not present on this occasion, on 26th October and informed him that the Board was resolved to recruit a senior manager to lead and coordinate all functions. A '*chief general manager*' would be appointed, accountable to the Board for all aspects of running the business according to its strategies and policies. Garraway would retain his responsibilities for operating and engineering, and his external links to the Association of Railway Preservation Societies, the Association of Minor Railways and the Great Little Trains of Wales marketing panel, and would report to him, as would the Commercial Manager. The appointee would be responsible for personnel, publicity, general administration, new works and planning. Smith was to see Garraway to explain the Board's proposals.

Whilst it was obvious at the time that there was a problem with Company/employee relations, especially if the move to unionise was taken as an indicator, it was also true that the Board was perceived by the staff as being remote from reality. Equally, since the Deviation had been started the financial position had been getting out of control, even with the eventual payment of compensation by the CEGB, and responsibility for that could be more firmly laid with the Board. It is not obvious which problem the Board thought it was trying to resolve by inserting someone into the chain of command above Garraway, but it is understandable that he was upset by the move. He had given over 20 years of loyal service to the Company and it must have seemed that just when it looked as though the Company's major objective of all that time was going to be achieved, he was going to be pushed out. He must have been devastated.

Staff relations were discussed again on 21st November. Some 39 employees were reported to be members of the NUR and four had joined the Transport Salaried Staff Association, that organisation now requesting negotiating rights. In a discussion Routly commented that the only competitor from the Company's funds apart from staff wages was a small amount for capital objectives. Bank interest represented 5% of the wages bill.

Eaves estimated that the year's cash outflow would by £94,000, as against £99,000 budgeted. Inflow was

Blanche *with a down train on the up line at Tan-y-bwlch in June 1978.*

Alan Bowler

£64,000 over budget due to grants and the expanding travel agency business. There had been overspending on the tunnel, £40,000, and the power station bridges, £8,000. The aim for 1978 '*could*', he said, be to equate inflow and outflow.

This last point was picked up when the 1978 budget was discussed. The objective of repaying loans, £150,000 at the time of the meeting, had been modified due to the overspend mentioned. Arising from the discussion, Broadbent was to investigate the likelihood that 59 permanent staff were envisaged for 1978. Smith was to investigate the building budget; all items would require his approval. Boston Lodge had allowed 15% of its budget as a contingency fund. Discussing shop profitability, an on going concern, Garnock suggested lines should be cut, mark-ups increased and stock reduced; Garraway reported that tea-making was being reorganised. The publicity budget was being increased, including £2,500 for a special train in May for the opening to Tanygrisiau; HRH the Prince of Wales was being asked to perform the opening, with John Noakes in reserve. A grant was to be sought for coach No. 119; if obtained the vehicle should be put back into the budget. It was agreed that there was no immediate need for a share issue.

Peak borrowing was likely to be £250,000 in May, declining to £100,000 in September, compared with £190,000 and £80,000 in the current year. Finally, Eaves expressed concern at the tendency towards over-optimism on revenue budgeting and a freer rein on expenditure in recent years.

When Garraway summarised the year-end's traffic figures in January 1978 they were all increased, as shown in the table, but still substantially down, he noted, on the early 1970s; figures from outside agencies were still awaited.

	1977	**1976**
Journeys	377,839	372,310
Bookings	207,717	202,623
Fares	£243,138	£190,298
Sales	£132,593	£115,129

There was £14,654.48 in the bank and the loan account stood at £190,000.

On the Deviation, MSC personnel had graded the line up to the valve house (penstocks) crossing in December and in January had proceeded towards the Cwmorthin bridge, reported Garraway. He acknowledged the significant contribution made by the Dee & Mersey and Lancs & Cheshire groups in screwing down the track to the Stwlan crossing and aligning it ready for ballasting and tamping. Additional work was needed on the tunnel lining before it would be approved for regular passenger services.

At Boston Lodge *Blanche* and *Mountaineer* received attention to wheelsets. The latter passed its hydraulic test, again! Repairs to Merddin Emrys included attending to the fuel tanks and pipes to eliminate blockages arising from the use of thick fuel. The new *Earl of Merioneth*'s cab was under construction, its dome covers and pan plate skirting and shielding completed; work on its bogies was in hand. Work continued for British Rail on the Vale of Rheidol oil-firing conversion; No. 7 was commissioned in March.

By the time the Board met on 10th February, the loan account stood at £220,000. Eaves had submitted a revised budget in December that was approved. He reported that borrowing was likely to peak at £15,000 more than the currently agreed ceiling. Additional items highlighted were £10,000 on the tunnel, £9,000 wages/stock less a grant, £4,000 for *Mountaineer*'s boiler and £4,000 to deal with the Penlan rock fall; the Company was to buy the freehold of the site for £3,500 including fees. Whilst approval was given to sealing the Deeds for the Harbour station freehold, Smith was to investigate if the payment could be deferred. Concern was again expressed about the commercial department's stockholding; Garraway was to try and get the figure down to £25,000.

Dick Hardy was concerned that Garraway had implemented a pay rise that might have breached government policy. Broadbent had received a letter saying that the Company was compliant in 1977 and would seek approval for the current move, totalling 10%. Routly insisted that the increase was to apply

Vale of Rheidol Equipment Ltd's Orenstein & Koppel 0-8-0 had arrived on the FR, by rail, in 1972. It left by road in 1978.

Geoff Hall, FR Archives

Opposite: *Perhaps* Blanche *was ailing on this occasion in June 1978, when it was double heading with* Upnor Castle *on what does not appear to be an excessively long train.*

Alan Bowler

to basic rates only. Salaries were also to be increased by 10% when approval had been received.

A request for the Prince of Wales to open the line to Tanygrisiau having been turned down, suggestions were sought for an alternative, the Board adopting Freddie Laker as first choice and the Chairman of British Rail, Peter Parker, as second; neither accepted the invitation. Peter Johnson (Society publicity officer, the author) was to handle publicity in the enthusiast press whilst Doug Jackson, of the Manchester-based City Press Agency, was to handle the national and regional media.

By 17th March good progress had been made in the Tanygrisiau station area, with the car park and platforms almost complete.

The Board's relationship with Garraway had not improved by the time it met on 7th April. Routly and Smith had met with him but afterwards he was still uncertain about the best course of action and had taken legal advice. The options put to Garraway were: (a) underpinning with a deputy, or the appointment of a chief General Manager, depending upon the maturity of the candidate, with Garraway agreeing to retire at the age of 55; (b) the appointment of a chief General Manager with Garraway accepting different duties; or (c) redundancy. He did not commit himself; Routly and Smith agreed to meet his solicitor.

The Secretary of State for Wales had been invited to open the line to Tanygrisiau between 9th and 20th June. A special train was to be run from Porthmadog and a golden spike ceremony held at Tanygrisiau.

On 13th April Garraway submitted a report showing the previous 15 years' passenger miles, which he said represented the growth of traffic.

1962	817,118	1970	2,956,423
1963	933,514	1971	3,048,973
1964	1,007,608	1972	3,182,500
1965	1,077,000	1973	3,348,208
1966	1,272,899	1974	3,419,274
1967	1,614,446	1975	3,334,876
1968	2,390,559	1976	3,199,906
1969	2,584,177	1977	3,400,000

Blanche had returned to traffic, its place in Boston Lodge being taken by *Linda*. The latter's wheelsets were removed and sent away for new axles to be fitted. The axleboxes, motion, drawgear and tender running gear were overhauled.

Looking forward to finalising arrangements for the Blaenau Ffestiniog terminus, Garraway had been dealing with the Education Authority concerning the boundary of the school built on the GWR goods yard site. The school wanted screening from the Railway and was not prepared to give up unused land to the Railway's advantage because it would be deemed substandard and ineligible for grants. Garraway took the line, he said, that the Railway did not want a substandard terminus.

On the Deviation, tunnel remedial works were nearly completed and track laying was in progress at Llyn Ystradau and over the Cwmorthin bridge. Garraway and Deviation Project Leader, Michael Schumann, had noticed that the proposed guest list for the opening to Tanygrisiau omitted the names of the Railway's neighbours Rhys and Aneurin Davies and Norman Evershed.

Major Olver conducted an inspection of the new line on 7th and 8th June; he was happy for the official opening to take place on 24th June, subject to certain unspecified stipulations, and was prepared to allow regular services to commence as soon as the tunnel was finished and cleaned. Garraway thought that if volunteer support continued as promised and there were no mechanical problems 24th June could also be the public opening day. He also reported that: '*Major Olver stressed the necessity of completing outstanding signalling work at Tan-y-bwlch and Minffordd and bringing the latter up to standards necessary to cope with present-day levels of traffic. This he feels essential before we get involved in any further signalling schemes.*'

Olver also looked at '*the problems in Blaenau*', particularly with reference to clearances under the Dorfil Road footbridge, and commented that the Railway would be better off terminating at Stesion Fain.

During the week ending 9th June there was a hiatus with the locomotive fleets. *Blanche* failed with leaking crown stays and flue tube and *Merddin Emrys*'s cylinder joints failed at one end. In the works, problems occurred with reassembling *Linda* because the connecting rods had been incorrectly adjusted by a contractor, also described by Garraway as '*due to errors of preparation of components*'. When Linda was tried out a week later its axleboxes ran warm. *Blanche* also needed attention to its firedoor ring before it was returned to service, and *Merddin Emrys*' problem was resolved only after removing its bottom end cylinders.

At this date there was £9,271.82 in the bank, revenue year-to-date was £38,804, compared to £27,236 the previous year, and the loan account had crept up to £260,000.

The public opening to Tanygrisiau took place immediately after the official opening on 24th June, as Garraway had hoped. The event went well, despite extremely heavy rain. There were two special trains, the first for the deviationists hauled by *Blanche*, the second for invited guests hauled by *Merddin Emrys*. Despite the Board's hopes for a celebrity to open the line, it had settled for Dewi Rees, Director of the Manpower Services Commission; there is no comment on this choice in the Board minutes. The first public train left Porthmadog at 15.00.

The following week's operations were very busy, satisfactory according to Garraway, with some '*mammoth*' double-headed trains needed to carry the increased loads. Despite fare increases income rose by £4,000 and sales by more that £3,500, both figures compared with the previous week; the current account was £6,890.87 overdrawn. Business dropped off slightly during the second week of Tanygrisiau operations but whilst the bank account was back in the black, by nearly the same amount, the loan account had gone up to £270,000.

When the Board met on 14th July it agreed, in recognition of the tremendous efforts of all staff in completing the extension, to pay, in lieu of overtime, a bonus of £50 to all full-time permanent staff and a further £10 to supervisory staff. There was some discussion on how and when pay increases could be implemented without putting the Company in breach of government pay policy and thereby putting further grants at risk. 5% had been paid already but 10% had been promised; it was agreed to pay the second 5% from 1st August, the payments to be retrospective to 1st January. Supervisory staff was being transferred to salaries paid monthly, reducing overtime payments; Garraway was given permission to be flexible in agreeing the final amount, presumably if necessary to secure concurrency, subject to Routly's final approval.

Consultants had been appointed to advise on the

Merddin Emrys *takes water at Tanygrisiau on 15th September 1979. The water tank, oil tank, on the far side of the line, and the loop were removed after services were resumed to Blaenau Ffestiniog. The goods shed is all that survives of the original station.*

Author

Company's senior management structure, visiting Porthmadog and meeting Garraway. The Board accepted recommendations made, including the appointment of a Chief Executive. A contract with Garraway was subsequently ratified.

Hardy reported that he had agreed a negotiating structure with the NUR. Three departmental committees were to be set up, covering mechanical; traffic, commercial and administration; and S&T, electrical, building and civil engineering. Two higher levels of negotiation were also to be established. There were to be no restrictions on non-union members dealing with either their head of department or the General Manager. Volunteers could be represented at departmental level if required. The disciplinary procedure had been adjusted to bring it into line with BR practice.

Little was said about the financial position except that the 1979 budget should allow a £25,000 loan repayment and departments should be given an indication of the likely level of resources available, so their expenditure budgets could be drafted within realistic limits.

A period of consolidation was called for before extending to Blaenau Ffestiniog and it was felt to be unlikely that work could start before the end of 1979. City Press's bill of £600 plus £159 expenses for handling and promoting the Tanygrisiau opening was agreed, with Garnock commenting that he hoped that at the next such event the press coverage would be better.

Back at Porthmadog there was a fresh disagreement with the South Snowdon wharf developers, despite Bourne's withdrawal from the scene. This time it was over access. Smith reported that he had threatened that the FR would take action under section 34 of the 1959 Highways Act on the basis that access to the wharf was a public right of way. It was thereby anticipated that the FR's access would be secured because the developers would not want to risk having a public right recognised.

Traffic on the extended line continued to be busy after the excitement of the opening had died down. There was much overcrowding and prospective passengers were turned away, particularly at Tanygrisiau. On 14th July Garraway was calling for more carriages but in the short term radical measures were called for.

The answer, put in hand before the end of the month, was the 'early bird', a 09.00 departure from Porthmadog, Monday to Thursday, half fare for all, diesel haulage and bookable in advance. It was an immediate success and was sometimes fully booked up to two days ahead! A 17.00 departure was added to the timetable too. To encourage passengers originating from Tanygrisiau to travel later in the afternoon cheap fares were made available on the 17.13 and 17.43 departures; they could return on the 19.00.

The week before the August bank holiday 28,958 journeys, 15,355 bookings, were made, generating £24,854.04 traffic revenue and £10,221.98 sales income. Garraway regarded the week as record breaking, although he did point out that 29,000 journeys had been surpassed on two occasions previously, in 1972 and 1973. There was £25,790.70 in the bank and the loan account had been reduced to £180,000.

The financial situation was the first item on the agenda at the 20th September board meeting, held at Combermere Abbey, Garnock's Shropshire home.

Eaves explained that the £50,000 overspent on finishing the tunnel and the power station bridges had been committed after securing a further £30,000 borrowing facility at the beginning of the year. In the event only £20,000 of the additional borrowing had been needed, an achievement made possible by deferring expenditure; the Harbour station freehold was given as an example. '*Unexpectedly good*' summer revenue had compensated for the overspending, restoring the financial position to the level originally projected. The overdraft was presently £140,000. Eaves said that the current facilities would be required in 1979 also.

There was also, he said, no danger of the Railway being liable for tax in the immediate future, as £60,000 was, at around £15,000 per year, currently available to be set against any likely liability. 90% of the Deviation costs had been accepted as '*replacement costs*'.

Eaves went on to say that, in his opinion, the Company should budget for a contingency surplus in 1979 and that £10,000 on loan from the Society should be designated to a specific project. He also suggested that any future Tory government might stop the grants currently available to the Company and therefore every effort should be made to take advantage of the Railway's eligibility in the short term. Eaves and Garraway were to brief Routly and Garnock on the overspending so that an approach could be made to the Wales Tourist Board for a supplementary grant.

Under the heading of '*Chairman's Report*' it was agreed that whilst '*Ff*' should be used in the Welsh translation of the Railway's name, the English version should retain the single '*F*' for the time being.

Garraway expressed concern about the possibility of relations with the local authorities deteriorating because of the difficulty in meeting the Railway's requirement for two tracks between Glan-y-pwll and the proposed new central station. It was agreed to settle for one track but obtain provision for two in the overbridges.

At the next meeting, on 8th November at the National Westminster Bank training centre in London, payment of a £25,000 grant from the Development Board for Rural Wales was reported. The award was for signalling work carried out at Tan-y-bwlch; there had been some concern that it might be lost because the project had not been completed on time.

The headhunting firm being used to find a Chief Executive had submitted an account for £2,000, which was accepted. Legal expenses of £688 had been incurred in connection with Garraway's contract. Garraway reported that it was expected to reduce sales stocks by £10,000 during 1979. Eaves commented that whilst most creditors had been paid to date he anticipated substantial outstanding bills by May if the bank's borrowing limit of £270,000 was to be adhered to.

Routly announced that his legal partnership had taken over the Company's pension scheme and that any commission due to him would be donated to the Trust.

Completion of Glan-y-mor carriage shed and development of works' offices were victims of spending restrictions. Garraway was concerned about the lack of progress on the former but it was agreed that the office space was more important. Carriage No. 120 was to be included in the 1979 budget.

Meanwhile, the building gang was already demolishing the Boston Lodge chimney in preparation for the building of the office extension. Sheffield group members carried out work on the carriage building.

Inside the works the Alco had passed its hydraulic test again and would therefore be available for emergency use. Its new boiler had been completed and tested. *Blanche* was the beneficiary of a winter overhaul; work was proceeding, slowly, on Prince's frames, its tender was being rebuilt and pan plates were being manufactured for it. Pan plates had been made for a Vale of Rheidol Railway loco and dimensions were awaited from British Rail before another could be made. Amongst the carriages, No. 14's interior was being overhauled and work continued on building Nos. 119 and 120.

In his end-of-year report, dated 5th January 1979, Garraway commented that, apart from 26th December, traffic had been disappointing; the weather had been wet and had turned cold, rendering mountain roads difficult or impassable. The running totals for the year, which would be missing figures from coach tour operators and BR, were:

	1978	1977
Journeys	399,402	385,076
Bookings	237,598	213,201
Fares	£342,988	£244,899
Sales	£177,134	£141,434

There was £7,984.31 in the bank but the loan account had now increased to £240,000.

Princess *on the Railway's ERF low-loader at Minfordd yard on 7th September, 1975. The vehicle was maintained and operated by the Society's White Rose area group, based in Leeds.*

M.F. Haddon

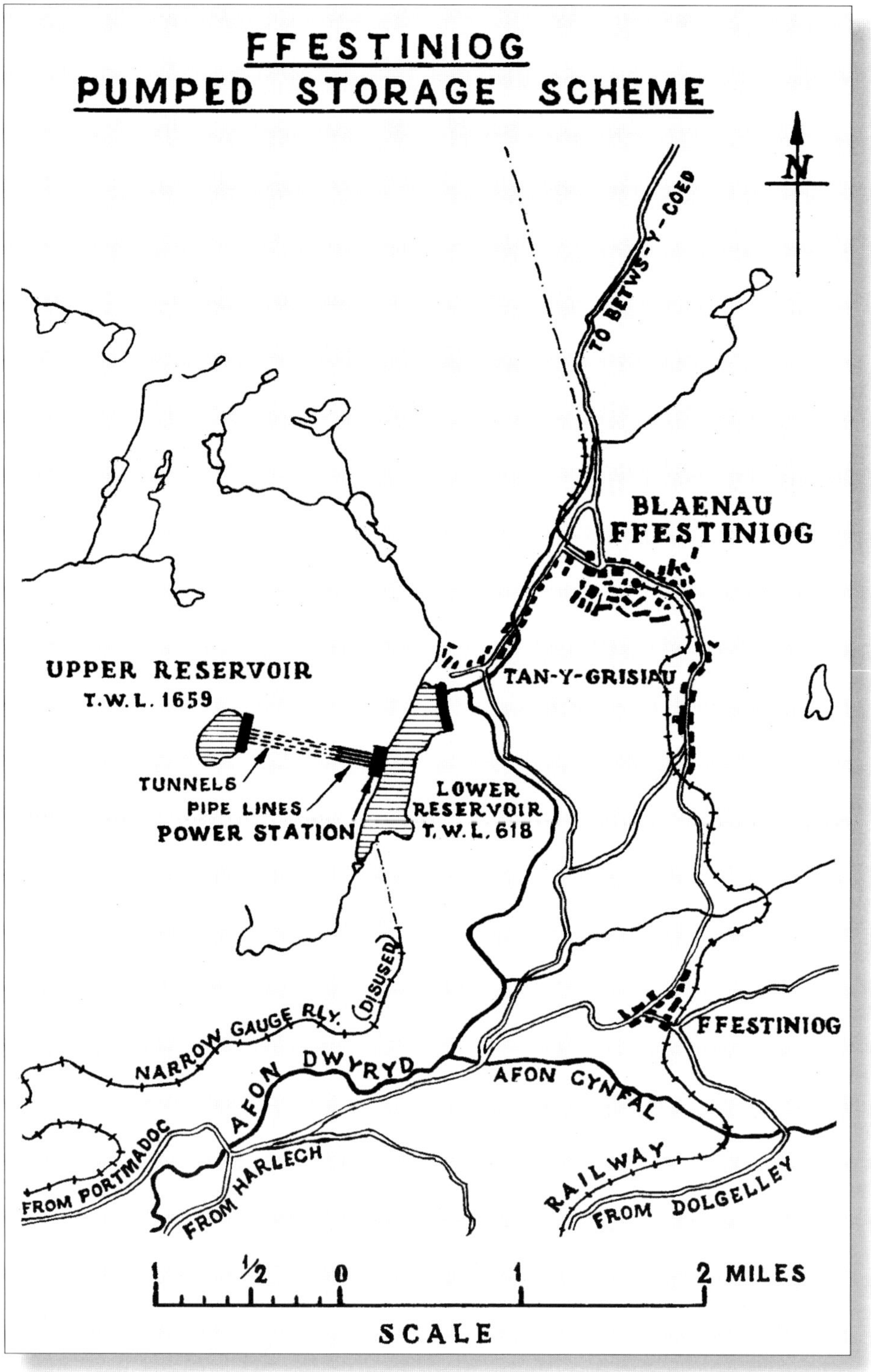
FFESTINIOG
PUMPED STORAGE SCHEME
N
TO BETWS-Y-COED
BLAENAU
FFESTINIOG
UPPER RESERVOIR
T.W.L. 1659
TAN-Y-GRISIAU
TUNNELS
PIPE LINES
POWER STATION
LOWER
RESERVOIR
T.W.L. 618
NARROW GAUGE RLY. (DISUSED)
FFESTINIOG
AFON DWYRYD
AFON CYNFAL
FROM PORTMADOC
FROM HARLECH
RAILWAY
FROM DOLGELLEY
1 ½ 0 1 2 MILES
SCALE

Interlude 2

The Electricity Board and the Deviation

1952~1978

The saga of the appropriated trackbed and its replacement ran throughout most of the period covered by this book. The story has been told before, notably by Brian Hollingsworth in 'Ffestiniog Adventure', but with the benefit of entrée to material not previously accessible, fresh insight may be brought to it. In the interest of continuity the threads of the Deviation story have been brought together here.

On 7th February 1952, Cynon Evan Davies had written to Fred Gilbert:

> *'I should have mentioned in my letter that a notice has been served by the solicitor to the British Electricity Authority (BEA) in connection with the North Wales Hydro-Electric Power Scheme of the intention to apply for an Act of Parliament giving compulsory powers to acquire or use certain lands and/or premises in the counties of Caernarvon and Merioneth. Scheduled to this notice so far as this Company is concerned, are the Tanygrisiau station building; including the house, stores, shed and garden; and in addition the railway track, sidings, footbridges, underbridges, rail bridges, tunnel and airshaft between Blaenau Festiniog and Dduallt, (west side of Moelwyn tunnel); also between Glan-y-pwll Blaenau Festiniog and the track leading to Oakeley Slate Quarries; also to the quarry of Messrs J.W. Greaves & Sons.*
>
> *No steps to object to these proposals have been made. . . . In any event, this Company has no funds with which to pursue any objection by way of petition or otherwise.'*

The public notices about the scheme had been published on 3rd December the previous year. It was intended to provide a network of reservoirs and hydroelectric power stations that would have covered large parts of Snowdonia. Budgeted at £4½ million, it had first been devised by the North Wales Power Company (NWP) in 1944 to reduce the need for coal for power generation. The proposed Ffestiniog station and works envisaged an enlargement of Llyn Conclog and Llyn Cwmorthin and the creation of *'a reservoir in the said urban district to be formed by a dam across the Afon Ystradau at or near the junction of that stream with the Afon Cwmorthin'.*

There would have been two generating stations, one at Conglog, the other located on a 13¼ acre site in the Ystradau valley west of Tanygrisiau. The new reservoir would have been much bigger than that eventually built, flooding both the site of the present Tanygrisiau station at its eastern end and the former reservoir that had powered the FR's 1836 Moelwyn incline at its western end. The Railway was not mentioned in any of the scheme descriptions. It seems that neither NWP nor BET consulted or informed anyone likely to be affected by these schemes during their planning stages.

At least one would-be FR supporter saw a possible silver lining, though. On 21st January 1952, Alan Lowry Porter, in Blaenau Ffestiniog, had referred to it in a letter addressed to *'The Secretary, Ffestiniog Railway Society'*, saying:

> *'As you are no doubt aware, the proposed hydro-electric projects in this district would terminate the existence of the Ffestiniog Railway as a rail link between Blaenau Ffestiniog and Portmadoc, and in view of the adequate bus service, this is not likely to have any effect on the issue. However, I think that the railway has thus a better chance of survival. The owners have completely lost interest, but once they have realised the compensation that will be paid by the BEA for the flooding of and other damage to their property, they will then be more amenable to allowing the remainder of the property to pass into the hands of some body wanting to run it as a railway. The line is now so derelict as to make even scrapping*

A feature of the deviation's early days was use of hand-propelled trolleys to transport materials from Tan-y-bwlch, uphill, to Dduallt, especially before 1968; in this view of a gang at Tafarn Trip project mastermind Gerald Fox wears the plaid shirt. In the background the lighter ballast indicates the renewal of track.

FR Archives

unprofitable and only a labour of love can do anything, but as such labour is forthcoming that presents a smaller problem. A shorter line would be cheaper to run and maintain, and the new lakes would offer a considerable tourist attraction if the line ran as far as Dduallt station, and under the new schemes a road would connect such a railhead with Blaenau and Maentwrog.'

Porter was later instrumental in establishing the Llanberis Lake Railway.

Davies's letter stirred Gilbert into action, for on 11th February, signing himself *'Hon Sec Legal Committee, Ffestiniog Railway Society'*, he wrote to (Blaenau) Ffestiniog UD, Deudraeth RD and Portmadoc UD Councils:

'Ffestiniog Railway Society and the Festiniog Railway.

The above Society, a non-profit organization is very actively engaged in endeavouring to find ways and means in acquiring complete control of the Undertaking, reinstating the track, locos and rolling stock and re-opening the whole line to passenger traffic at least during the tourist season.

It has just been brought to my knowledge by Mr C.E. Davies, the Secretary of the Festiniog Railway Company that they have been served with a notice. Is your Council doing anything by way of protest, if so, I should be glad to hear if we can do anything to assist, as the essence of our scheme rests upon being able to work the whole line and in conjunction with British Railways, to tap the holiday traffic from the North Wales holiday coast resorts, thus bringing trade to your town and revenue to us. . . .'

The recently formed National Parks Commission

said, in its objection to the Bill, that it would prefer all schemes, except Ffestiniog, to be turned down although it was prepared to accept proposed extensions to two existing power stations, including Maentwrog, and an Afon Rheidol scheme. The logic for being prepared to accept the Ffestiniog proposal appears to have been that the landscape was already seriously disfigured by the tipping of slate waste, notwithstanding the proposed site was, when the park was established, within it!

When the Bill received its second reading on 1st April 1952 it came in for some severe criticism; one of its most vociferous opponents was West Midlands MP Gerald Nabarro, later to be involved with the Severn Valley Railway, who said the scheme was extravagant and did not use financial resources to best advantage. Shortly afterwards the British Electricity Authority decided to proceed only with the extensions, at a cost of £$^1/_2$ million, saying that it could not afford the capital investment for the remainder; royal assent was given to the truncated scheme on 1st August 1952. Apart from the National Parks Commission's willingness to accept a power station at Tanygrisiau, which may not have been public knowledge, there was no indication that the BEA considered it to be a live scheme.

Details of a new pumped-storage scheme, and particularly its effect on the FR, had become public knowledge only after the local authorities' responses appeared in the local press in July 1954. In addition to flooding the line between the tunnel and Tanygrisiau, the railway would be breached by the power station access road at the site of the former LNWR exchange station in Blaenau Ffestiniog. This road had the effect of bypassing Tanygrisiau and was later adopted by the Highways Authority.

The Company decided not to object to the scheme in principle but asked for a diversionary route to be provided. It became clear that the BEA did not take the Railway seriously and convinced itself that the restoration scheme was merely undertaken as a means to obtain compensation from it. The FR was unable to gain any substantial support for its objection; Ffestiniog UDC, for example, had written to the BEA *on 28th September 1954 that:*

The first deviation site developed was the embankment approaching the proposed Rhoslyn bridge. The first mechanisation on site was photographed on 31st July 1965.

P.J.G. Ransom

The foundation stone that marks the start of work on 2nd January 1965. Colonel Andrew Campbell (middle distance, wearing a white shirt), Merioneth County Council's solicitor and owner of Dduallt Manor, also possessed a licence to handle explosives; here he starts to retreat from a blast site.

Geoff Hall, FR Archives

'. . . . it was resolved to give full support to the proposed scheme, which it is expected will provide employment for a large number of inhabitants in the area, during its construction, and after its completion. . . . Although my Council are sorry that it will not be possible to have your scheme as well as the opening of the Ffestiniog Railway, part of which is to be submerged under your scheme, they have no hesitation in supporting the hydro electric scheme. They are prepared to give every support possible in order to secure the proposal.'

Merioneth County Council gave its support to the scheme on 19th January 1955, having first objected, although it had been told that the BEA was *'investigating the possibility of permitting the Railway to operate from Portmadoc to Blaenau Ffestiniog.'* Even the local Lodge of the North Wales Quarrymen's Union did not object.

Trevor Bailey wrote to the BEA on 14th September 1954:

'We are extremely disturbed by the appearance in the press of details of the Ffestiniog Hydro Electric Scheme which appears, at the present stage, to be cut and dried and clearly has a very serious effect upon our railway. We were already aware that a scheme of some form was in hand, the first intimation having been given to the Secretary of the Festiniog Railway Preservation Society in the most arrogant fashion by one of your authority's employees engaged on a survey of the area last month, and we have subsequently learned more details from other sources. At no time, as far as we are aware, have we had any official notification of the scheme from any quarter. . . .

It appears to us clear at this early stage that the continued operations of the railway would appear to be an embarrassment to the hydroelectric scheme and we can only assume that it is this fact which has been the cause of the attempt to steamroller a smaller concern out of existence.

You may not possibly be aware that the Parliamentary Secretary to the Ministry of Transport stated in Parliament last May that the Minister had been pleased to authorise one of his inspecting officers to inspect the Festiniog Railway with a view to advising on the measures necessary to reopen it to passenger traffic . . . . it is the intention of this Company to introduce trial running over the portion of railway between Tan-y-bwlch and Blaenau Ffestiniog in the very near future. . . .'

He received a reply dated 20th September 1954 from the Chairman, Lord Citrine:

'I have now had an opportunity of seeing your

letter of the 14th September . . . .

I have spoken on this matter to the divisional controller in charge of our operations in North Wales, and he informs me . . . . the first discussions concerning the authority's proposals were held with the county and local authorities who were likely to be affected, and these preliminary discussions were concluded only on Friday last, the 17th September.

He expressed the opinion, with which I agree, that discussions with these authorities should take precedence over any discussions with other interests, but he assures me that your Company is on the list of organisations next to be informed. There is some little difficulty in this matter as so many bodies have or claim to have interests that it is not easy either to meet them collectively or to decide on the order of precedence in which they should be met. You may take it however that a meeting would have been held with your Company before any final decisions were taken, and that we are quite prepared to explain our proposals to you as soon as a mutually convenient date can be arranged. This meeting can be held in London, if it is of advantage to your Company, and if you would care to suggest a few dates convenient to you, we will do our best to arrange an early meeting at the above offices.'

The attitude that the State utility would first consult with local authorities and others before communicating with those directly affected by its activities was undoubtedly common at the time. The meeting took place on 3rd November 1954 with seven persons from the authority facing Alan Pegler and Bailey. The authority kept the minutes:

'Mr Eccles welcomed Mr Pegler and Mr Bailey and expressed his regret if they felt that they had been treated other than courteously. There was a lot of preliminary work to be done in connection with a project of this magnitude and the view was held that the first approaches should be to the Local Authorities and River Boards after which it was intended that other interested parties would be informed of our proposals. To be perfectly frank about the matter, however, the Festiniog Railway Company would probably have been approached as landowners rather than as a railway company. . . .

Mr Bailey stated that the work of rehabilitation was not such a problem as some people seemed to imagine. Indeed they hoped to be working stretches of the line next year. The major engineering constructions were sound and the permanent way would be renewed stage by stage. Many people were prepared to give their services for nothing in helping to clear the permanent way and some were even prepared, as a hobby, to repair the engines free of charge.

Mr Pegler thought that the Railway might be of

Dduallt, looking towards Tan-y-bwlch and the site of the Rhoslyn bridge in 1966. The new embankment approaches the bridge site from the left and the temporary track rises to meet it.

Geoff Hall, FR Archives

Much of the rock and earth moved over the first three-quarters of a mile of the new route was loaded by hand.

Chris Noel, FR Archives

The Tunnel Mess, located by the entrance to the old tunnel, was brought into use at Easter 1967. It could accommodate up to 24 persons. The track from Dduallt remained in situ to service the mess.

Geoff Hall, FR Archives

some advantage to the authority in carrying materials necessary for the construction of their scheme but Mr Cooper explained that the weight of the equipment and also other factors made this an unlikely possibility and one that would not appeal to our contractors.

A general discussion then ensued during which the following points were made:

(a) the surveyor of the Railway Company had in mind a diversion of the existing route by using the old incline or tramway to the west of the present railway. This might necessitate another tunnel but it would shorten the existing route and it might be that a cutting would suffice. The question of the gradient would need serious consideration. . . .

(g) It would not be a practical proposition to stop the Railway short of Blaenau Ffestiniog as it was essential for the Railway to link up with British Railways in that town and so enable circular tours to be made. The use of motor buses to bridge the gap created by the flooding of part of the Railway was not favoured by the Company.

Mr Eccles then summed up by saying that the Authority were planning to go ahead but they were not sure yet whether they would get the bill. The authority were willing, as good neighbours, to do what they could but he did feel, personally that he would be dishonest were he to say that he felt the Railway Company could make a success of their scheme, having regard to all the circumstances. . . .

Mr Bailey pointed out that it would not be very satisfactory were the Company to be told in 1963 that the Authority were proposing to 'turn on the taps'. He went on to say that the reopening of the Railway was no new idea but had been under consideration for at least two years, and added that the capabilities of the Company and its financial support should not be underestimated. . . .'

The Bill was introduced to Parliament later the same month. The Company's surveyor, C.R. Lowe & Company, wrote to the Authority's Merseyside and North Wales Division on 12th January 1955 proposing:

'. . . . (a) Resiting the proposed dam to a position further north, lowering the water level some 15ft which would bring the Railway line above water level some 150ft from the tunnel entrance, and then to have water-retaining embankments for the remaining 150ft.

(b) To lower the water level by blasting away some of the protruding hillside so as to give a similar, or approximately similar quantity of water but at a lower level.

The extent of work seen from the air in November 1968.

M.B. Dane, FR Archives

(c) Raising the level of the line from the BEA's proposed water level so as to keep the line above water level up to the existing tunnel, making a cutting through the hill and relaying the track above the tunnel and joining up with the present line beyond the southern end of the tunnel.

As regards a diversion of the line, Mr Smith replied . . . . that he thought that, if the BEA were prepared to divert the line, the Railway Company would have no objection.

We have reported to our clients on the above lines, and, as regards the previous paragraph, we understand that they would agree to a suitable diversion. . . .'

The Company's petition against the North Wales Hydro Electric Power Bill was submitted on 4th February 1955; Sharpe, Pritchard & Company was the parliamentary agent. The FR objected to the compulsory purchase powers sought insofar as they affected the Railway and asked either that the Ystradau dam be modified to protect the Railway from flooding or that any works necessary to protect it, including diversion, should be constructed at the BEA's expense. Bailey and John Routly, as Directors, and Bill Bellamy, as Secretary, signed the petition over the Company's seal.

The FR was not the only railway affected by the proposals, for the limits of deviation and compulsory acquisition were quite wide ranging, enough indeed to seal off the access to the former LNWR station at Blaenau Ffestiniog! The British Transport Commission therefore also petitioned against the Bill but was quickly able to come to an agreement and withdrew its objection.

A meeting, held with representatives of the BEA on the 5th February, which the Company's representatives seem to have left under the impression that agreement to protect the Railway had been reached, was considered by the Board on 23rd February 1955. It was reported that the Company's petition against the Bill had been submitted and it was considered that vigorous action would probably have to be taken to oppose the Bill before the next Board meeting. It was, therefore, agreed that Routly, Bailey and Les Smith jointly should be empowered to take any necessary steps in the meanwhile. It was felt that there was a strong need for greater publicity and that this should be sponsored mainly by the Society. Broadbent agreed to consult with Routly with a view to securing the services of influential people willing to assist in this connection.

On 3rd March, Sharpe, Pritchard wrote to the authority's solicitor, Dyson Bell & Company, proposing an amendment to the Bill that would empower a deviation of the Railway, saying that acceptance would result in the FR withdrawing its objection.

The authority denied that any agreement had been made so Sharpe, Pritchard responded by explaining the background, writing on 15th March 1955:

'Adverting to your letter of the 9th March our clients inform us that it was their understanding that at the meeting on the 5th February it was agreed that the most practical proposition would be to divert a part of the existing railway track of the Company which would be flooded if the proposed reservoir, work No. 3 is constructed. In fact the British Electricity Authority's engineers themselves suggested this course and the site, which they had in mind for such a diversion of the railway, was inspected. This was not workable owing to the gradients being somewhat too steep but the engineers were, it was understood, going to prepare a

Linda *propels a train of track-laying materials over the Rhoslyn bridge in 1973. The sleepers to the left of the track were used as a temporary platform for the councillors' visit on 7th July 1973.*

Norman Gurley, FR Archives

revised scheme. If that scheme has now been prepared our clients would be most grateful if you would let us have particulars of it as it is obviously a matter of considerable importance to them and there is not now much time before the Bill will be in committee.'

This was to no avail and the House of Lords Select Committee considered the Bill over four days from 29th March 1955. A feel for the BEA's position regarding the Railway can be had from this extract from the authority's Counsel's opening remarks:

'We say regretfully that this Railway no longer justifies itself and there is no likelihood of it ever being fully maintained as a railway in the future. In those circumstances it would not be a wise way of spending public money to deviate its railway so as to avoid it being submerged. If the Bill goes through, the Railway Company will, of course, have a full claim for compensation. If this Bill means that the Railway must close down, then the Company will get compensation. It is important that we should have that point firmly in mind. No individual will suffer loss, and the compensation will cover the prospective value that the Railway might have if my learned friend is right in saying that it can be reopened.'

Given that the authority later made clear that it considered the Railway undertaking to be worthless the claim about compensation being payable may be considered fatuous.

Pegler gave evidence the next day. During examination he accepted that the practical way of preserving the Railway, providing the scheme went through, was not by alteration of the reservoir site but by deviation. He told the committee that the

The annual convention, the end-of-season dialogue between Company and Society, for several years included a journey towards the head-of-steel for the delegates, an incentive for participation. Blanche *was in charge on 5th November 1973.*

Norman Gurley, FR Archives

main attraction of the Railway was its connection with standard gauge lines at each end, enabling circular tours through Snowdonia to be made. He said that he thought the line could be made operable for much less than the figure of £25,000 quoted.

Faced with the BEA's scepticism the Company had devised another clause for Alan Pegler to promote; by this means it hoped to establish its bona fides, proposing that if the Railway was opened for passenger traffic to Tan-y-bwlch by 1st January 1958, as certified by the Ministry of Transport, a deviation should be provided at the authority's expense. There followed some interrogation to establish the Company's value, compared to the cost of the proposed Deviation, it becoming obvious that not only was there was no business plan for the Railway but that Pegler was not even briefed with the latest accounts.

During his examination of Pegler's evidence the FR's own barrister suggested that most interest in the Railway might be shown by '*old gentlemen*' or children, as well as '*quite ordinary, middle-aged persons*'! In his summing up the Railway's barrister observed that in a scheme costing some £15 million the estimated £123,000 required to divert the Railway was insignificant, regardless of the Railway's value. In his cross-examination of Pegler, the BEA's QC tried to establish if the FR would be anything like the railway portrayed in the film '*The Titchfield* [sic] *Thunderbolt*'!

A consultant from Freeman, Fox & Partners gave evidence that a large number of sleepers were in bad condition, the drainage was defective at some points, three underbridges required reconstruction and footbridges were in a bad condition, some stone embankments were weak, in need of reconstruction – obviously not restricting himself to the section affected by the power station – and '*considerable expense would in any case be required to put it into good condition*'. He also gave evidence about a deviation route. No plan was produced but the estimate provides a few clues.

It was estimated that the new formation from Tanygrisiau to the power station would cost £9,000; the power station viaduct – £17,500; the extra cost of constructing the power station while the Railway was operating, including temporary timber trestles – £11,000; the new formation from the power station to the north tunnel portal and at the south end of the tunnel – £9,000; new 2,200ft tunnel – £55,000;

Temporary trackwork in place while the tunnel's south cutting was excavated. The 1836 incline is behind the site.

FR Archives

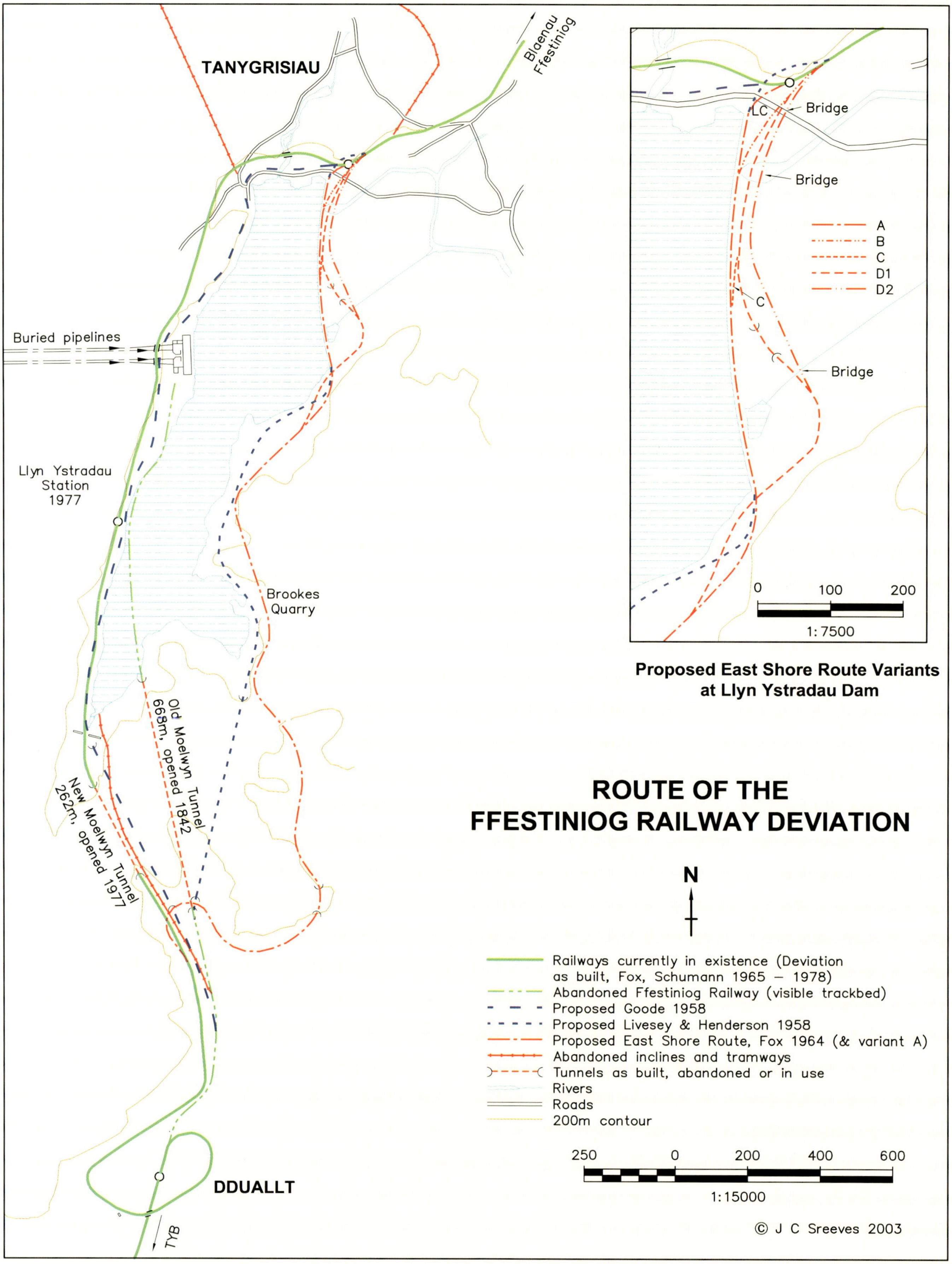
TANYGRISIAU
Blaenau Ffestiniog
Buried pipelines
Llyn Ystradau Station 1977
Brookes Quarry
Old Moelwyn Tunnel 668m, opened 1842
New Moelwyn Tunnel 262m, opened 1977
DDUALLT
TYB
LC
Bridge
Bridge
A
B
C
D1
D2
C
Bridge
0 100 200
1: 7500
Proposed East Shore Route Variants at Llyn Ystradau Dam
ROUTE OF THE FFESTINIOG RAILWAY DEVIATION
N
Railways currently in existence (Deviation as built, Fox, Schumann 1965 – 1978)
Abandoned Ffestiniog Railway (visible trackbed)
Proposed Goode 1958
Proposed Livesey & Henderson 1958
Proposed East Shore Route, Fox 1964 (& variant A)
Abandoned inclines and tramways
Tunnels as built, abandoned or in use
Rivers
Roads
200m contour
250 0 200 400 600
1: 15000
© J C Sreeves 2003

Above: *The Smalley excavator was the first item of new plant to appear on the deviation. An appeal for Green Shield trading stamps was launched to buy one but a visiting plant hire contractor heard of the appeal and offered to supply the machine on free loan. It was photographed on 20th August 1973, on the occasion of its formal presentation to the project.* Below: *Setting the first shots to bore the tunnel, August 1975.*

Both Geoff Hall, FR Archives

The pilot bore seen on 7th November 1976.

Author

To handle the stone emerging from the tunnel an extensive range of sidings was developed at its south end, where the stone-crushing equipment was sited.

FR Archives

culverts – £5,000; fencing – £2,000 and new track – £14,500; making a total of £123,000. He estimated that it would cost at least £25,000 to put the rest of the Railway into running order again; possibly as much as £50,000, depending on the standard of the work.

The Authority put pressure on Pegler to say how the Railway's revival and restoration was going to be financed. It also wished to have the previous year's balance sheet produced as evidence, something the FR's barrister knew would serve no useful purpose. He covered both points in his closing remarks:

> *'My learned friend asked for a balance sheet of last year and I have got it in my hand. I confess that it is quite unhelpful to anybody for this reason. It was dealing with the year ending 31st March, 1954, and as your Lordship knows, Mr Pegler only came into the matter in August. If your Lordship would like to look at this document you are very welcome to do so, but I want to be perfectly frank about this. The way in which the capital in the future is to be raised has not been decided. . . .*
>
> *It is sometimes said that you do not employ an elephant to hatch a pheasant's eggs. When the elephant seeks to nestle down upon the eggs it is not with the object of doing good to the progeny, and I ask your Lordships to say that it is not reasonable that the British Electricity Authority at this stage, for the purposes of stopping our enterprise, should make us give and tell your Lordships exactly how we hope - not how we have got - to raise capital. In my submission that is unreasonable and an unfair thing to do, and I would ask your Lordships' indulgence in saying that it is a reasonable thing that this matter should not be pursued any more by my learned friend. It is obviously meant to be harmful to us, and in my submission it is so. . . .*
>
> *I should add that the way that BEA have dealt with us has been extremely cavalier. They appeared to be going to discuss the matter fully with us. It was left on an entirely agreeable and friendly basis that they should submit to use the line of deviation. Your Lordship has seen that correspondence. Then it suddenly closed down. . . . The negotiations, which were going on perfectly happily and on a perfectly friendly basis, are suddenly closed down by someone fairly high up in the British Electricity Authority, and no more negotiations take place. . . .*
>
> *For the purposes of this case I am obliged to take . . . . the view that I cannot challenge what they say, namely, that deviation is the only possible way, but with great respect I should be very surprised, if this were put upon them, if they did not consider whether it might not be cheaper to build, for example, a wall across what will partly be mud flats on the extremities of the reservoir, so as to narrow the extent of the reservoir and save my railway altogether. Yet this was something that we never discussed together because they closed down on the negotiations. I perfectly agree that I am not in a position to challenge their engineers, but if they assert that their method of deviation is more expensive, then my answer is that it may be but is that the only way of dealing with it? Engineers can do remarkable things when they are pressed. . . . I shall ask your Lordships to consider whether people, who have been as cavalier as they have been in dealing with the negotiations, should not be asked to consider whether there is not a cheaper way out when it comes to the point of deviation when you know that by merely putting on the line an extra 100 yards of tunnel, which is quite unnecessary, they add £8,000 to that cost. It may be by making some other arrangement they may make some other change upon their figures. I am obliged to take the matter as it stands, and I am saying that I am entitled to have it, provided I show my bona fides at the end of the period. That is what my clause is designed to do.'*

One of the Authority's engineers, engaged in planning the transmission route to Hawarden, had given evidence that he was ready to *'fall over backwards'* in being cooperative and sympathetic to those affected, prompting the FR's QC to comment:

> *'But so far as my Company is concerned, I do not mind whether he falls over backwards. What I want him to do is be slightly forthcoming, and that he has certainly failed to be.'*

The BEA's QC cast doubt on the FR's intentions when he said:

> *'It is the practice of Parliament when statutory undertakers are suggesting to Parliament that they are going to be able to do this,* [raise capital to build the deviation] *. . . . that the committee*

The Ffestiniog goes under . . . .

Left: *The concreting train at tunnel north, 1977.*

Eric Hubbard, FR Archives

Opposite top left: *Drilling inside the tunnel.*

Paul Francis Photography, FR Archives

Right bottom: *The tunnel south portal photographed when newly completed early in 1977.*

Geoff Hall, FR Archives

Below: *With Robin Daniels at the controls, the battery loco emerges from the tunnel with a wagonload of stone.*

Geoff Hall, FR Archives

The Atlas Copco mine loader was a compressed-air-powered machine designed to load skips in confined spaces; it was used to clear rock from the tunnel.

Geoff Hall, FR Archives

Drilling the rock on the site of the north cutting for the new tunnel. The breach in the 1836 dam can be seen behind the machine operator.

FR Archives

should be satisfied whether from the financial point of view there is any real likelihood of them being able to do so. Your Lordships may recollect the speculative railway days of the last century when that sort of thing was always one of the things very closely considered, and another was whether the promoters were really bogus people - I am not suggesting that these people are engaged in this business. But that commonly happened in the last century and the committee looked into those matters with the greatest care.'

He also commented that the Authority could not be faulted if an Ordnance Survey map it had seen indicated that the Railway was disused; surely it should have checked the position for itself.

The objection was fruitless and the resulting Act contained no protection for the FR. The irony is that the Electricity Authority must have spent considerably more than £123,000 on legal fees combating the FR's claim before it was settled.

The BEA's attitude towards the FR seemed to be that it was functioning for the state, by extension therefore, for the people, and could therefore do what it wanted; it was probably not untypical of a state-owned authority at the time. It was undoubtedly this attitude that eventually produced legislation that allowed such matters to be dealt with by public inquiries, appeals and counter-appeals.

So far as the BEA was concerned the FR was all but worthless and could not be further reduced in value if a part of it was removed. It clearly thought that the mere existence of its scheme would inhibit the FR's restoration to Blaenau Ffestiniog and refused to take the Railway seriously. For its part, the FR did not help its own case by not only not having a business plan for the Railway but by not having even attempted a financial case for the Deviation; the BEA's advisers and barristers must have found it very easy to score points at the FR's expense. Whilst no one really knew if the revived FR would be a success or not, a plan could have been produced based on pre-war figures, with post-revival figures being brought in, and extrapolated, as they became known. As it will be seen, it was not until 1963 that the Railway and its assets were valued and its maintenance liability established; then the situation began to improve.

On 20th April 1955, the Board agreed that Routly should prepare a case for counsel regarding the compensation to be claimed but a month later it was agreed to defer a decision on a petition, presumably on the grounds of cost, although Pegler's appearance at the select committee can't have given much cause for confidence.

By 14th June, a meeting with Lord Citrine was being sought, whilst '*in the meantime, no concessions should be made to the CEA to enter upon this Company's land*'. Pegler and Routly met Citrine before the 9th August Board meeting; it had been agreed that both sides should appoint a valuer for the purpose of deciding the compensation to be paid for the severance; T.S. Dulake was appointed to represent the FR.

In pursuit of the information needed by Dulake, the Board agreed, on 5th October 1955, to pay Robert Evans £21 for his services in connection with a statutory declaration of the Company's ownership of its land and buildings, identifying them on a large-scale Ordnance Survey map. This effort came to naught, however, when Citrine wrote to Pegler on 5th December 1955 saying that the two parties' valuers could not reconcile their views and that as the Authority's advisers could not accept that '*equivalent reinstatement*' was applicable, he thought no useful purpose would be served by continuing the discussion.

The Railway was served with a notice to treat, covering the line between Tanygrisiau and the tunnel, by the Authority on 2nd February 1956, the notice of entry being served the next day. Bellamy acknowledged these notices on 17th February 1956, reserving the right for the Company to remove any fixtures and machinery, including track, which had not been removed when the Authority took possession.

When the Board met on 17th April 1956, it agreed that '*it is most necessary to improve the appearance of the whole Railway in order to strengthen the Company's case*'; that negotiations with the CEA should be treated as strictly confidential and that the Company should maintain to the outside world its definite intention to complete the link to Blaenau Festiniog and to establish public interest in its completion.

The Electricity Authority's valuer, at Vigers & Company, wrote to Dulake on the same day, rehearsing the valuation of any compensation, saying this could be achieved by either of two ways, in both cases assuming that the Railway was not a commercial venture. Firstly, this would be by estimating the value of the land, associated houses and properties and of the wayleave rentals received from slate companies: only a small sum, he thought, especially if the quarries ceased to

Back on the operating railway . . . .

Linda *passes the down colour light home signal as it leaves Penrhyn in the 1970s.*

Alan Bowler

Whilst the deviation was progressing, the rest of the Railway functioned as normal. Here, under the watchful eye of the signalman Merddin Emrys *leaves Porthmadog during 1977. The groundframe 'horticulture' was the result of the efforts of Charles King, then the station cleaner.*

Geoff Hall, FR Archives

No. 26 in its 1977 Silver Jubilee livery, and Mountaineer *await departure.*

Geoff Hall, FR Archives

use the line in Blaenau. Secondly, the Railway could be valued before and after the severance, where he said that the best guide to pre-severance value was the £3,000 paid by Pegler for 85% of the share capital with an allowance for restoration work carried out. He said he was prepared to recommend that the Electricity Authority pay more than the Railway's cash value but that it would be wasting time talking about reinstatement.

In consequence the Board decided, on 25th July 1956, to prepare a series of alternative schemes, each to be surveyed and costed.

The following year the Authority was pushing for the claim to be settled, leading to a decision, on 11th April, that:

> *'Every possible step should be taken to establish that no part of the Railway undertaking has been abandoned but that the Company has every intention of reinstating the whole Railway. In particular it was decided that all timetables issued by the Company must include the names of all stations up to Blaenau Ffestiniog, showing the words 'services temporarily suspended' against those stations to which services have not yet been resumed.'*

Following receipt of a chase-up letter Francis Wayne wrote to the CEA on 27th June 1957:

> '. . . . *Our delay with this matter has been entirely due to our desire to see a fair and proper solution to this problem. This in turn implies that the diversion, which the Company has always been, and still is, determined to build, will follow the best route and will be built at minimum cost.* . . .'

The Board discussed the issue on 1st July 1957 concluding:

> *'The alternative routes were discussed, it being emphasised that a new tunnel in the neighbourhood of the old incline, on which the Company's detailed survey was based, would be operationally more difficult than the former route owing to the limitations emphasised by the steeper gradient.'*

Details of these proposed early alternative routes have not as yet come to light but the Company's preference seems to have been for a line to the west of the reservoir.

A scheme for the Royal Engineers to undertake all earthworks except the tunnel over a period of about three months was considered on 1st August. Colonel Evill, of the 24th Engineering Group, who was prepared to do this work, also examined the possibility of the RE building the tunnel and laying the track!

The Company's plans were being reviewed by its consulting engineers, Rendel, Palmer & Tritton. However, by 5th February 1958, Livesey & Henderson had been appointed to this position; Henderson had been at Cambridge with Routly. Brian Hollingsworth recorded that the Railway rarely received a bill from his company.

Vigers & Company's Walter E.A. Bull was eventually pressed into forming an opinion on the Railway's value, writing to the CEA's legal department on 11th February, 1958 '. . . . *I do find myself in some difficulty in giving you a valuation.* . . . .' and valuing the property taken at £1,345, made up of £1,000 for Tanygrisiau station building; £150 for the shed adjoining; £120 for Blaenau Ffestiniog station shed and £75 for 3.76 acres (at £20 per acre).

After speculating that volunteers would be unable to maintain 13 miles of railway he went on to guess that the value of a fully restored line might be worth £15,000 as '*a plaything for a rich enthusiast*' and concluded that the line between the long tunnel and Blaenau Ffestiniog might, therefore, be worth £5,000.

On 9th April, 1958 he wrote again, correcting an error he had made, including property in Blaenau Ffestiniog twice, reducing the valuation by £120. His calculation on the amount of land involved varied from the authority's engineer because, he speculated, he used a map, where the thickness of a line could be critical, whereas he assumed the engineer had the benefit of a survey. He accepted the latter's figure of 2.96 acres and valued it at £60.

When the Board met on 26th April 1958 it was reported that L&H had resurveyed the Company's route and had found an alternative, which might be viable. The report was submitted on 30th October 1958 (see Appendix 5 Vol. I).

Towards the end of 1958, Routly informed the Board at a meeting held on 30th December, the CEGB made an application to the Lands Tribunal for a ruling on the applicability of rule five regarding reinstatement. In due course the hearing was set for 2nd July but was then postponed because of the

The route behind the power station – pouring concrete for the concealed penstock bridges in 1977. The site compound can be seen in the distance, slightly left of centre.

Norman Gurley, FR Archives

Right: *Given the restricted clearance for access clearly demonstrated in the previous photograph it was perhaps not too surprising that on one occasion an error of judgement led to a lorry overturning in June 1977.*

Norman Gurley, FR Archives

In advance of the tunnel's completion work was started on preparing the formation alongside Llyn Ystradau. Blaenau Ffestiniog plant contractor and quarry owner Eifion Williams loaned equipment and labour for use on this section during 1975.

Geoff Hall, FR Archives

A temporary bridge was built across the culvert through the dam that powered the incline on the railway's original route. Rock from the tunnel's north cutting was transported over the bridge to form an embankment beyond it.

Geoff Hall, FR Archives

Laying track between the two level crossings at Tanygrisiau.

Geoff Hall, FR Archives

CEGB's failure to comment on the FR's deviation proposals and its statement of agreed facts, the latter having been submitted as long ago as 27th January.

At its meeting on 11th July 1959 the Board considered correspondence between L&H and Freeman, Fox, the CEGB's surveyors, in which the latter had suggested that to obtain the necessary clearance above maximum water level in the reservoir, the gradient of the diversion route should be increased to 1 in 62, instead of the 1 in $67^1/_2$ suggested by L&H. The Board had accepted a variation from the line's traditional 1 in 80 ruling gradient with reluctance, having been told that to insist on it would involve unreasonable cost and it did not want to be unreasonable in its demands. The Board wanted the engineers to examine if the gradients could be eased through the proposed new tunnel, saying that 1 in 62 would be impracticable.

It was nearly a full year later, on 11th–13th May 1960, that the FR's claim for reinstatement of the route appropriated by the CEGB was dealt with by a hearing held under the Lands Tribunal Act of 1949. Chairman Sir William FitzGerald MC QC visited the FR on 30th May, saying he wished to get an idea of the atmosphere it generated. He was given a ride up to the Moelwyn tunnel on *Taliesin*, the first time the locomotive had been there for about 21 years, Garraway reported; the locomotive of choice, *Prince*, had shed a piston cotter on the way up.

The Company claimed the cost of building a deviation around Llyn Ystradau was £180,000; Pegler and Wayne were the FR's witnesses. During the course of the hearing Pegler said that he knew about the earlier hydroelectric scheme in 1951 but he thought that it had been dropped, saying, '*I took the view, rather naively perhaps, that lightning never strikes in the same place twice and if there had been a scheme and it had been dropped presumably one was absolutely safe.*' As the CEA had not declared its intention to take note of the National Parks Commission's declaration that it was prepared to accept a power station at Blaenau Ffestiniog, although in fact Tanygrisiau, Pegler's attitude was hardly surprising.

Once again much play was made of the existence of a map indicating the FR as an 'abandoned railway'; this was surely a little disingenuous as when the North Wales Power Company first prepared its Ffestiniog scheme in 1944 the FR was operating most weeks, even if not daily; the prospect of revival cannot have been unknown to the Authority when the pumped storage scheme was being developed either.

British Railways' Chester-based District Traffic Supervisor, Harold Young, was examined on the use of the FR to BR. He explained that the FR restored to Blaenau Ffestiniog would be beneficial to BR runabout ticket-holders and that BR badly wanted the traffic.

Wayne was able to cite the case of the Loch Aber power scheme, circa 1930, where the Aluminium Company had, in raising the level of Loch Triog by about 25ft, also paid for the diversion, including a short tunnel, of the adjacent West Highland line for about a mile. He suggested that these works were carried out without, so far as he was aware, any suggestion being made that any extra benefit was required to accrue to the LNER.

In his decision, released on 18th July, FitzGerald summarised the background to the case, rehearsing the legal arguments put to him. He closed by saying that he thought the CEGB's QC was on sound ground to argue that the cost of reinstatement in relation to the value of the undertaking was a relevant consideration and that if that cost is out of all proportion to the value then it would be unreasonable to order reinstatement. In conclusion he said that taking Pegler's acquisition of the controlling interest for £3,000 and the most optimistic estimate of the Railway's growth he was forced to conclude that the cost of the proposed deviation would be a sum larger than the total value of the business and, that being so '*Rule 5 of Section 2 of the Acquisition of Land (Assessment of Compensation) Act, 1919*' was not applicable.

So that, on the face of it, was that. The business was not worth enough to justify the investment. Wayne, at least, must have known that his claim that in the tribunal's rules the word '*may*' should have been interpreted, as 'must' was unlikely to prevail; on the other hand he knew that any compensation payable on the basis of the land's value and interruption to the business would be minimal. On the CEGB's behalf, MacKenna had certainly been unreasonable when he asserted, contrary to evidence, that the FR would only go ahead with the Deviation if it won its claim.

The Board met immediately after the reading of the judgment with Wayne and the legal team in attendance. An Appeal on a point of law was possible, the Board was advised, and it decided to pursue that course of action.

At the Appeal hearing, heard by Lord Justices Ormerod, Harman and Pearson, the CEGB's barrister claimed that:

> *'A claimant for compensation was entitled to full compensation for his pecuniary loss. That was the fundamental principle . . . . The principle of reinstatement could not apply where the cost of reinstatement exceeded the value of the business. It was an axiom that the part could not be greater than the whole. The Railway Company could not be in a better position than if the whole business had been taken from them. Their business must be judged by commercial standards.'*

The Company might have wondered about the bench's neutrality when Harman asked '*Why should the British taxpayer finance the hobby of running a few little puff-puffs?*' adding '*All this is curiosity, that's all.*'

The appeal was dismissed on 19th December but it was not until 2nd February 1962 that the judgement was published. The next day, the Railway Inspectorate's Colonel Woodhouse submitted a note for file, requesting that Colonel McMullen and Colonel Robertson, the Chief Inspecting Officer of railways, see it. '*I think this is the end of it*', he declared briefly.

When the Board met on 7th February 1962 it agreed that no further purpose would be served by an Appeal to the House of Lords. Wayne was asked to arrange informal discussions with the CEGB to ensure that each side appreciated the viewpoint of the other and to find common ground. It was further agreed that there was no question of abandoning the hope or the intention of restoring the link to Blaenau Ffestiniog,

The Company's options were considered at the 7th March Board meeting. It was agreed to discuss the feasibility of other routes with L&H and to continue discussions with the Royal Engineers on construction and accepted that it was highly desirable that the route on the west side of the reservoir should be considered further. Wayne was also to try and sell any rock extracted during construction! A minute of the 24th July Board meeting makes it clear that it was still expected that the CEGB would pay for a diversionary route to be built.

As approaches to the CEGB had got nowhere by 20th February 1963, the Board agreed to prepare another claim for the Lands Tribunal. Smith reported that in spite of the recent weather a survey party of nine had been working in the hills and had discussed several routes between Dduallt and Blaenau Ffestiniog and was working out possible alternatives.

There was a breakthrough at the 9th April meeting, when Smith reported on a survey carried out by Gerald Fox and friends. This was the now-infamous spiral route. A report on the financial implications of restoring the line to Blaenau Ffestiniog was to be prepared by Wayne and accountant Martin Barradell (see Appendix 9 Vol. I); Smith was to obtain detailed plans and estimates of the cost of restoring the line by the proposed route.

On 22nd May, the Board recorded its appreciation of Fox and his assistants' work. It was decided to accept the route with a ruling gradient of 1 in 80 and with a short, curved tunnel of about 90 yards, the gradient being compensated on curves and all curves being transitional. The final decision to go ahead was deferred until a detailed estimate had been received; Smith was authorised to spend up to £100 in obtaining an expert opinion on costs. It was agreed to initiate enquiries with the Ministry of Transport with a view to obtaining a Light Railway Order for the route. In order to assist in the final decision the Secretary and Accountant were asked to recast the accounts of the Company on a more reasonable basis which would show the true assets and liabilities (see Appendix 7 Vol. I); it was agreed to accept their suggestion that the accounts should include as an asset the claim for severance and disturbance and that the estimated cost of the new route should be treated as a liability.

By 18th June, Smith was proceeding with negotiations for the purchase of the land. Fox's report was completed in August. In common with many documents produced by those involved with the Deviation, it seems, it was undated (see Appendix 8 Vol. I).

Writing on 6th September Wayne, probably trying to avoid too much bureaucracy, told Colonel Robertson '*this is not a question of lengthening the Railway so much as restoring another section*'! Against it Robertson scribbled '*No. It is a deviation on a completely new alignment.*'

On 27th September 1963, Smith reported that L&H had had discussions with Fox and had studied his detail survey. They were still checking the details, but would write a confirmatory letter in due course. Regarding land purchase, Wayne reported that a Mr Evershed had offered to sell the first section of land for a nominal consideration, and Smith expressed the hope, very optimistic it transpired, that negotiations that he had initiated with the owners of Glan-yr-afon and Dol-y-moch would reach a reasonable outcome. It was also reported that Robertson was to inspect the proposed route shortly and that no difficulty was anticipated over the grant of an LRO – more optimism. On the same date the CEGB's North Western Region told Fox that:

> '*The Board are unable to consent to siting of* [the] *railway on the west side of the power station and it would appear that the only feasible route left would be to construct the railway across the Tanygrisiau dam or alternatively, downstream of that dam.*'

The conditions the Board laid down for the use of the dam were, from the Railway's perspective, quite onerous. The CEGB required access to vehicular and pedestrian traffic at all times; the train service could be suspended at any time by the Board, without notice, for operational and/or maintenance reasons; any maintenance attributable to the Railway Company would carried out by the Board at Railway Company expense; the Railway would be responsible for diversion of any rights of way!

Colonel Robertson visited Allan Garraway on 29th September. On 11th November he wrote to the Assistant Treasury Solicitor, A.H. Kent, for advice:

> '*As you will know the Festiniog Railway Company lost part of their line by flooding when the CEGB built the Tanygrisiau dam. The Company are trying to get compensation out of the CEGB and one of the arguments they are using is that they propose to build a deviation line connecting the two severed parts of the old line and need the money for this purpose. How the Company will fare vis-à-vis the CEGB we do not know but negotiations are proceeding and, in the meantime, the Company have asked us for approval in principle of the new line . . . .*
>
> *We are not too happy about the Festiniog Railway Company's plan to extend their railway in this way. They have a very narrow financial margin as it is and are sometimes tempted to work unsafely to keep the traffic moving and the passengers' cash coming in. . . . What we feel we must guard against is the possibility that they may exhaust all their financial resources in extending the line and have nothing left to run it safely.*

A test train to the temporary terminus at Llyn Ystradau was hauled by the tunnellers' battery electric locomotive, May 1977.

Norman Gurley, FR Archives

We therefore officially sought enlightenment on how the Company proposed to run and maintain the railway when extended . . . . The first reply to this . . . . was pretty airy-fairy . . . .

Of those concerned Mr Broadbent has his feet closest to the ground and I have written to him. . . . This will I hope elicit an official reply . . . . which may give us what we need. In the meantime I shall be grateful for your advice on:

(a) Whether the LRO if made could apply to the deviation only, have no connection with that of 1923, and have a number of safeguards not present in the 1923 order built into it.

(b) What the position would be if the Company obtained compensation from the CEGB and this was conditional on the deviation being built but in our view was insufficient to cover the cost of the actual line plus the increased stock etc. needed to work it safely.'

Kent replied on 15th November:

'As regards question (a) one would normally amend the LRO of 1923 under Section 24 of the Light Railways Act 1896. There is no reason why the Order should not be drastically amended to incorporate new safeguards and the only trouble is likely to be the opposition of the applicants.

As regards question (b) I doubt whether you can do much about the final arrangements of the applicants. The position as I see it is that it is for [you] *to lay down your safety requirements and leave it to the applicants to find money. In an extreme case you might threaten to refuse to make an Order on* [the] *ground that the obligations under it could not be carried out by the applicants but you might possibly find it difficult to do this in this case.'*

The Board met at Pegler's home, Forest Lodge, Blyth, on 18th November, discussing particularly various alternatives for crossing the main access road at Tanygrisiau; the provision of double check rails or other safeguards at certain points; whether it would be cheaper and simpler to buy from Mr Evershed the area of land to be enclosed in the spiral east of Dduallt station, thereby reducing the cost of fencing and farm access; and details concerning the LRO and planning permission.

Wayne's and Baradell's report was dated 19th November (see Appendix 9 Vol. I). With great cordiality Woodhouse submitted his comments on it to Robertson with a handwritten report dated 15th November, surely an error. His lack of enthusiasm for the FR to both win its case against the CEGB and to complete the restoration to Blaenau Ffestiniog is all too obvious: *'I've studied the Festiniog submission with much care. . . . I must say I still look on their forecast as exceedingly optimistic . . . .'*

The Board met again on 25th November and considered the Wayne/Baradell report in depth (see Appendix 9b Vol. I).

Robertson submitted his report to Colonel Denis McMullen, who had inspected the FR in 1954 and who had recently been promoted to be Chief Inspecting Officer of Railways, on 25th November 1963.

'. . . . the Festiniog Railway Company officially asked us for approval in principle to the issue of a LRO for the construction of a new deviation line to connect up the two parts of their railway below and the Llyn Ystradau reservoir. . . . The cost, excluding land to be bought, is estimated at £135,000 and they hope to get this in compensation from the CEGB. . . . It seems quite clear . . . . that they want the approval in principle from us for use as a bargaining factor in their negotiations with the CEGB.

I have consulted [the] *Treasury Solicitor and you will see . . . . that we cannot really question their ability to find the money – I think it follows from what he says that we must also accept that they can do what they claim they will be able to do by way of maintenance, restoration of engines, construction of coaches, etc. We cannot withhold a LRO on grounds of safety if they can successfully negotiate all the other pitfalls of land purchase, public inquiries, etc. . . . As regards use of the new line we can write into the amended LRO our usual paragraph that the deviation shall not be used for the carriage of passengers without the permission in writing of the Minister first being obtained: we can then make it quite clear that the Minister would not give permission until he is satisfied that the new line has been properly built and that proper resources for safe running over the line as a whole have been assembled. . . .'*

On 4th December Wayne wrote to McMullen with a formal application for a LRO, although it was not in compliance with the rules, and a response to queries on the Wayne/Baradell report.

McMullen replied in January 1964:

'. . . . I am to stress that at this stage it is not possible to say in advance whether or not the Minister would grant such an application. . . . I am however able to say at this stage that the technical details of your proposal have been considered very carefully by the Railway Inspectorate and that no objections to it are seen from the point of view of public safety . . . .'

He closed by asking to see a copy of the draft LRO when available. Wayne wrote back on 21st January assuring McMullen that *'every aspect of this operation has been considered most seriously in every possible detail'* and enclosing a copy of the report he and Baradell had prepared and a copy of L&H's summary estimate (see Appendix 10 Vol. I).

During the Inspectorate's internal deliberations the costs were considered in some depth, complete with advice obtained from British Railways' Southern Region's civil engineers. The latter thought L&H had underestimated the quantity and cost of excavating in peat on both counts by a factor, in cash terms, of three and that the cost of building the tunnel would be £12,000 rather than £9,250. BR SR also thought that PW costs had been underestimated by 25%; Robertson thought they had got this wrong – perhaps it was the price of new materials, as used on the SR?

On 8th March, Garraway reported discussing the missing bridge over the Dolrhedyn road at Tanygrisiau with the Clerk to Ffestiniog UDC. He said the bridge had been removed by McAlpine's, with FR permission, during construction of the power station. The Council later, with Smith's verbal approval, removed one abutment and realigned the road. Whilst McAlpine denied all knowledge of its involvement, despite Garraway supplying details of correspondence, the Council accepted responsibility for it, pointing out that if the bridge was to be replaced on the original alignment the road would be passable only by pedestrians and small vehicles. The Clerk suggested that the bridge site could be bypassed by using the CEGB's Stwlan dam road. Garraway said he had told the Clerk that as the Railway was planning a deviation the Council should develop plans for the bridge whilst it still had plenty of time. In the event this Council did nothing and the matter was left to Gwynedd County Council to resolve after 1974.

When the Board met on 27th October it was reported that Norman Evershed and his brother had offered to donate about four acres required for the first section of the spiral at Dduallt. The Board considered Fox's proposals for establishing a volunteer civil engineering group to begin work on construction. In approving the proposal it was agreed that the group would be responsible to Garraway, with whom Fox would work out all the details; the proposed expenditure should be incorporated into Garraway's budget, to be presented at the next Board meeting which could also consider suggestions for an appeal for funds. '*In the meantime the Company would probably consider making available between £300 and £500 for setting up accommodation and purchase of tools.*'

On 15th November, Garraway reported that Fox had had a party at work on Colonel Campbell's barn, at Dduallt Manor, which was to provide volunteer accommodation, also on collecting materials from the old tunnel for use at Dduallt, and digging out in the cutting below Dduallt station.

By the time of the 9th December Board meeting the route on the land, offered by Evershed, had been staked out. Addressing the need for works trains to deliver materials to site about 200 sleepers had been replaced above Tan-y-bwlch. The Board agreed to complete the purchase of the land and other formalities as soon as possible; to allocate £1,000, plus any donations received for the 'Blaenau fund' towards immediate expenditure on the new route, including up to £250 for the purchase of the land; and to proceed as rapidly as possible with the new construction.

The first sod was cut formally, near the site of the present Rhoslyn bridge, on 2nd January 1965. Some boundary walling was demolished and used as fill in the bog, leaving Garraway to comment the next day: '*I query though whether it is a good move to start removing our already deficient boundaries until things are a bit more finalised.*' This was the start of an ongoing battle of wills over control of the Deviation; despite the Board's decision in favour of Garraway the deviationists wanted to run things their own way and only deal with the Board. On 14th February Garraway was complaining about a report submitted by Fox that he had received via Wayne, saying '*I understood from the Board meeting that Gerald Fox's organisation was to be under my control, and that the allocation of labour as between new line and existing work was to be my responsibility, in which case I feel that much of this report is of purely internal interest . . . . in any case I feel that the report should have been submitted to me and from me to Les Smith, who is the Director responsible. . . . I feel it very important that the proper procedure is very carefully adhered to with Fox or my position will be completely intolerable.*' It was in fact several years before a reliable modus operandi was established between Garraway and the railway builders.

The delay in settling the compensation claim was discussed when the Board met on 24th February. With $8^1/_2$ years elapsed since the CEGB had broken the route, the Board decided it was time to push for a settlement. Rhys Davies of Glan-yr-afon and Aneurin Davies of Dol-y-moch were to be offered £100 each for the land the Company needed; the latter was also to be offered a cash payment of £15 to settle other outstanding matters. Planning permission was held up awaiting a discussion between Clough Williams Ellis, the Company's landscaping consultant, and the CEGB's consultant; the delay seems to have been with Williams Ellis. The Board confirmed again that Fox was to be responsible to Garraway.

Garraway recorded the first use of explosives during the week ended 17th April and by 12th May about 60 yards of formation had been completed.

The Company's plans continued to exercise the Railway Inspectorate, with Robertson once again writing, on 1st June, to the Treasury Solicitor: '*I cannot find that in the draft LRO . . . . any attempt has been made to fulfil the two conditions . . . . which were conditions on which RI were prepared not to object on safety grounds, and thus not to kill before birth, the proposal to re-link the two severed portions of the Festiniog Railway. . . .*' He further emphasised yet again that the two conditions, that services were not to be run without the Minister's approval and that

The first steam train to Llyn Ystradau was hauled by Mountaineer *on 28th May 1977; the same formation was used for Major Olver's inspection the next day.*

Norman Gurley, FR Archives

the Railway should be subject to Section 1(1)(a) and (c) of the Regulation of Railways Act, were essential in the LRO.

In summarising the Inspectorate's position, Robertson clearly demonstrates his loss of confidence in the FR. His claim to have '*caught*' the FR running passenger trains without use of continuous brakes might not have been strictly true, although it is clear that the Inspectorate suspected that *Linda* had been used without them in 1962 there is no evidence surviving that it knew this was the case. His concern about the use of the Tanygrisiau – Blaenau Ffestiniog section without inspection overlooked that all previous re-openings had been preceded by an inspection carried out at the Railway's request.

By 1st August Fox had work in progress on two sites.

The Board, on 13th October, resolved that '*the common seal be affixed to a three-year tenancy agreement from Colonel Campbell of part of his house at Dduallt for accommodation for civil engineering group volunteers at a rent of £35pa from November 1964.*'

The planning application for the remainder of the route had not gone smoothly, as the preferred route, by a bridge in front of the lower dam, had been rejected due to the CEGB's objection on the ground of visual amenity. Another route – the minutes do not give more details but it might have been on the top of the dam – had been approved, but as the CEGB had introduced post-application restrictions on it the Board decided to appeal against the refusal.

On 24th October *Prince* hauled a works train to Dduallt; directors and others witnessed blasting and

On 15th June 1977 a special train hauled by Merddin Emrys *was run to Llyn Ystradau for filming by the BBC's 'Go with Noakes' TV programme; it was photographed emerging from the tunnel.*

Norman Gurley, FR Archives

inspected the workings and the mess and helped to load a skip.

L&H inspected the works during the latter part of the year, with particular regard to the steps needed to ensure the stability of foundations in soft or waterlogged ground. The consultants' report was accepted on 24th January 1966 when the Board agreed to take steps to ensure that the works met with their approval. With this in view the Secretary was to write to Fox to expedite his suggestions for future working.

The latest report from Dduallt, to Garraway and forwarded to the directors on 6th February, told of an average of 20 truckloads of rock dug out every week, with a maximum of 40 during one weekend. It stated that improvements were being made to the tipping arrangements to comply with the consulting engineers' requirements and also referred to the drains which were dug across the peat, as well as the method of blasting out the peat and filling with stone. By 21st February 590ft of work had been done.

On 28th March, Les Smith informed the Board that agreement had been reached with the CEGB's surveyor on part of the claim. The solicitors were to be instructed to apply for the sums concerned without prejudicing the main claim. The draft LRO was expected to be published in April, with Smith confidently expecting it to be made in May! Ffestiniog UDC was concerned about the delay in restoring the Railway to the town and offered to help; the Railway asked for help in dealing with the landowners, Rhys and Aneurin Davies; the latter was to prove extremely intransigent, probably because he had lost his home at Buarth Melyn to the CEGB. Garraway undertook to supply a compressor to the work site by Easter.

Smith reported, to the Board on 23rd May, that he had arranged for all the trees and shrubs at Dduallt to be retained. Rock would be taken from the land at the back of the trees to make an additional track, leaving an island platform.

Chairman John Routly shares a bottle of wine with, from left, Michael Schumann, Bob LeMarchant, Pete Hughes, Robin Daniels and Dafydd Elis Thomas MP on 25th June 1977.

Liverpool Daily Post, FR Archives

It was reported that, during the course of very friendly informal discussions with members of Ffestiniog UDC, they had expressed the hope that the FR terminus would be at the old GWR station where there would also be room for a car park and a bus station, which might be on the former FR station site, while the FR would now run into the former GWR goods yard. It was noted that this was a further development since the minute of October 1964. The Board expressed complete willingness to consider whatever proposals were made by the UDC and to conform as far as possible with its wishes. The new proposals would have been extremely simple to carry out had it not been for the CEGB access road and the new BR line, but it was assumed that the extra cost arising from the imposition of the new factors would not fall on the FR.

The LRO application had been made by the 25th July Board meeting, any objector having until 31st August to lodge objections. Notice of planning appeal had been given in respect of the planning application; it was withdrawn later in the year, without prejudicing the Company's right to make a fresh application at a later date. It was agreed to seek the cooperation of the CEGB with a view to agreeing a reasonable route for the line in the vicinity of the dam.

Aneurin Davies had agreed in principle that he was prepared to sell the land needed for the new construction, but a price had not been agreed.

Broadbent emphasised the importance of the civil engineering work being of a standard acceptable to the consulting engineers with a view to minimum permanent way maintenance.

Garraway reported on 4th September:

'The last quarterly report tells that there is a trend from using pneumatic rock breakers to drilling and blasting as the workers get more proficient. On site 1 wall demolition has been completed, track lifted and the footpath made good. Working the quarry to supply rock for the embankment has now begun after difficulties in getting track materials available. The site is far more complex than any yet worked, but will enable end tippers to be loaded at once. The peat is being blown from the embankment by toe shooting and this will become the main working site in future. Progress on site 3 is slowing down as this is becoming more difficult to work and it is hoped to continue it over Rhoslyn bridge when this becomes practicable. Two unfenced shafts over the [old] *tunnel have been covered with wire grills and a TA unit is looking into the possibility of blowing them up as a final solution. Work has also commenced on the building of a private siding* at Dduallt mess for Colonel Campbell's use, as he has acquired two private locomotives and we are making arrangements for him to have running powers down to Tan-y-bwlch, working his siding as an intermediate siding with an intermediate staff instrument and training Colonel Campbell as a qualified FR driver. Lack of accommodation at Dduallt is at times proving difficult, similar to the problem elsewhere.'*

As the number of volunteers willing to help in construction frequently exceeded the accommodation available in the hostel at Dduallt farm, the Board noted on 26th September that Smith had made enquiries regarding the use of temporary huts.

Two letters were sent to the CEGB on 17th and 18th November asking for its valuation for part II of the Company's claim and for an assurance that the necessary land for the new route would be available. No reply to these letters had been received by the time the Board met on 28th November; Smith was therefore to proceed with the LRO application for the route from Brookes Quarry to Tanygrisiau.

A meeting took place between the Railway, represented by Pegler, Routly, Smith and Garraway, and the CEGB at the power station on 6th January 1967. The CEGB was represented by H.W. Golding, station superintendent, C.N. Marston, Plant Superintendent, E.R.M. Roberts, District Lands and Wayleaves Officer, R. Savinson and J.S. Rose, solicitor's department. During the meeting the CEGB laid down the ground rules by which it was prepared to allow the FR onto its property. A further meeting was held on 9th January, with Garraway and Fox representing the Railway and Golding, Marston and Roberts the CEGB, when the rules were refined following a site inspection.

The 30th January Board meeting recorded considerable progress. The big news was that the LRO inquiry had been adjourned and, a draft protective clause having been agreed, the CEGB had formally withdrawn its objection. Agreement was also reached with landowners Rhys and Aneurin Davies, whereby the Company agreed to provide three level crossings, two footpath crossings, five cattle creeps of 4ft each

* The turnout was installed by 11th September.

and one overbridge of 4ft at agreed points; provisions regarding method and programme of work; payment to Aneurin Davies of £750 and £85 costs for land and payment to Rhys Davies of £400 and £45 costs for land. The Board agreed to push for the LRO to be made and Smith was to start work on the Brookes Quarry – Tanygrisiau order.

Relationships with neighbours were a concern and it was agreed that a record of complaints be kept and reported to the Board.

Members of the civil engineering group had offered to lend £400 to finance the building of additional hostel space near Dduallt. It was agreed that the money should be repaid not later than August 1968.

In February Garraway reported 'encounters' with Aneurin Davies on the deviation land; it was subsequently reported that Davies had refused to ratify the agreement made at the adjourned public inquiry.

On 13th March Garraway was instructed to see that full normal precautions were made to give warning when blasting took place at Dduallt.

When the Board met on 8th May Routly reported that Aneurin Davies had still declined to implement the agreement reached at the public inquiry. The matter was being actively pursued, he said. It was anticipated the Rhys Davies would withdraw his objection and complete the sale of his land; it was agreed that in this event the Company would contribute 15 guineas (£15.75) to photographic expenses incurred by him and permit him to remove the timber on the strip of land to be conveyed and to transport the timber from the site to a road.

The Board agreed to give Fox a centenary medal as a token of the Company's appreciation of his work.

Concerns about blasting and other procedures on the Deviation were evidently justified when, on 13th August, Garraway reported that:

'The deviationists had a large blast in the cutting below Dduallt and have filled it with about 50 tons of rock burying several of their tipper wagons and, I believe, damaging some that can be seen. They have also blown down fences in the vicinity. I understand that this work is in connection with the foundations of the bridge. I do trust that the whole question of this bridge has been cleared by the consulting engineers and that proper supervision is being given to the work and that they have not just started it without reference to anyone.'

The explosion also damaged Rhoslyn house, aggravating the already fragile relationship with its owner, Aneurin Davies.

At the 13th September Board meeting it was noted that the CEGB had still not replied to Smith's letter of 17th November 1966 despite reminders. The Company's solicitors were therefore in touch with the Lands Tribunal to try to speed up proceedings.

Smith reported that it was hoped to have Dduallt station ready for the laying of the run-round track by February. A compressor had been acquired for use on the Deviation and this was at Boston Lodge awaiting repair – six months after Garraway had been told to supply it! In the meantime, Smith had authorised the hire of a compressor until the General Manager could arrange for the repairs, if necessary making use of a local garage to do the work. Smith would examine the problems of future maintenance. The delivery, and operation of, the compressor to the Deviation was apparently quite a saga, which is only hinted at in the minutes and Garraway's reports. On 24th September he reported:

'. . . . there was a derailment of the compressor etc on Tuesday just above Garnedd tunnel which damaged the trackwork and the compressor and apart from the time spent in rerailing it and getting it back to Portmadoc, further ripping out cannot take place until the machine can be got through to Dduallt.'

The compressor was on-site by 1st October.

The CEGB replied to the 17th November letter on 21st September that '*the Board dispute the whole of part II of the Company's claim*'. The FR Board, on 17th October, expressed surprise and deep concern that a reply in this form should have taken over ten months when the claim had now been over 11 years awaiting settlement. It was agreed that a reference to the Lands Tribunal should be progressed as rapidly as possible.

Work over the winter was suspended for $2^1/_2$ months due to an outbreak of foot-and-mouth disease. Resumption of work highlighted a disciplinary problem, as Garraway reported on 25th February 1968:

'We have arranged with Colonel Campbell to

The concrete-carrying wagon being loaded at the penstocks road crossing before ferrying its load to the tunnel for shotcreting purposes, early 1978.

Norman Gurley, FR Archives

make use of his loco between Garnedd and Dduallt whilst the line is blocked by work at Garnedd. On Friday night, 23rd February, the usual train was left by the bottom portal of the tunnel, consisting of No. 1 van, the compressor tool wagon, compressor, No. 63 and Colonel Campbell's engine, the starting handle of which was locked away; a stop block was placed on the track below the van, which was also locked and braked. The quarrymen had four holes to drill, after which the compressor was to be taken to Dduallt for use on the loop.

When the PW staff and quarrymen arrived on Saturday morning they found the compressor, No. 63 and the engine missing, and these were found at Campbell's siding, having been taken there during the night.

It is bad enough trying to prevent vandalism and interference with equipment, but this sort of thing by our own people is criminal; the train they took had an unbraked heavy compressor wagon at the rear, which, if it had become unhooked, would have caused considerable damage. Work at the tunnel and getting the compressor to Dduallt was considerably delayed, and Colonel Campbell is very annoyed at the misuse of his engine and it being started by illicit means.

The incident was reported to Mr Broadbent, and whilst I appreciate the deviationists' transport problems, it is behaviour like this incident, the wanton carelessness in damaging Rhoslyn and other incidents over the last few years which has caused so much friction with these people.'

The LRO was made on 9th February and came into

effect on 21st. It described the authorised railway as:

> *'A railway (No. 3) 1 mile 7 furlongs and 9 chains or thereabouts in length commencing by a junction with the principal railway at a point immediately to the north of Dduallt station passing thence round the hill to the east of the said station crossing the principal railway at a point 10 chains or thereabouts measured in a southerly direction from the point of commencement thence proceeding in a westerly, northwesterly and northerly direction to Coed Dduallt, thence in a northeasterly direction towards the principal railway thence in a northerly direction along the west side of the principal railway thence in a northeasterly and easterly direction crossing the Moelwyn tunnel forming part of the principal railway thence in a southeasterly and easterly direction to Clogwyn thence in a general northwesterly and northerly direction to and terminating near Brookes quarry on the eastern side of Llyn Ystradau.'*

It would have been much easier to have said '*a railway (No. 3) 1 mile 7 furlongs and 9 chains or thereabouts in length as indicated on the deposited plan by the line coloured pink*'! Railway No. 1 was the 1832 route and railway No. 2 the 1923 junction railways, legally two railways, connecting with the WHR. The order permitted the abandonment of the spur between Dduallt and the old Moelwyn tunnel and included compulsory purchase powers. No part of railway No. 3 was to be used for the public conveyance of passengers without the permission in writing of the Minister of Transport and the Company was required to comply with any conditions that might, from time to time, be prescribed for reasons of public safety. The remarkable thing about the order is that it permitted the Railway to be built to, effectively, the middle of nowhere, when there was no indication that the FR would ever have either the resources to build onwards or be able to agree a route to Tanygrisiau. It might be that the LRO application was the trigger the CEGB needed to become amenable to the railway's approaches; was it coincidence that it was not too long after the Order had been made that the CEGB became agreeable to the idea that the deviation be routed along the most practical route, behind the power station?

The Board agreed on 12th March to press on with the second LRO application as soon as the route to be used could be settled in detail. An undated report dealing with the options for crossing the dam was probably produced sometime earlier (see Appendix 11 Vol. I).

A messy job! Concrete spraying in progress, 17th March 1978.

Norman Gurley, FR Archives

The relationship between the Deviation and the operational railway was defined more clearly at the 7th May Board meeting, when the Board agreed that there was to be no rail connection between the FR running lines and the deviation tramway; that no vehicles were permitted on the running lines unless approved and authorised by Garraway; that rail access to Dduallt was only by means authorised by Garraway and operated by approved drivers; there was to be better liaison between permanent staff and the civil engineers' group; and a clerk of works or project manager was to be appointed. The latter, and not more than three section leaders, were to form the communications channel with the General Manager.

On 20th June the Board was notified that Rhys Davies had agreed to implement the agreement reached at the public inquiry and draft contracts were awaited. It was hoped to arrange entry onto the land in about three to four weeks. Aneurin Davies was not prepared to implement his verbal agreement and notice to treat, compulsory purchase proceedings, would therefore be served as soon as the purchase from Rhys Davies was completed.

Garraway was asked to contact Mike Schumann, who had become Project Engineer, with a view to ensuring that all future traffic movements connected with the Deviation construction conformed to regulations.

The relationship had clearly improved by the 10th September Board meeting, when the Board *'put on record their very favourable impression of the work done on the Deviation. In particular the General Manager expressed the warm appreciation of himself and the permanent staff of the cooperation received by John Grimshaw* [a deviationist].' The Board regarded as urgent the provision of adequate compressed air for drilling, and the acquisition of more land.

During the autumn the CEGB was asked again to consider diversion of the railway to the west of the reservoir.

Arising from representations from the civil engineering group it had become clear that the work on the construction of the Deviation had become an increasing administrative burden on the Company, the Board noted when it met on 3rd November. It was therefore agreed to divide the work between two directors. Smith was therefore to be responsible for: all matters relating to the route, the acquisition of land, adherence to LRO conditions and insurances. Gerry Fiennes was to be responsible for safety, supplies and services, liaison between the Deviation and railway staff, budgets and making other resources available if required.

Early in 1969 preparations were made for the construction of Rhoslyn bridge, with Garraway reporting, on 5th January, that materials and supplies had been ferried up from Tan-y-bwlch to Dduallt.

Conveyance of a plot of land owned by the Davies brothers had been completed by 11th February, but access had only been obtained after a £60 bond in their favour had been obtained.

It was noted on 10th June that the Board had received a report from Schumann setting out proposals for constructing the Deviation on the Fox route up to Gelliwiog and thereafter by the west side of the lake. It was reported that:

> *'It was appreciated that Mr Schumann's proposals would have considerable advantage over the proposals for crossing the valley on or near the CEGB dam, and that up to 1958 all discussions and proposals for the Deviation had been based on the west side route. It was, however, recalled that at some time in 1958 (the year in which the Company reopened its passenger services to Tan-y-bwlch), the CEGB had decided to oppose any proposal to build the Deviation to the west side of the reservoir. Furthermore, Mr Smith reported that the CEGB have recently confirmed by telephone that they would refuse to allow the use of this route. The decision of the CEGB to oppose the west side route had been taken in 1958 without consultation with the Company and no explanation had been given to the Company either in 1958 or since then. It was therefore regrettable that Mr Schumann's proposals could not be taken any further at the present stage. It was hoped that the CEGB would give at least some explanation of their opposition.'*

On the same occasion it was reported that the Lands Tribunal had agreed a total price of £675 for the purchase of $1^1/_2$ acres of land from Aneurin Davies.

Routly consulted, he reported on 13th September, the accountants Peat, Marwick & Mitchell on the loss-of-profits calculations. PMM introduced new elements into the calculation, including deferred maintenance, extracting details from the Company's records to calculate an appropriate multiplier.

Early in October the project was subject to vandalism when the tool store was broken into, the mess water pipe broken, and jubilee track and six wagons were tipped over the embankment.

Despite being rebuffed over the question of using the route behind the power station as recently as September, the Board considered Schumann's route again when it met on 11th November, the minute recording that '*This route had been considered some years ago but the CEGB have only recently agreed to discuss it as a result of an approach to their Chairman. The route had been discussed recently with Mr Golding (CEGB Station Superintendent) and Mr Marston his deputy, both of whom agreed that they saw no operational difficulties from the CEGB viewpoint.*' This was tremendous news for the FR, especially as no really practical route had been determined either on or in front of the reservoir dam.

Garraway met the Railway Inspectorate's Major Olver on 28th November to discuss the tunnel, after which the latter reported:

> '. . . . *In particular Mr Garraway proposes that there should be ample clearance between the train and the top of the tunnel to enable smoke and fumes to be rapidly dispersed. He hopes that by this method it will be possible to eliminate the necessity for providing ventilation shafts. I stated that we could not make a decision on this matter until we had seen plans showing a detailed proposal for the tunnel.*'

Chief Inspecting Officer Robertson responded:

> '*My first reaction is that we should not accept a tunnel and the length without ventilation shafts – with steam traction on a steep gradient.*'

No ventilation shafts were built.

The revised compensation claim, £70,537 plus interest, had been lodged on 24th December 1969, the Board was informed on 18th February 1970. Ffestiniog UDC had given agreement in principle to the west side route; plans for an LRO were awaiting planning approval, with every indication of support from the UDC, the planning authorities, and the landscaping consultant; land purchase was awaiting the agreement of Aneurin Davies; negotiations regarding Dolrhedyn bridge were in hand; the siting of Tanygrisiau station was being discussed with the tourist Board and the CEGB; William Edwards, MP for Merioneth, was supportive and was keen on developments at Tanygrisiau. It was agreed to make an announcement in the Society magazine.

Finally, on 10th March it was reported that the CEGB had signified its agreement to the planning application for the route behind and above the power station and that the Company had completed the purchase from Aneurin Davies of the first section of land up to the old incline, while negotiations were in hand regarding the continuation up to the tunnel by the route now proposed; as Davies had advocated this previously no difficulty was anticipated.

In advance of the Society's AGM on 25th April Garraway sent the directors a '*news flash*', presumably so they were briefed on recent events when meeting members! He said:

> '*At Dduallt the tracks at the end have been realigned onto the new alignment ready for the laying of more permanent way around the spiral to Rhoslyn bridge this summer. The CEGB press forward with construction works at many sites practically up to the old inclines. This work should be considerably enhanced this summer through the appointment of a full time site foreman (Bunny Lewis) who will be taking up duties during May.*'

Despite the CEGB's cooperation on the ground it was still taking its time to deal with the compensation claim, the Board being advised, on 8th September, that it had asked, twice, for a further two months before proceeding to the next stage of the claim. The request was granted despite the fact that the land was taken 14 years and four months ago; the Board was plainly pained by this statistic. Also, it was agreed that the 1971 budget should allow for a 50% increase in expenditure on the Deviation, due to all the delays.

At the end of February 1971 good progress at various sites was reported. Bunny Lewis had also succeeded in catching red-handed one of a party of three youngsters who broke into the Moelwyn mess, and handed him over to the police. As a result the police were able to trace those involved in other incidents and some money was recovered.

As the Rhoslyn bridge was substantially completed, the beams had been put in place in January, a problem manifested itself. Should the site beneath the bridge, the 1836 route, be considered new works or not? If yes, it did not comply with Ministry requirements on clearances. Garraway was left to sort it out, writing to Major Olver on 1st March:

> *'I am . . . . enclosing an official letter to the organisation, regarding Rhoslyn bridge. At the moment we are only concerned with this from the aspect of a structure over the existing line, but obviously we shall need to have it fully approved eventually for the opening of the new route.*
>
> *These designs should of course have been submitted to you before construction ever commenced. The original design for this bridge had been for a stone arch of conventional style, but when the design was changed, I assumed that all the necessary checks and approvals had been obtained, ... I was somewhat horrified when I discovered otherwise. Consequently I have now been left holding the baby to get it cleared with your people, but at present we are unable to trace L&H's deliberations, and the people concerned have moved elsewhere.'*

Olver replied on 16th March that the design should have been submitted but that provided L&H's design calculations were sound he was sure that there should be little difficulty in obtaining approval.

Meanwhile, the Board had met on 9th March, considering the comparative costs of the east and west shore routes submitted by the Company's new consulting engineers, Donald Halstead & Partners. The estimate for the west shore route was £224,132 and that for the east shore one £242,110. The west shore estimate included £97,000 for a tunnel, for which a separate estimate from a J.H. Dallison was costed at £47,181. Dallison also estimated for a cutting in place of the tunnel at £42,335. It was agreed that no further consideration should be given to the east shore route and that Smith and Fiennes should continue to plan the west shore route with particular attention to reducing the cost of the major works.

The Lands Tribunal hearing scheduled for 5th July was postponed until 4th October, the postponement being requested by the CEGB due to the size of claim! The tribunal President visited the Railway on 20th July; normally he would have visited during the course of the hearing but the Company was anxious that he saw the Railway at its best, when it was busy.

Before the end of September the Company did receive some good news from the CEGB, in the form of a letter dated 20th September agreeing to the route behind the power station and confirming the conditions to be imposed.

On 24th September 1971 Garraway reported:

> *'During the summer 528 man days have been put in by organised groups, 279 by weekend parties and 368 by individuals. Embankments both sides of Rhoslyn bridge have been earthed and seeded. Barn site cutting has been virtually completed. Dingle/Midge embankment has been levelled and an excellent sheep creep completed. Cutting back into hill, felling trees, and finishing off waterfall culvert along Midge has continued. Dragon/New Moon cutting has broken through and is being finished to correct level and width. With the aid of the excavator Bluebell has made great progress and is nearly complete.'*

The report illustrates one of the features of the Deviation's first phase, the often-whimsical names given to the sites by the deviationists. Only Rhoslyn predated them.

The Lands Tribunal hearing took place on 4th–8th and 11th November and the decision was given on 19th November. The Company claimed for £152,061, broken into three sections: loss of profit after 40% tax – £138,511; capitalised value of additional cost of alternative (longer) route – £8,322; preliminary expenses incurred in establishing the alternative route – £5,228. The CEGB claimed that the second two items were not allowable and calculated the loss of profit at £51,448 before tax. In the event the tribunal's Chairman, H.P. Hobbs, calculated the loss of profits after tax at £59,693; he disallowed the claim for the capital value of the new line and allowed the claim for the preliminary works, awarding the Railway £65,000. With interest, the Company received £107,000.

Planning permission for the west side route had been received by the time of the 11th November meeting and, taking into account the 20th September letter from the CEGB, the Board formally adopted the route. Smith reported on the next significant objective, the Dolrhedyn bridge at Tanygrisiau, saying that in his opinion it was the local authority's job to resolve the matter of clearances underneath it. He also reported on the cost of a cutting in comparison with a tunnel. The length of the tunnel would be 230 metres and the anticipated cost £60,000 whereas a cutting would cost £65,000. The matter was left to lie on the table.

Another Board meeting was held on 29th November,

Merddin Emrys *arrives at Llyn Ystradau with a ballast train during the spring of 1978, probably the first train through the tunnel since the completion of shotcreting.*

Norman Gurley, FR Archives.

when Smith called for a decision on whether or not a cutting or a tunnel was to be used, the want of it holding up LRO plans. Smith stated that Schumann expected to be able to reduce the length of the tunnel in his construction work. Routly asked if the Company was employing the 'best brains' on the problem. Broadbent pointed out that if an outside firm were asked to investigate, it would only lower five boreholes of 5in diameter for some 60ft in order to obtain rock specimens. He also stressed the need for a tunnel on safety grounds, because sheep would fall into a cutting. After further discussion, the Board gave approval to the tunnel. At the same meeting the Deviation budget for 1972 was set at £2,855.

When the Board met on 14th March 1972, Garraway asked for details of the programme for rebuilding the line to Blaenau and how the equipping of it was to be financed, drawing attention to a statement made at a Society area group meeting by a director that Blaenau Ffestiniog would be reached by 1978. Broadbent, David Garnock, Fiennes and Garraway were to meet to formulate proposals for the rebuilding of the next $4^1/_2$ miles and Garraway being asked to prepare a paper for circulation to the Board.

The question was also raised in respect of the location of the station at Blaenau Ffestiniog and Routly asked all members to visit Blaenau to acquaint themselves with the neighbourhood, so that the matter could be discussed at a later date! In the event it was Fiennes who produced a paper and it was discussed on 9th May. Broadbent was to be asked if his contacts with the Royal Engineers would enable him to ask if the Army would be interested in constructing the new tunnel. Publication of the programme was to be delayed until after a joint meeting with the Society Board scheduled for 4th July.

Approval was given for the expenditure of £2,600 on the blasting of the north cutting by the contractors, Rock Services (Midland) Ltd with payment being made in two equal instalments. A second dumper truck was also authorised at a cost of £400.

Considerable concern was expressed at the contents of an advertisement that had appeared in the Daily Telegraph under the aegis of the '*Society for Individual Freedom*'. Headed '*The Festiniog Case*', the advertisement had outlined the Railway's relationship with the CEGB since 1956 and called for a change to the law dealing with compulsory purchase; after Fiennes had reported on the implications that it had on CEGB officials, with whom the Railway had to deal, the Board formally disassociated the Company from the SIF, leaving Fiennes to '*convey this conclusion to the right quarters*'. Former Company Secretary Francis Wayne was involved with the Society.

Smith reported, on 14th September, on the LRO's progress; the CEGB had objected to inclusion of a clause defining an arbitration procedure, he said, explaining why it was necessary to safeguard the Company's interests. Aneurin Davies' claim had been settled satisfactorily, Smith also reported, the Board approving settlement of £1,200. Fiennes reported on the £5,025 budgeted for the Deviation and intimated that there was no allowance for the tunnel in that amount. The south cutting was included and might be brought forward.

The site of the Company's station at Blaenau Ffestiniog was discussed and Garraway commented on the desirability of the station being sited at Glan-y-pwll, for operational reasons. The Board supported his proposals and asked him to produce a formal scheme.

Garraway raised the question of Rhoslyn bridge and the certification required by the Department of the Environment was also raised. Smith later reported that he had discussed the matter with Major Olver and had been advised that until a public passenger service used the bridge there was no urgent requirement for the certification.

Broadbent reported, on 6th February 1973, on the necessity for deciding on whether new rail or second-hand rail was to be bought for the Deviation and the restoration of the line from Tanygrisiau to Blaenau Ffestiniog. It was agreed unanimously that new rail should be bought in view of the labour saving that new rail would give over second-hand rail. The quantity to be bought was 100 tons.

In a request dated 17th April, Schumann appealed to the army for help with the tunnel, Cwmorthin bridge, three culverts, excavation of 3,500 cubic metres and formation of 850 metres of embankment. Such support would have been of great value but nothing came of the request.

Permanent track was laid as far as Barn cutting and a temporary platform laid to accommodate a special train on 7th July; the train carried members elected to the new local authorities that were to take effect from 1st April 1974.

Donald Halstead submitted a report on the effects of wind pressure on railway operations at the Cob, Cei Mawr and Rhoslyn bridge, in May 1974. After studying the highest gusts recorded at Trawsfynydd between 1965 and 1971 (the highest was 72 knots in 1966), the structural engineers had concluded that a 75-knot wind would overturn an empty coach and suggested that, allowing for a 10% safety factor, operating trains in wind speeds of over 65 knots would create a degree of risk. Such a wind might occur once or twice a year, during the winter months, and conditions requiring trains to cease operating would be extremely rare. Some additional, concealed, props were applied to Rhoslyn bridge as a result.

It was also in May that the works were shown to the Railway Inspectorate, Garraway writing:

> '*Colonel I. McNaughton visited the line on 15th May and travelled on* Linda *to the head of steel, walked over to the head of the incline and had a quick look at the whole railway. A beautiful day helped the friendly atmosphere; I showed him the site of the proposed terminal at Blaenau etc en route* [to] *Llandudno Junction. He has agreed to all my requests for rationalisation of speed restrictions and seemed favourably impressed with all he saw.*'

In December, Schumann submitted a report to the directors on the options available to build the tunnel. It was considered by the Board on 2nd January 1975, when Ben Ball recommended use of a direct labour scheme subject to the Board being aware that he felt an estimate of £50,000 was more appropriate than the figure of £40,000 given in the report. The Board approved this in principle provided satisfactory external supervision was arranged. The approval was also subject to the Wales Tourist Board confirming in writing its verbal undertaking to grant-aid the project.

The CEGB had agreed to grant the Company a 99-year easement, based on £10 per annum, commuted to a lump sum of £71, for the use of its land behind the power station, the Board was informed on 7th April. A similar agreement had been reached in respect of the Tanygrisiau station site, although the lump sum was £70 in this case.

A deficiency in the transitions of curvature on the spiral had been established, requiring the line so far built to be resurveyed to accommodate 200ft radius curves. The most notable evidence of this work is the width of Barn cutting, originally much narrower. The survey, by Brian Hollingsworth, and modifications were carried out in the spring of 1975.

Major Olver inspected the spiral on 13th May, preparatory to the introduction of a shuttle service between Dduallt and Gelliwiog that commenced on 17th May. The site was visited by HRH Princess Margaret and her children on 25th July.

When the Board met on 11th September the tunnel bore was 20ft long. The three miners, Robin Daniels, Peter Hughes and Bob le Marchant, were being paid £1 per hour (for a 60-hour week) plus £3.33 each per metre progress and a terminal bonus of £750 each.

A meeting was to be held with the CEGB on 19th September to discuss the use of volunteer labour and the possibility of a loop at Buarth Melyn. All tunnelling equipment was on site except for a battery-electric locomotive, which was being overhauled.

A different complexion was put on the Deviation on 13th November, with the announcement that the Manpower Services Commission had agreed to fund the employment of 12 otherwise unemployed men for 12 months on it, leading to grants of nearly £27,250 payable to the FR; this was the first project to attract support from the newly created Manpower Services Commission, established only in September. At the Board meeting held on the same day it was reported that the CEGB had intimated that trains would probably be allowed to terminate at Buarth Melyn on a temporary basis.

In 1975 the deviationists had moved 10,085 skip loads of rock and earth plus 2,073 skip loads of rock from the tunnel. Volunteers contributed 3,087 man-hours (up 200 on 1974) and the Deviation work required 4,000 loco-miles.

The tunnel had attained a depth of 160 metres by 19th January 1976 – '*124 metres to go*', commented Garraway. The bore was expected to be completed by Easter, when opening-out would commence.

It was noted on 21st January that three MSC grant-scheme employees were being taken on every three weeks, with the peak in employment expected as the weather improved.

A representative of McAlpines' had visited the power station site on 5th January and details were awaited to enable a new MSC grant application to be made. The contract made with Sir Alfred McAlpine & Son (Northern) Ltd required that company to act as main contractor and provide an agent and foreman. The works were specified as: four reinforced concrete bridges over the pressure pipes leading to the power station requiring excavation of 3,300 cubic metres of rock without blasting, transport and compaction of material into embankments, construction of two road/rail level crossings, ducting for cables, one culvert and fencing. Subsequently £100,000 was received from the MSC. Smith reported that the level crossings could be built to Major Olver's requirements for a total of £5,000.

Garraway produced a report that included reference to the crossings on 18th March. A meeting had taken place with representatives of the Railway, Railway Inspectorate, CEGB, police and county planning and highway departments present. It appears that the CEGB had expected gated crossings to be installed and was unhappy, citing safety, to learn that the Railway was planning to install open crossings. Major Olver was persuasive that open crossings were common on railways operating at much higher speeds and carried the day. The position was complicated because there had been no resolution concerning the avoidance of the Dolrhedyn bridge by road traffic, which could be dealt with by adopting part of the Stwlan dam road and building a very short new road into the village, due to local authority procrastination; if the road was adopted the CEGB would have no interest in the crossing arrangements on it. Perhaps Olver's assertion that as a statutory Company the Railway could reinstate the bridge without the need for planning permission, and therefore regardless of whether road vehicles could pass underneath it, was reported back with good effect.

Garraway also wrote about the rock coming out of the tunnel that was to be used as ballast. He had been concerned about its size but PW engineer, Fred Howes, had told him that continuity of supply was the chief problem. There was concern about the economics of converting tunnel stone to ballast as the need to wash it had not been foreseen – the rock was very dusty and left untreated the dust set like concrete after rain. '*On the credit side,*' Garraway said, '*very many tons of ballast has been put down on the new line, which would have cost an awful lot of money to buy and haul up from Minffordd – and labour to lay. Most of the rest of the ballast coming out will likewise go to the spiral, which from Fred's aspect is getting it ballasted at no cost.'*

The tunnel was pierced on 1st May. Judged by the lack of comment, either by the Board or by Garraway, tunnelling seems to have been relatively trouble-free. The same claim could not always be said of operations outside the tunnel, however. On 23rd April a train of skips ran away and ended up in the shuttle platform at Dduallt and on 30th April the diesel locomotive *Jane* ran into a stop block near the tunnel mouth; it was being driven by unqualified MSC personnel, reported Garraway, and the driver was slightly hurt.

By the 28th July Board meeting there were only 70 metres to go with reaming the tunnel and it was expected to be completed by the end of August; rock bolting was expected to be completed a month later. The recouping of expenditure on equipment was expected to start soon with the sale of the stone crusher and screen.

Although neither Garraway nor the Board commented upon it, the beams of the Cwmorthin river bridge at Tanygrisiau, arguably the Deviation's largest visible structure, had been craned into position on 26th July; the abutments had been built by the deviationists at Easter.

Garraway reported, on 6th August, on discussions with the power station manager, Golding, over public access to the proposed temporary terminal at Buarth Melyn. Golding had told Garraway that he expected to have new security arrangements for the power station completed imminently, so he would be less concerned regarding the presence of the public near the lake or on the footpath. There would not therefore be any opposition to foot access from the footpath or Buarth Melyn station, and the provision of a platform for limited access to and from trains. As the footpath was an existing right of way Golding surely had no control over its use; his influence would have been limited to access over the CEGB's land for railway purposes, particularly if the easement granted to the Railway made no provision for a station. By the time of Garraway's report, dated 8th September, the temporary terminus had been renamed Llyn Ystradau. The reason for the choice of the name was that the public might know what a 'Llyn' was and be attracted by it as well as being able to pronounce at least that part of the name!

There was at this time great concern amongst the Company's employees about the money being spent on the Deviation and its effect on the stability of the business and, therefore, their jobs. A meeting was held between the directors and heads of departments on 18th September following which an extract of details, reviewing the current position, was circulated to all staff under the heading *'Building back to Blaenau'*. Highlights not previously covered included the cost of the power station project which was estimated at £247,000, while the Tanygrisiau–Blaenau section was estimated at £40,000. £100,000 had been received from the CEGB as compensation and the Manpower Services Commission would pay labour costs plus 10% towards materials, about £100,000. The Wales Tourist Board was to pay £40,000 towards other costs (plus £20,000 for Tanygrisiau–Blaenau Ffestiniog). Thus the Company had to find £117,000; of this £50,000 would be a 12-month interest-free loan from the National Westminster Bank that did not need to be repaid for several years. The Company had allocated £25,000 a year from profits to the project but anticipated cost reductions by favourable arrangements with plant hire and because cheaper rail had already been obtained.

The WTB grant had to be approved by the Welsh Office and this approval was awaited. However it was planned to start work in October, whether or not this approval was forthcoming, as it related only to the last £10,000 of the grant.

The local authorities were concerned that if the railway terminated at Stesion Fain the full economic benefit to the town would not be realised. Blaenau Ffestiniog District Council and the County Council had approached the FR with a view to establishing a terminus at the old Central (GW) station. The Company told the Council that there was no finance available for such an extension, but the Welsh Development Agency had offered to prepare the site and the Council had offered the building at present incorporating the information office. The FR had suggested that BR might extend its passenger line to the Central station and this possibility was being taken up with BR. Duffws station was too short for present-day trains but would serve as a station car park.

Dolrhedyn bridge would be reconstructed at the expense of the County Council; the Railway was in a position to insist that the work was done. The Penlan rockfall was also a hurdle; arrangements were in hand to purchase the extra land required for a diversion and the District Council was obtaining legal opinion on whose responsibility the matter was.

Three years previously, the WTB had calculated

Preparing the reinforcing for concreting the Cwmorthin bridge foundations, spring 1976.

Paul Francis Photography, FR Archives

Tanygrisiau station under construction, March 1978.

Norman Gurley, FR Archives

Major Olver's inspection train crosses the Cwmorthin bridge on 24th June 1978.

Norman Gurley, FR Archives

that the FR would make £90,000 per annum profit when running to Blaenau Ffestiniog. The (unaudited) operating profit for 1976 was likely to be over £40,000. Assuming that operating profits were maintained at £40,000 or more over the next two or three years and assuming that about £20,000 or £25,000 had to be applied to the completion of the line to Blaenau Ffestiniog, there should be considerable amounts available for improvements to the existing railway, including the annual half mile of track renewal, although it would not be possible to do everything thought desirable.

The cash-flow forecasts had been approved by the bank, the WTB and MSC. The maximum borrowing would be £125,000. The financial value of the volunteer element was estimated to be of the order of £60,000pa excluding the deviationists and the directors, so it was recognised that the Railway was not viable without substantial volunteer effort.

Approval of the Wales Tourist Board grant in October was the signal for work to start behind the power station. There were two significant features to the work: the four underground bridges over the CEGB's high-pressure pipelines and the requirement to remove a large volume of rock without using explosives; the former seems to have been quite straightforward apart from the CEGB's nervousness, but the rock-bursting machine used to deal with the latter proved to be extremely temperamental.

In January 1977 the consultants had called, unexpectedly, for the tunnel roof to be lined to between 4in and 6in depth by sprayed concrete, the 'shotcreting' method (the old tunnel had been unlined). Agreement was reached for the work to be carried out in two stages, before and after the short period that trains ran through to Llyn Ystradau; once again it took a while for a satisfactory modus to be established.

Track laying through the tunnel was extended into the north cutting and on 2nd February the first train, consisting of the Hunslet mines locomotive *Moel Hebog* with wagons of rails, traversed the tunnel to Llyn Ystradau. The portals were being prepared for concreting. Cleaning down the bore and the floor was in progress. At the power station the penstock bridge foundations were being excavated.

On the 4th March Routly reported on his writing to the MSC, asking for permission to use its labour on the tunnel and at Penlan; MSC personnel had previously refused to work in the tunnel but had consulted a trades union after which they agreed to work there in return for an additional 5p per hour!

On the same date Garraway reported that work was in hand fitting mesh for shotcreting. The tunnel sides were being cleared and a drainage ditch put in. The portal areas had been cleared and foundations poured. The second penstock pipe had been exposed and one foundation concreted.

By 1st April he was reporting that portal work had made slow progress and likewise the complete erection of mesh reinforcement inside. Progress improved subsequently and he hoped that the Easter holiday would advance matters sufficiently for completion about 26th May, forecasting an inspection on the 28th, deviationists' special on the 29th and public services during the following week.

The tunnel portals were up to schedule, reported Garraway on 13th May, but the shotcreting continued to cause problems. Representatives from all the firms involved were on site and the Railway took the line that they must find a method of making it work – or say that they could not do it by their method. By 20th May the portals had been completed and the five poor places were being shotcreted; the system was at last working better, though some technical difficulties had to be overcome.

The first steam train, hauled by *Mountaineer*, ran to Llyn Ystradau to test clearances on 28th May; the same formation was used for Major Olver's inspection the next day. More work was required on the tunnel, though, before public running could commence. Dispensation was obtained, however, to run a special passenger train for the BBC-TV '*Go with Noakes*' programme through to Llyn Ystradau on 15th June. Although the official opening took place on 25th June it was not until the afternoon of 8th July, following a two-day inspection by Major Olver, that the public was allowed to travel to the temporary terminus.

Acting on the advice of the consulting engineers, the tunnel was inspected daily, before the first train; an additional, more thorough, inspection was undertaken on Friday nights. An undertaking was given to the Railway Inspectorate that the Dduallt–Llyn Ystradau section would be worked on the one-engine-in-steam principle.

Work proceeded on the penstock bridges during the summer, although pouring the foundations of the third was delayed after the concrete lorry slid over the side of the embankment. At the beginning of August the fourth was delayed because the concrete company closed for holidays!

Volunteers worked on the Tanygrisiau station site during August, completing rough levelling and widening of the formation and removing surplus rock by the end of the month. The formation to Tanygrisiau was completed by December, when grading and ballasting commenced.

Shotcreting recommenced in January 1978; in February Garraway reported slow progress with equipment failure and arctic weather adding to the difficulties. The Board thought, on 10th February, that nothing had been learned from the previous year's experience. The importance of finishing the tunnel was stressed – both to utilise MSC labour and to enable the forthcoming timetable to be operated. Garraway was to apply for an MSC grant extension. A total of £1,000 a month was being paid to McAlpines for a foreman; Broadbent was to assist in finding and recruiting a replacement.

Garraway sounded confident on 17th March when he reported that work on grading the two level crossings had been completed, subject to CEGB approval. Both the car park area and the Tanygrisiau station platforms were virtually completed and cable ducts and upstands for Cwmorthin bridge were being constructed. Some clearance of the south end of the tunnel had taken place. The tunnel '*makes better progress with the advent of FR staff*', he said. A very successful open day for both the press and technical representatives was held on 17th March. The Guardian newspaper published a photograph and an article on the event three days later. Spraying had passed the halfway mark and digging out and clearing up was progressing.

For some of April and May Garraway reported the amount of concrete sprayed: 14th April – 34 cubic metres, another poor week with plant and equipment problems and labour sickness; 21st April – 48½ cubic metres, a better week; 5th May – 27½ cubic metres, only four working days; 12th May – 32½ cubic metres but supplies of accelerator awaited.

Major Olver visited on 8th June and Garraway said he was very praiseworthy for what had been achieved. He was happy to allow celebrations to take place on 24th, subject to certain stipulations, and was also prepared to let regular services commence as soon as the tunnel was finished and cleaned, along with various other jobs to be completed. The track was put back in tunnel south cutting only minutes before he arrived; fortunately he was late.

Providing volunteers came as promised and that there were no breakdowns occurring with the shotcreting, Garraway considered that it should be possible to make 24th June the actual opening day to passengers. Spraying was completed in the tunnel by 16th June, but fencing, stiles, ballasting and tamping was still in progress.

The line was formally opened on 24th June, the first public train following one for the deviationists and one for invited guests. Despite the public opening, amidst great joy and very heavy rain, it was September 1979 before Garraway finished reporting on Deviation works. And the tunnel portals are still unfaced in 2005!

According to Brian Hollingsworth, the Deviation had cost £610,000 plus £180,000 in volunteer labour. Funding came from the Wales Tourist Board (£178,000), the Development Board for Rural Wales (£42,500) and the Manpower Services Commission (£142,000). Although £107,000 compensation had been received from the CEGB it will be seen elsewhere in this book that much of it was applied to other capital projects. The remainder of the funding came from loans, leaving the Railway heavily indebted to the bank and with no resources available to complete the restoration to Blaenau Ffestiniog.

Chapter 10

Back to Blaenau - the Final Years

1979~1983

Having completed the Deviation and opened the line to Tanygrisiau the Company was faced with the problem of fettling up the route, nearly two miles, to Blaenau Ffestiniog when it had borrowing of some £250,000 to support and no resources available to allocate to extension work. It had been caught unawares, moreover, when it found out that the volunteers who had contributed so much to building the Deviation were not interested in restoring the Railway to its ultimate terminus. The local authorities, on the other hand, were keen for the Railway to terminate in the centre of the town but there was no indication of the cost to the Railway. The Deviation still needed some attention, too, and a resolution to the Penlan rock fall was sought.

The candidate for the post of Chief Executive, P.R. 'Dick' Wollan, was introduced to the Board on 22nd January 1979. A former ICI executive, he was to take up his three-days-a-week appointment from 19th April. In the meantime he hoped, he said, to visit the Railway and to get to know it and the people.

At Blaenau Ffestiniog, the Board was told, the Countryside Commission was expected to buy Isallt, a Victorian merchant's house, and sub-let part of it to the FR for terminal use; Allan Garraway had already reported that he didn't think the premises suitable but was unable to secure an alternative. The European Economic Commission was mentioned as the source of funding for the Blaenau development for the first time.

Moving on to the budget, Hugh Eaves forecast a peak-borrowing requirement of £300,000 and was concerned that projection into 1980 made no provision for a reduction, calling therefore, for further revisions. The following budget amendments were agreed:

(a) raising projected income to £420,000 (although John Routly and Eaves preferred to be more conservative)
(b) Further reduction in stock for resale to £51,000
(c) Reducing wages by 10% by staff reduction
(d) Allan Garraway to control spending commitments and staff engagement

Supplementary grants for the tunnel and power station bridges could not be relied upon. Routly also hoped to 'offload' the Penlan project from the Development Board for Rural Wales to the Welsh Development Agency by calling it a land reclamation scheme, thereby making £50,000 from the DBRW available for other work.

The Company's assets had been revalued for insurance purposes, revising the current total of £900,000 to £2,205,246; the increased figure would be taken into account when the next balance sheet was prepared.

Garraway sought clarification as to whether the 'new' *Earl of Merioneth* should be considered a new locomotive or a rebuild. The Society, when consulted, said it would prefer it to be classified as new. The idea of sending the old *Earl of Merioneth*, originally *Livingston Thompson*, to the National Railway Museum at York was first considered, favourably, by the Board on 2nd March.

On that occasion the Board decided that the Railway name could be spelled with one or two 'F's in either English or Welsh on signs or as the logo. The Board agreed with the Society to retain the archaic single 'F' in the Company's corporate name.

Following a site meeting with McAlpines the cost of strengthening the line at Penlan had risen from £180,000 to £210,000. The Board thought there were benefits in building a deviation in that the line would be founded on solid rock and further from residential property; residents had expressed concern about the possibility of further rockfalls when trains

After a long gestation the 'new' Earl of Merioneth *was named by Allan Garraway in a ceremony at Harbour station on 23rd June 1979. Alongside was* Merddin Emrys *carrying a headboard in celebration of its centenary.*

Author

resumed. It thought also that Manpower Services Commission labour could be used on a deviation and that it would be easier to get the work classified as land reclamation!

It was agreed to discontinue the use of the cottage at Bron Turnor and accept Lady Ball's offer to have exclusive use of a cottage at Tanygrisiau for £500 per annum from July.

The Company's public liability insurance cover was increased to £5,000,000; it was hoped that this amount would be adequate for the requirements of the CEGB, with which body the Company was about to complete a licence for the use of CEGB land on the Deviation.

A £300,000 overdraft limit had been agreed with the bank and the Company was £10,000 below the cash-flow forecast, but only because some suppliers had not been paid. This was putting relationships with suppliers under stress: '*there was a danger of getting a bad name and a need to improve supplier relations next winter*'. The £300,000 limit was reached by 6th April.

The achievement in building the Deviation was recognised by the wider railway preservation world on 27th January, when the Association of Railway Preservation Societies presented the Society with its annual award, being presented '*to a member society which it considers has made an outstanding contribution to voluntary railway preservation*'. Society Chairman, Gordon Caddy, received the award, which was a London, Brighton & South Coast Railway royal train headboard, with project engineer Michael Schumann, at the Association's AGM in York.

In Boston Lodge *Merddin Emrys*'s winter overhaul had been completed by 30th March although modifications to its steam brake were in hand. Work on *Earl of Merioneth*'s bogies, identified as C and D bogies, continued. *Prince*'s firebox was being fitted, its superheater header was being fabricated, work on the tender body was in hand as was that on the smokebox. A new radiator for *Moelwyn* was being made. In April new steamchests were being made for *Mountaineer*.

When the Board met on 14th March 1980 it recorded that:

'EEC grant application assumed three train set operation to Blaenau Ffestiniog by Easter 1982; this was to meet the requirements of the railway inspectorate. Tan-y-bwlch and Minffordd may only be used for crossing works trains and emergencies. Loops would become limiting factor on traffic (rather than carriages) in about 1985 so increased traffic (over and above hourly 10–12 coach trains) would require signalling at Minffordd and Tan-y-bwlch and possibly Llyn Ystradau, for which considerable resources would be needed after 1982.'

Porthmadog ground frame and Dduallt signalling installation were handed over to the traffic department by 4th May.

Wollan's duties were confirmed when the Board met on 11th May. He was to maintain and improve budgetary control procedure so that expenditure and commitment of both capital and revenue were contained within limits approved by the Board; he was to submit reports, not less than monthly, to keep the Directors informed of progress, indicating variance from the budget in financial terms and in regard to practical achievement, with reasons; and he was to endeavour to work in close harmony with the Society and the volunteer movement generally. In his first report, on the same date, Wollan said that whilst there was still a problem with outstanding creditors the Inland Revenue was not pressing for the £12,000 owed, which was helping cash flow!

The 25th anniversary of the Company's change of control was discussed. The press would be invited to travel on 23rd June and a dinner would be held in the evening. Alan Pegler would propose 'the Company', Routly to reply; Les Smith would propose 'the guests' with a reply by Gerry Fiennes or Francis Wayne. The Society, meanwhile, was making arrangements to celebrate its own 25th anniversary in September.

By 8th June No. 23 was repainted, at the Society's suggestion, in ivory and green to mark the anniversary, although it did not have the red ends of the 1950s livery.

Earl of Merioneth was ready for steam testing at the same time. It made its first trip across the Cob on 12th June and on 23rd June was formally named by Garraway at Porthmadog. *Merddin Emrys* stood alongside carrying a headboard recording its centenary. By 13th July a weighing rig had been constructed and the loco's balance adjusted. Tests carried out on Tan-y-bwlch road bridge, with both Fairlies, indicated that the structure was in need of strengthening, work that had been deferred earlier when the local authority

Just before Earl of Merioneth *was completed, in January 1979, a new superheated boiler was delivered for* Mountaineer. *Built by Danks of Netherton the boiler was designed, at Boston Lodge, to be capable of being installed in the Hunslets, a theory that has yet to be put to the test. By 1st August 1983* Mountaineer *had been thoroughly overhauled, with new steam manifold, pony truck, driving axle boxes and smoke box; it had piston valves, instead of slide valves, and its frames had been strengthened.*

FR Archives

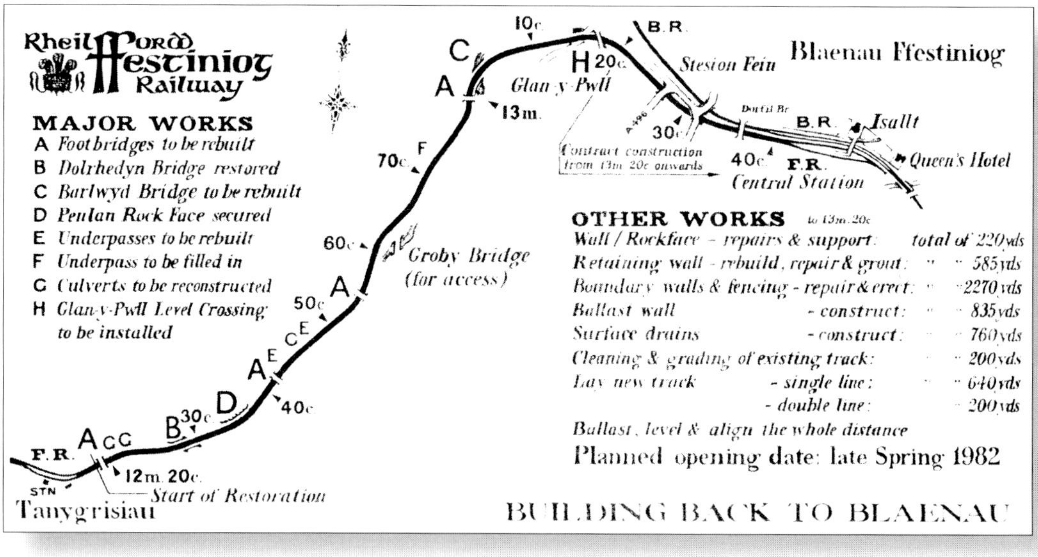

Upnor Castle *passing Llyn Ystradau with the 16.30 ex Porthmadog for Tanygrisiau on 27th August 1979.*

John Scrace

was considering widening the road. Its first trip to Tanygrisiau was with 12 carriages on 28th June and it entered service after a press launch on 19th July.

The report of the first meeting of the safety committee was received at the 6th July Board meeting, held at Combermere Abbey. The committee comprised Paul Dukes (Works Manager) – Chairman; Martin Duncan (S&T fitter) – NUR representative; Arthur Lambert (Society Managing Director) and Ralph Taylor (Company electrician) – Company representative. On this occasion most of the departmental heads were present and made presentations.

Alan Heywood, Traffic & Commercial Manager, said that the FR needed tidying and growth was constrained by insufficient carriages; four new vehicles in seven years were inadequate and two due '*this year*' had not been delivered; three carriages were life-expired. The business should diversify and raise off-peak business.

Paul Dukes said his objective for 1980 was to have six steam, two diesel locomotives and 26 carriages available for service. He needed four additional staff of the right calibre and a new long-term locomotive project would be highly desirable. He saw a need to stockpile fuel at a cost of £40,000 in 1980 (compared with £28,000 estimated in the current year) and suggested that a return to coal firing might be viable in the future. The use of larger engines on longer/fewer trains might save fuel, too. He also warned of the danger of the proliferation of paperwork and the resulting bureaucracy.

Permanent way engineer Fred Howes said his staff and volunteer input was reducing; trackwork was maintained at the expense of fencing. He hoped to keep the existing rail going as long as possible with an annual programme of half a mile renewal and half a mile heavy maintenance.

Wollan summarised, saying that the aim of balancing expenditure with income, leaving a £25,000 debt-repayment surplus, was possible with an increase of two staff for civil engineering.

Financially, revenue was £4,000 down on the budget by the end of June; payments were £22,000 down on the budget because of delay in implementing the pay rise! The DBRW had agreed to grant £50,000 for the Penlan reconstruction/repair.

Following on from the ARPS award to the Society in January, recognition of another sort came in June, with the announcement in the Queen's birthday honours list that Garraway was to receive an MBE, the first time that such an award had been made to someone involved in railway preservation.

Blanche broke a driving axle on 6th August, discovered at Penrhyn on the evening train; a

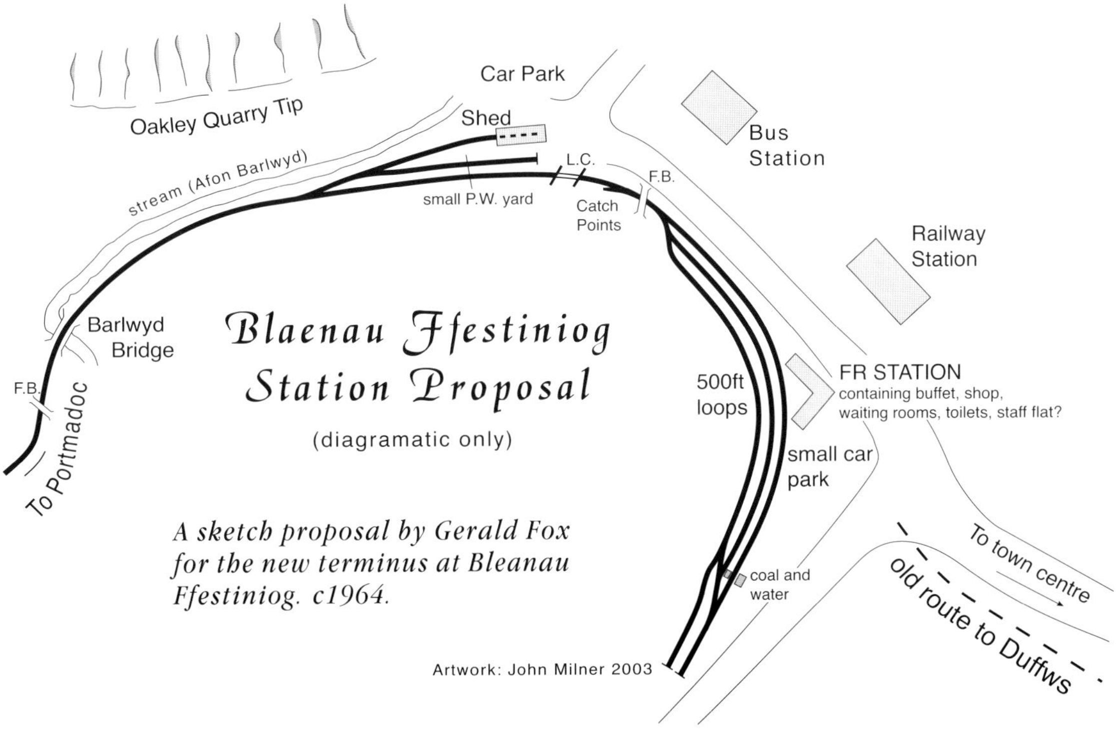

A sketch proposal by Gerald Fox for the new terminus at Bleanau Ffestiniog. c1964.

Left: *The Penlan stabilisation required a considerable scaffold installation, complete with lift, 14th May 1980.*

Author

Below: *The contractors moved onto the Blaenau Ffestiniog station site in 1980; surveying the FR route was one of the first tasks carried out after installing the site offices.*

Geoff Hall, FR Archives

Onwards to the Final Phase

Above: *Before services could be extended to Blaenau Ffestiniog the trackbed required at great deal of attention. Clearance and some track laying had been carried out from 1974. After the reopening to Tanygrisiau the outstanding civil engineering was broken down into identifiable mini-projects that were taken on by groups and individuals with varying degrees of success. By June 1981 the timbers for the Barlwyd bridge were in place.*

Arthur Lambert, FR archives

Left: *Norman Gurley, second from left, supervises a track-laying gang near Tanygrisiau.*

FR Archives

Right: *Early in 1981* Blanche *returns to Tanygrisiau having brought up a train of ballast.*

Author

Left: *Clearing the station site during 1981. The FR formerly ran where the excavator stands.*

Geoff Hall, FR Archives

replacement was obtained within a week. The loco was returned to traffic but then failed with a broken eccentric. This was replaced but then another one broke. Although *Blanche* was '*running satisfactorily*' before the end of the month its leading crank pins ran warm during September.

Mountaineer's leaking tubes were reported on 31st August; it had given another season's useful service, said Garraway, but '*unless serious failures occur it is not expected to be used again*'. It would be kept serviceable until Prince was completed.

Notwithstanding the Society's concerns about the strategy for returning to Blaenau Ffestiniog – it had been told the scheme was likely to cost £950,000 – the Company Board confirmed, on 10th September, that its policy was to get the project through before financial aid was curtailed. The BR layout had been changed, with the effect of allowing the FR to achieve its own proposed layout.

The year was not a good one for traffic. At the time of the meeting journeys stood at 328,676, down from 359,988 the year before. Income was up, £342,739 versus £307,310 on traffic, but only because of inflation and fare increases. The budgeted fare income had been £420,000 but it was more likely to be £385,000. Only 1980's peak fares would be increased, with a projected income of £460,000 on 1979's traffic.

There was concern that the overdraft limit would be reached by February because of the decline in traffic. However, Wollan thought that £23,000 in non-budgeted grants might become available; in addition, if an extra, unbudgeted, £20,000 was spent on Penlan a further £27,000 would become available. The cash-flow situation required obtaining any grants available and the acceleration of the sale of land at Minffordd and Porthmadog, the slaughterhouse field, the latter first mooted for sale in 1955!

The Society's 25th anniversary event, held on the weekend of 15th/16th September, was intended to celebrate 25 years of achievement and to recruit volunteers for the next 25 years. It focused on Boston Lodge with a wide range of relics, equipment and activities demonstrated or exhibited; the programme listed 55 items. *Moel Hebog* operated a shuttle service from Porthmadog to the old loco shed with No. 110 in

Left: Merddin Emrys *emerges from the 'new' tunnel with the 15.50 from Porthmadog on 28th May 1980.*

John Scrace

A view of Glan-y-pwll (lower right), Blaenau Ffestiniog (centre) and Manod seen from the Oakeley quarry tips. The new tunnels for the FR had been built and the associated roadworks nearly completed although the Stesion Fein water column still remained, 1981.

Author

faux push-pull mode. Unlike subsequent gala events the normal train service was not otherwise augmented. Some 1,780 return bookings on the shuttle testified to the event's success, although it was to be several years before a similar event was held again. One benefit for the Railway was that Boston Lodge was subjected to a massive tidying-up session!

Civil engineering consultants Ove Arup had surveyed Penlan and proposed a simpler, and therefore cheaper, solution of bolting the rock face. When the Board met at the Great Northern Hotel, King's Cross, on 8th November a preliminary report had been received with an indicative price of £55,000 plus preparatory work, drainage, stone facing and site clearance. The Company had bought the cottage affected by the rockfall and it was duly demolished. A grant from the EEC would be sought.

Eaves pointed out that the cash-flow shortfall was broadly balanced by money budgeted for Penlan but unspent. (The previous week Garraway had reported the current account overdrawn by £1,037.89 and the loan account standing at £130,000.)

A link with the past was lost over the Christmas holiday, when lifting the line between Dduallt and the old Moelwyn tunnel was completed.

1980 got off to a good start with the news, notified to Garraway on 9th January, that the Welsh Office would support the Blaenau Ffestiniog station scheme. The work was expected to be completed in June 1981.

There was good news, too, from Boston Lodge, with the steaming of *Prince* on 10th February, the first steaming for the Railway's oldest locomotive since 1968. The Society had taken the initiative in moving its overhaul forward in 1974 and much of the work since had been carried out by volunteers. The locomotive had been made to fit the modern FR, being longer, wider, higher and heavier than before. It had been equipped with oil firing equipment, a superheater, mechanical lubricators and steam sanding and drain cocks. On 16th February it satisfactorily hauled a test train of ballast wagons, needing only minor adjustments afterwards. Those who saw it might have thought they were seeing a ghost as it was still in grey primer. A trip to the paint shop beckoned.

There was less good news, however, for the Board to review at its 28th January meeting. The 1979 volume of traffic had been down by $5^1/_2$% compared with the previous year. This was considered reasonable in the light of a $7^1/_2$% decline in the British leisure industry generally. Indebtedness had been reduced by £23,000. When the Board said that it wished to be kept informed on what had been achieved for the money spent, Wollan reported that the permanent way was a little behind schedule due a shortage of volunteers, priority given to grant-aided work had distorted Boston Lodge's programme and that a serious backlog in the S&T department had attracted adverse comment from the Railway Inspectorate. The possibility of reorganising S&T management was discussed and appreciation was expressed of Norman Pearce's contribution, as volunteer head of department.

A 35% pay claim, to allow for inflation and progress towards parity with the average of selected industries, had been countered by departments being asked to identify savings in non-wage expenditure. The deferment of £21,000 of expenditure was agreed and an offer of 5% payable from 5th January plus 5% payable from 5th July and backdated to 5th January was made. The employees' response was awaited; they had proposed that the 35% increase be financed by increased fares.

The new joint station at Blaenau Ffestiniog would be authorised by an LRO covering both standard and narrow gauge railways. It having been discovered that the 1975 LRO, whilst authorising borrowing of up to

BR brought in its track materials for its new Blaenau Ffestiniog station by rail, on 1st May 1981 using 40 141.

Author

Merddin Emrys *decorated in connection with Portmadoc's carnival on 18th August 1973. The human disguises conceal Evan Davies and Phil Girdlestone and others.*

John Alexander

Linda *passes above Tanygrisiau in 1978; one of the reconstructed footbridges can be seen on the right.*

Geoff Hall, FR Archives

GADEWCH I FREUDDWYDION EICH PLENTYNDOD DDOD YN WIR
LET YOUR CHILDHOOD DREAMS COME TRUE
You could realise your ambition and learn to drive or fire our engines. Our railway runs on volunteers.
Become an engine driver, fireman, guard, signalman. Work in the restaurant, maintain the track, use your skills in our well equipped workshops, or perform a hundred other vital tasks.
Join the Festiniog Railway Society now.
Members enjoy travel concessions and a quarterly magazine. Local society groups around Britain take parties of volunteers to the line. Apply to: Festiniog Railway Society, Harbour Station, Porthmadog, Gwynedd LL49 9NF
F R
If you would like to join Bill on the footplate, come and start your training now.
We need all the help we can get!
FESTINIOG RAILWAY SOCIETY
FESTINIOG FESTINIOG RAILWAY SOCIETY
FESTINIOG RAILWAY SOCIETY

By Narrow Gauge Train through the Mountains of Snowdonia
Rheilffordd Railway Rheilffordd Railway
Ffestiniog
Rheilffordd Railway Rheilffordd Railway
Special inclusive tickets from British Rail Stations. Please ask for details
Trains run daily from the end of March until early November. Also limited winter service. Information from: Ffestiniog Railway, Porthmadog, Gwynedd
Telephone: Porthmadog (0766) 2340/2384.
One of the Great Little Trains of Wales
BLAENAU FFESTINIOG
Buffet service of light refreshments. Parking.
Connecting bus service to Llechwedd Caverns and Gloddfa Ganol.
Llandudno
Stwlan Dam
Tanygrisiau
Connecting bus service to Stwlan Dam.
Tan-y-Bwlch
Buffet service of light refreshments. Picnic Site, Nature Trail and Parking.
Pwllheli
PORTHMADOG
Self-service restaurant. Parking.
Penrhyn
Minffordd
Barmouth
Holyhead
Bangor
Liverpool
Chester
BLAENAU FFESTINIOG
PORTHMADOG
Pwllheli
Barmouth
Aberdovey
Aberystwyth
WALES
Shrewsbury
Newtown

Linda *at Llyn Ystradau in 1977.*

John Hunt

Merddin Emrys *at Tanygrisiau during 1979; the loco carries a headboard commemorating its centenary. The high vantage point shows the facilities installed to equip the station as a temporary terminus.*

Geoff Hall, FR Archives

The Dolrhedyn road bridge under construction in 1979.

Geoff Hall, FR Archives

On 16th February 1980 Prince *hauled a ballast train up to the Moelwyn tunnel, a fine trial after its protracted overhaul. It was in traffic by the end of April.*

Geoff Hall, FR Archives

Top left: *Seen from the Garth, a train sets off for Blaenau Ffestiniog in 1983. The photograph shows just how much the Railway's environment has changed since the 1950s. Houses on the wharves, dinghies and cruisers in the harbour, the Britannia Foundry replaced by an office block.*

Geoff Hall, FR Archives

Left bottom: *Perhaps the first time they had double-headed,* Merddin Emrys *and* Earl of Merioneth *cross the Cob on 4th May 1980; the train had been organised by the society's Lancashire & Cheshire area group.*

John Alexander

Above: *Coach No. 119 fresh out of the paint shop in 1980. The carriage seated 32 in a 3rd class saloon; the white window obscures a toilet compartment.*

Geoff Hall, FR Archives

Left: *In contrast, an earlier photograph taken in 1973 showing coach No. 116 at Boston lodge with* Mary Ann, *which was then fresh out of the paint shop and newly fitted with a pagoda cab roof.*

Geoff Hall, FR Archives

The opening of the new BR platform on 22nd March 1982.

Author

25th May 1982, the day the FR resumed operating to Blaenau Ffestiniog.

Author

Conditions were often very extreme but work continued in the snow in January 1982.

Arthur Lambert, FR Archives

£500,000 by mortgage and/or debentures, did not permit borrowing by overdraft, the new Order would also be used to regularise the borrowing position and to increase the borrowing limit to £750,000.

Another piece in the Tanygrisiau–Blaenau Ffestiniog jigsaw, the Dolrhedyn bridge, was virtually completed, whilst two more tenders were awaited for Penlan; McAlpine had already bid £85,000, in the event the only tender received. Wollan was to agree with Routly and Smith the scheme of work needed to achieve the reopening by permanent staff and volunteers. Projects were to be offered to the Society groups. The EEC grant for Blaenau Ffestiniog included for the Penlan work, too. The contract price was ultimately settled on 14th March at £85,000 plus £175 per extra hole if required.

During the first three months of the year *Linda* and *Blanche* were overhauled, *Prince* was painted, *Moelwyn*'s engine was overhauled and *Upnor Castle* was given a 'new' engine. Steel-bodied carriages Nos. 119 and 120 were brought to an advanced state of completion, the former being in service by 4th April, the latter a week later.

When the Board met on 14th March the directors had met Lord Parry, the Wales Tourist Board's Chairman. He had told them that although he was in favour of an additional payment being made for the tunnel and power station bridges, his Board was not. He would try and locate other sources of funds for the Railway.

Routly had secured a renewal of the overdraft facility. He had told the bank that '*reduction of borrowing may not be possible for one or two years in view of the government scheme for Blaenau Ffestiniog central and the Company's need to respond*'. Eaves commented that resale stock levels had reduced, creditors had fallen over the year and financial control at Porthmadog had improved.

The pension fund's trustees reported that the higher rate of inflation, than the $8^1/_2$% assumed in the fund, required a higher rate of funding and indicated the high cost to the Company. It was agreed to bring this benefit to the attention of the employees.

By 9th May, the bank holiday week, traffic was comfortably in front of 1979's. Journeys were nearly 4,000 up and fares revenue over £10,000. On 10th May a fire that started near Cei Mawr and crossed the line near Trwn-y-garnedd before spreading up the hill was still putting the Railway at risk the next day, leaving a train stranded at Tanygrisiau, the incident leading to the author's first and last duty as a double-engine fireman when the train was returned to Boston Lodge on 12th May.

The Board had met on 9th May. Although it was not recognised as such, the highlight of the meeting was surely the news that the slaughterhouse field had at last been sold, to the slaughterhouse owners for £3,000! Perversely, within 10 years, in view of the interest then being taken in the WHR, the Company might have wished that it had not been sold after all.

Alan Pegler, Bill Broadbent and Dick Wollan inspect the site for the new Blaenau Ffestiniog station on 25th October 1981.

Author

The FR was able to announce that it would resume services to Blaenau Ffestiniog on 25th May 1982 in time to send out invitations to those it had promised first trip/day journeys. A training train of passenger stock hauled by Linda, *with Allan Garraway at the regulator, was run to Blaenau Ffestiniog during the evening of 24th May. Here he removes the stop block that separated the operating railway from the extension at Tanygrisiau.*

Author

Norman Gurley photographs the FR's road crane offloading the water and fuel tanks on to rail vehicles for delivery to the new station in May 1982.

Geoff Hall, FR Archives

In July, *Princess* was returned from its sojourn in Blaenau Ffestiniog and volunteers engaged in stripping the Peckett. Garraway's reports become much more abbreviated during this year, with very little detail beyond the financial position.

The 11th July Board meeting was held at Netley Hall, Company Clerk Mark Wright's Shropshire home. The Board agreed a resolution in support of the Blaenau Ffestiniog LRO application.

Net of EEC grants the Company needed £100,000 – £140,000 to restore the line from Tanygrisiau to Blaenau Ffestiniog. The volunteer requirement for new works alone equalled the highest annual rate of input on the Deviation project; in addition an input equal to that for permanent way in 1978/9 was needed to maintain the existing Railway. The Society's Arthur Lambert had agreed to be Project Manager with Company employee Andy Putnam in charge of machinery; there was also a need for a site foreman. The DBRW was to be approached for financial assistance.

The weather was consistently poor during July and into August; on 13th August Garraway remarked, of week ended 8th August '*another week 20% down in journeys, which can largely be attributed to weather; Wednesday only had 1,053 bookings, Monday 1,986, on a week where 2,500 – 3,000 would be expected.*' After the August bank holiday the loan account had been reduced to £75,000 at the expense of the current account, £1,257.96 overdrawn, this being a response to the overdraft being contra the Company's statutes.

On 10th September Garraway reported on the impact of opening to Tanygrisiau in terms of bookings there and at Tan-y-bwlch.

Year	Total Bookings	Tan-y-bwlch	Tanygrisiau
1976	211,988	83,800	
1977	210,618	36,500	
1978	226,329	23,600	
		23,600*	
1979	215,408	14,400	34,200
1980	210,000	12,000	37,000

* from 24th June

In 1977, 18,000 members' tickets had been issued; following the restriction of the number of journeys, only 8,000 had been issued in 1978. In 1980 the child-free age was raised from under

The four overbridges between Tanygrisiau and Glan-y-pwll were repaired with cast concrete decks placed higher than previously to accommodate higher rolling stock. The loco is a 1948-built Planet named Ashover *in recognition of its original ownership by the Ashover Light Railway; its acquisition late in 1981 was made with the support of the Society's East Midlands area group, the group and its members having maintained their interest in its wellbeing ever since. Andy Putnam, right of train, joined the company in 1977. Groesffordd, May 1982.*

Arthur Lambert, FR archives

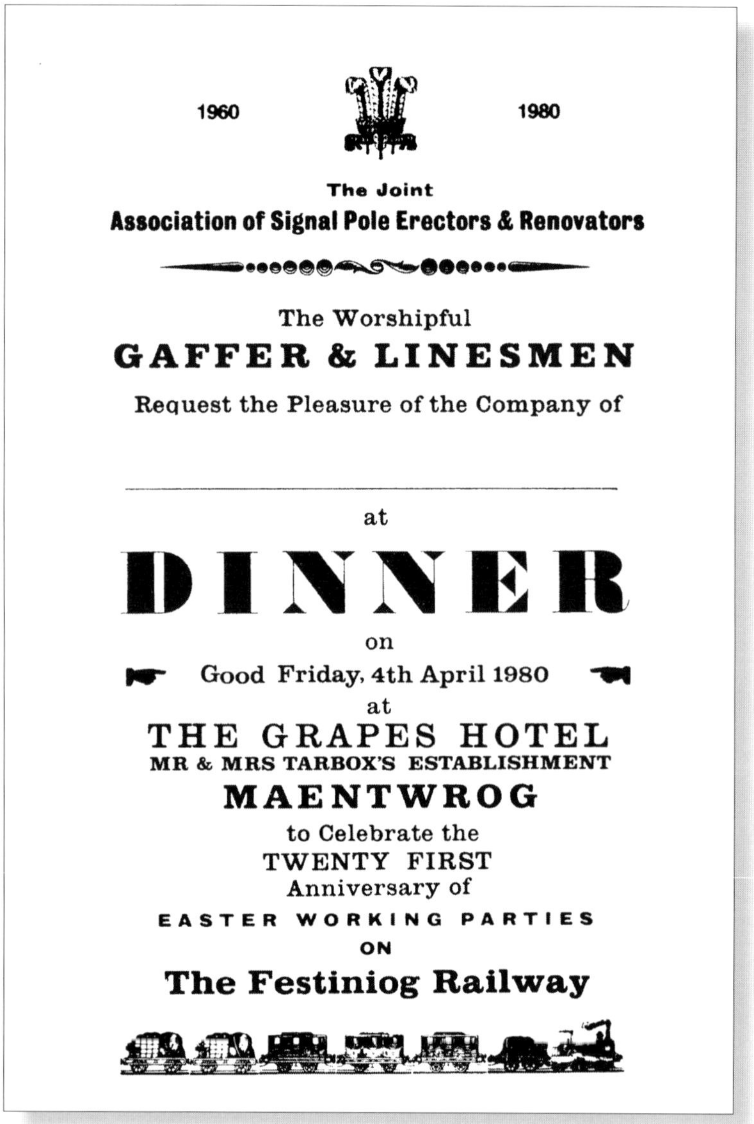

1960 1980

The Joint
Association of Signal Pole Erectors & Renovators

The Worshipful
GAFFER & LINESMEN
Request the Pleasure of the Company of

at
DINNER
on
Good Friday, 4th April 1980
at
THE GRAPES HOTEL
MR & MRS TARBOX'S ESTABLISHMENT
MAENTWROG
to Celebrate the
TWENTY FIRST
Anniversary of
EASTER WORKING PARTIES
ON
The Festiniog Railway

three to under five, which he thought would have accounted for 3% or 6,000 bookings.

A system whereby supporters could make loans, repayable on demand, to the Company was devised as a means of reducing interest payments. The minimum that could be loaned was £500; at the 12th September Board meeting Eaves acknowledged a loan made by Routly. By 24th October, £49,850 had been made available to the Company under this scheme.

The departmental managers made presentations to the Board in support of their budgets. In discussion Paul Dukes said that work at Boston Lodge was interrupted by ad hoc visitors and attributed productivity problems to the loss of the JGF (*jolly good fun* – Routly's phrase) factor; permanent staff felt unappreciated. The works needed a new structure to improve progress and quality of work, he concluded.

There was unhappiness about the proposals for Blaenau Ffestiniog station, which were now effectively out of the Company's hands altogether. Isallt was still deemed to be unsuitable and the consulting engineers had relocated the footbridge in such a manner that impacted on the structure gauge without even consulting the Railway or the County Council! The Railway, with BR support, was refusing to accept the move and the Council was considering the implications.

Garraway's last report for the year was for the week ended 31st October, which revealed that the current account then stood at £5,356.50, with the overdraft at £115,000 and private loans at £49,850.

The Board learned, on 14th November, that the Wales Tourist Board had declined to grant-aid construction of any further carriages.

When the Board met on 9th January 1981 it heard that the EEC grant due the previous year, presumably for Penlan, remained unpaid. Had it been on time 1980's income would have been above budget. Net income from the travel agency business was £19,000 against £12,000 budgeted.

The Company's offer of a $17\frac{1}{2}$% pay rise had been accepted by the staff and £55,000 budgeted for the increase. A further increase, calculated as 50% of performance over budget, would be paid in October. Wages grades had been reduced to three: skilled, semi-skilled and unskilled, plus a $12\frac{1}{2}$% supervisory allowance; there was a probationary grade for new entrants and most seasonal staff. Eight grades covered the salaried staff. There was no provision for length of service. Implementing the grading scheme cost £25,000. Not necessarily cause and effect, but a decision to reduce the pension scheme's funding rate from 12% to $10\frac{1}{2}$% was notified at the same meeting.

The Blaenau Ffestiniog (Central Station) LRO 1981 was made on 20th January. Broadly speaking it authorised a standard gauge line 482 metres long, effectively a deviation of the Trawsfynydd link line, which had never been authorised for the carriage of passengers, a narrow gauge line 636 metres long and an increase in the Company's borrowing powers to £750,000. Although the two railways and Gwynedd County Council made the application jointly, according to Article 18 the costs of obtaining the Order were the

The new BR platform opened on 22nd March 1982, when the FR 'just happened' to have Blanche *in the vicinity as the first train arrived. The DMU driver slowed down and the two trains entered the station together.*

Author

Linda *at the end of the line on 25th May 1982.*

Author

Brian C. Harris

Linda *passes above Tanygrisiau on 31st August 1982.*

responsibility of the British Railways Board!

The 1980 EEC grant, £73,000, had been received by the time of the 13th March Board meeting. A renewal of the £300,000 overdraft limit had been agreed with the bank.

Between Tanygrisiau and Blaenau Ffestiniog work had been carried out on culverts, walls and two of the four overbridges although funding to complete the project was still not in place. Wollan was quietly optimistic that programme completion dates would be met. Routly was optimistic of securing grants from the DBRW and the Wales Tourist Board: '*meanwhile the importance of achieving savings wherever possible in the programme was stressed*'. BR had started track laying but its S&T work was unlikely to be completed until November.

In a brief comment on industrial relations the Board expressed its appreciation of the management for improving the situation.

At Easter, 17th–20th April, traffic was the highest since 1974. However, to dampen the joy the following week saw heavy snowfalls above Tanygrisiau! The Company was also £183,334.89 overdrawn.

On 12th May, Wollan report that a survey on local craftsmen's wages revealed a 23% disparity with FR rates: 18 $^{1}/_{2}$% if public and private national-sector firms were excluded. He recommended making up the 23% difference over two years. The Board accepted this as an objective for skilled staff '*as soon as circumstances permit*'.

The draft accounts for 1980 showed that a profit had been achieved, despite putting 95% of wages costs in the operational account and the remainder under capital expenditure. Both Routly and Garraway had made loans to the Company.

The weather continued to be poor into the summer, with journeys down by more than 40,000 by 21st August. Crucially, both fares and sales revenue were also down, by a total of £15,758. When the Board had met on 3rd July receipts had been £50,000 under budget and a £25,000 shortfall was being forecast for the end of the year.

A change in locomotive working occurred around this time, with the removal of the last of the volunteer taboos, being that of driving trains. It had been realised that the utilisation of paid fitters as locomotive drivers was not necessarily making best or most productive use of their time. A few of the longer-standing volunteer firemen were therefore invited to train as drivers, initially on the basis that they would only be allowed to drive single engines. When qualified they found they were allocated the turns the paid drivers didn't want, the inconvenient ones; the author's informant on this was not polite! Eventually most of the driving came to be undertaken by volunteers and the restriction on the Fairlies was quickly removed when a driver was needed for an evening train scheduled for double-engine haulage and no other driver or locomotive was available.

When the Board met on 11th September it was agreed that trains would run to Blaenau Ffestiniog as soon as the line was completed and before the opening ceremony. Garnock was to consult with Buckingham Palace over an invitation to the Prince and Princess of Wales. It had been calculated that 850 people, including medal holders, would have the right to travel on the first day!

No firm response had been received to the Railway's invitation to the Prince and Princess of Wales when the Board met on 13th November but the Princess '*or the Prince on her behalf if the royal birth were to preclude her attendance*' would be invited to rename *Mountaineer* as *Princess of Wales*. Broadbent was to contact John Ransom to seek his approval. The restoration of services to Blaenau Ffestiniog, '*not to be called an opening*', was intended to take place on 25th May 1982, the 150th anniversary of incorporation.

To improve the cash flow some work had been deferred and the year would end with some staff vacancies and scheduled work incomplete. Wollan and Garraway had not claimed salary increases awarded earlier in the year. The sale of Tyddyn-y-bwlch, the Penrhyn crossing keeper's house, was approved; after it failed to find an 'internal' buyer at £15,000 it was put on the open market at £16,000. A 10% fare increase was to be implemented from the start of services in 1982 and a $6^{1}/_{2}$% pay award would be paid from January, with the addition of a review later in the season when the traffic turnout could be assessed. The Board restated its commitment to eliminating the 23% differential as soon as circumstances permitted.

The Company's 1832 Act of Parliament requiring a 'lodge' to be maintained at Glan-y-pwll level crossing was behind a decision to apply for an amending LRO, but the parliamentary agents were also to be instructed to include automation of Minffordd and Penrhyn crossings and an Article that would legitimise the operation of the travel business in the Order.

The Festiniog Railway home again . . .

THE CHAIRMAN AND DIRECTORS OF THE FESTINIOG RAILWAY COMPANY

In Association with British Rail,
Gwynedd County Council And Meirionnydd District Council
Request The Pleasure Of The Company Of

Mr P. Johnson

TO THE OFFICIAL OPENING OF BLAENAU FFESTINIOG STATION

BY THE RT. HON. GEORGE THOMAS, M.P.,
SPEAKER OF THE HOUSE OF COMMONS

ON SATURDAY, 30th. APRIL 1983 AT 11.30a.m.
And Afterwards To Travel To Porthmadog And Back On A Special Train
On Which A Buffet Lunch Will Be Served

Guests Are Requested To Assemble At 11.00a.m.

R.S.V.P.
(BY 28th. FEBRUARY 1983)

The official opening of Blaenau Ffestiniog station was performed by George Thomas MP, speaker of the House of Commons, on 30th April 1983. The loco headboard featured the speaker's coat of arms and his parliamentary catchphrase; after the speeches George Thomas signed the headboard.

Both Author

It must have been with a certain sense of irony that one local business, the electricity supply utility MANWEB, welcomed the Railway back to Blaenau Ffestiniog the year before. Not surprising, as their Branch Manager Richard Weir had previously, and subsequently, worked for the FR. The new station had opened for British Rail traffic only on 22nd March 1982.

Peter Johnson

After the 30th April ceremony both FR and BR trains departed simultaneously, when it appeared that the DMU tried to outdo Merddin Emrys *in the exhaust stakes!*

Chris Jones

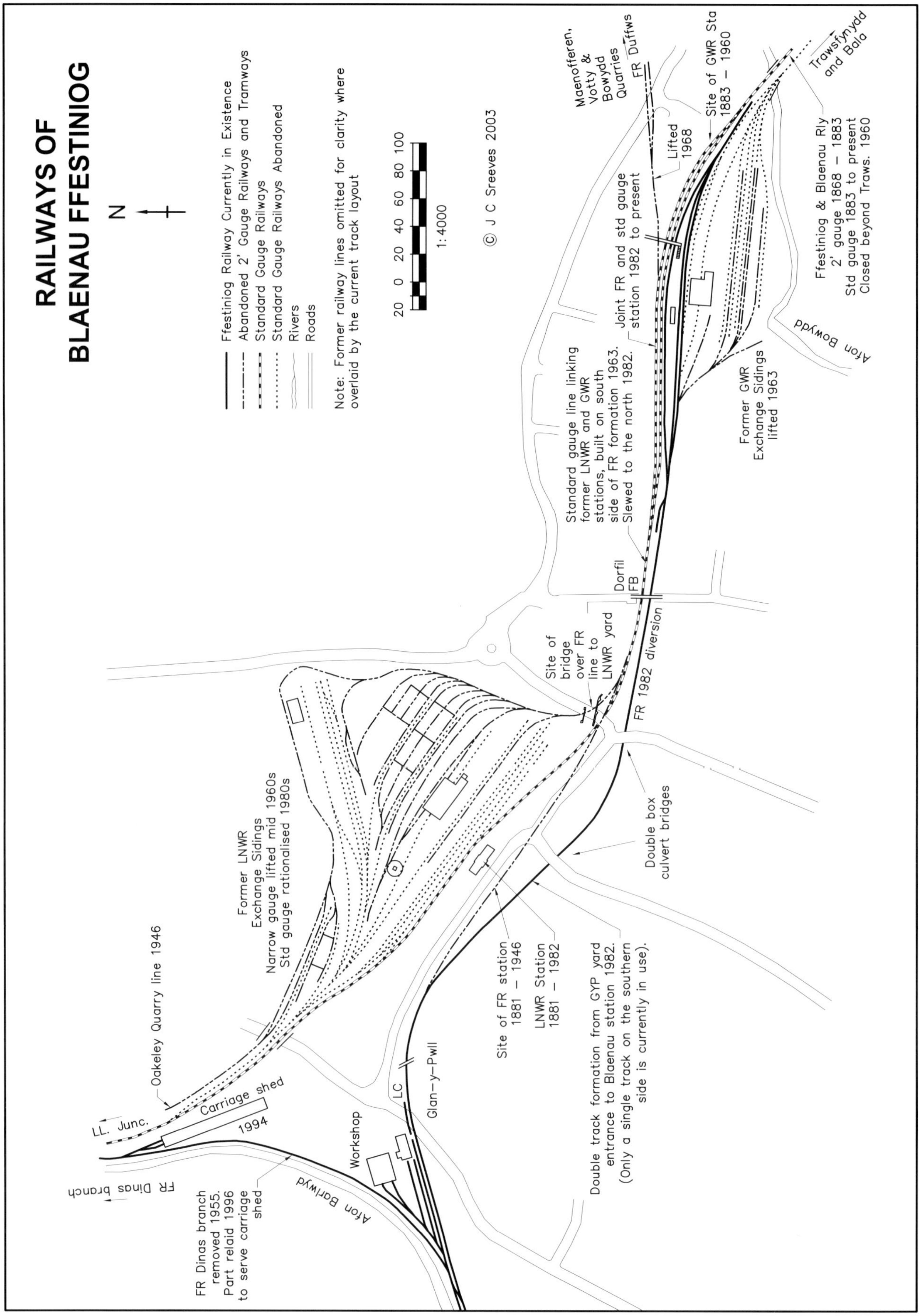
RAILWAYS OF BLAENAU FFESTINIOG
N
Ffestiniog Railway Currently in Existence
Abandoned 2' Gauge Railways and Tramways
Standard Gauge Railways
Standard Gauge Railways Abandoned
Rivers
Roads
Note: Former railway lines omitted for clarity where overlaid by the current track layout
20 0 20 40 60 80 100
1:4000
© J C Sreeves 2003
Maenofferen, Votty & Bowydd Quarries
FR Duffws
Site of GWR Sta 1883 – 1960
Trawsfynydd and Bala
Lifted 1968
Joint FR and std gauge station 1982 to present
Ffestiniog & Blaenau Rly 2' gauge 1868 – 1883 Std gauge 1883 to present Closed beyond Traws. 1960
Afon Bowydd
Standard gauge line linking former LNWR and GWR stations, built on south side of FR formation 1963. Slewed to the north 1982.
Former GWR Exchange Sidings lifted 1963
Dorfil FB
Site of bridge over FR line to LNWR yard
FR 1982 diversion
Double box culvert bridges
Former LNWR Exchange Sidings Narrow gauge lifted mid 1960s Std gauge rationalised 1980s
Oakeley Quarry line 1946
Site of FR station 1881 – 1946
LNWR Station 1881 – 1982
Double track formation from GYP yard entrance to Blaenau station 1982. (Only a single track on the southern side is currently in use).
LL. Junc.
Carriage shed 1994
LC
Glan-y-Pwll
Workshop
FR Dinas branch
FR Dinas branch removed 1955. Part relaid 1996 to serve carriage shed
Afon Barlwyd

Not used by passenger trains since 1975, the awkwardly sited loop at Penrhyn was removed during the month.

The 'inability' of the Prince and Princess of Wales to accept the Railway's invitation appears to have caused some distress when the Board met on 9th January 1982. Garnock circulated copies of the letter at the meeting and was deputed to discuss the refusal with the Wales Tourist Board's Chairman, Lord Parry. Routly, Smith and Garnock were to investigate alternative candidates for the 'opening'.

The $6^1/_2$% pay award had been refused by NUR members, who wanted a fixed mid-term increase backdated to 1st January 1982 and a fixed date for achievement of parity with skilled workers in local industries. The Board would not agree to this; Wollan, however, had '*reappraised the cash flow projections in the light of the year-end out turn and now considered that it was quite prudent to put forward a new package which would contain an element of back pay related to 1981 results, thus raising basic rates on to which the 1982 proposed $6^1/_2$% would be built, resulting in an effective increase of approximately $11^1/_2$% in 1982*'. It was agreed that Wollan could take this offer back, contingent on continued economies.

The content of the Society magazine editorials had become an issue – '*the problem of vetting editorials to prevent inaccurate and/or undesirable material being presented was again considered*'. *The Company view was 'of the need for accuracy and good public relations in the magazine editorials, which must be seen by most readers as a corporate publication, representing both bodies.*' Society Chairman, Gordon Caddy, had not raised the matter at the last Society Board meeting, so Routly would discuss it with him again. Routly subsequently wrote to Caddy with a suggested vetting procedure.

Under the heading of 'society liaison' it was reported that the possibility of renaming *Mountaineer* had not been received with any enthusiasm, but as the main reason for doing this no longer applied the matter ceased to be an issue; John Ransom had not therefore been approached.

At the Board's 12th March meeting it was noted that the LRO application would have to be sealed before 31st March. George Thomas MP, Speaker of the House of Commons, had been invited to perform the reopening ceremony.

Wollan reported that he had reached a settlement on pay that would cost £58,000. A lump-sum payment of 2% on the 1981 wages bill had helped to produce a $12^1/_2$–14% increase over the 1981 base rates. Part of the package was to be strict control on overtime worked, the 24% worked in 1978–1980 had reduced to 15% in 1981 and the target was now 10%.

1981's cash control was viewed favourably by the Board, which congratulated all concerned. Wollan endorsed the objective of returning to using bank borrowing during the off-peak only and reminded the Board that with the completion of the route to Blaenau Ffestiniog the Railway would have exhausted its access to large subsidies. Meanwhile, he said, the bank recognised that by holding to the £300,000 overdraft facility the Company had, in real terms, considering capital employed, shown an improvement over the past five years.

A new venture was announced at the end of the meeting with the news that the Company had been approached to provide a consultative service to Merseyside County Council/Liverpool Garden Festival for the development of a narrow gauge railway in 1984. The fee of £150 per day plus expenses was approved and Garraway was asked to deal with it.

British Rail commenced using its platform in the new Blaenau Ffestiniog station on 22nd March 1982. Just as its first public train came into view so did a short works train hauled by *Blanche*! The DMU driver played the game and kept pace with his steam counterpart who was stealing his thunder.

The Railway Inspectorate's Major Peter Olver was scheduled to make an advisory visit on 29th March but details of his observations have not come to hand.

The year's business got off to a poor start, with traffic revenue only just in front of the previous year's and the sales were trailing badly behind as well. Garraway noted a resistance to the fare increase but perhaps people were waiting for the resumption of services to Blaenau Ffestiniog. When the Board met on 7th May Wollan reported that, despite the poor sales, Olver's requirements could be met within the budget.

The prospect of providing a link between the Conwy valley and Cambrian coast lines, and thus speeding the service between the North West and the southern half of the Lleyn peninsula, had encouraged BR's Red Star parcel service to make the FR part of its network. Approval to advertising the service on the side of trains was given.

Whilst the railway had been opened to traffic there was still work to be done before it could be considered finished, as demonstrated by this view of Prince *passing between barriers of flags at the Glan-y-pwll level crossing.*

Author

The Society had agreed to Wollan vetting magazine editorials but a requested amendment had been ignored. Society Director, Bryan Chicken, present in lieu of Broadbent, was asked to discuss it with Caddy so that there would be no recurrence. The author thinks that he was responsible for the omission, recalling that the proposed alteration was received too late to be incorporated.

Under the heading '*other business*' it was recorded that compensation for outstanding claims up to 1973 by Aneurin Davies had been settled and an additional claim for £3,500 for further land and disturbance since then had been agreed; the payment was an unbudgeted item.

In discussing arrangements for the resumption of services to Blaenau Ffestiniog, it was agreed that Routly would write a congratulatory letter to staff. Management assured the Board that attention would be given to the standard of engine-crew dress.

Olver made his formal inspection on 17th May, submitting his report on 30th July. He observed that Dduallt – Blaenau Ffestiniog was to be worked as a single section, with the points at Tanygrisiau locked out of use. He commented on 20 items that required attention and agreed strategies for dealing with them with Garraway and railway personnel. He also met Peter Marston, Gwynedd County Council's deputy planning officer, who was to become planning consultant to the FR for the Welsh Highland Railway Transport & Works Order application, to discuss aspects of the site that lay within the council's purview, particularly specifying that 'a deterrent' be placed on the top of the

Opposite: *This photograph was taken on the deviation, at Gelliwiog, with a train that illustrates the FR's development – a new loco, observation car, with brake compartment door promoting Red Star parcels, steel-bodied carriage, buffet car, corridor connections and electric lighting, all additions to stock since 1954.*

Norman Gurley, FR Archives

boundary wall between the railway and the adjoining school, to '*prevent persons climbing over the wall or even sitting on top of it as at present*'. Commenting that the works '*appear to be complete in all respects and have all been well constructed*' he recommended that, subject to attention being given to the 20 points identified, the works should be approved.

During the evening of 23rd May, Garraway drove *Linda* to Blaenau Ffestiniog with a train of coaching stock for training purposes, the finest way to commemorate the 150th anniversary of the Company's incorporation.

Services were resumed two days later, fulfilling the dream of those who thought '*something could be done*' back in the 1950s. They could not have imagined, especially after the early trouncing by the CEGB, that the Railway's restoration would be partially financed by government agencies and an overdraft rising to £300,000. Despite the Board's efforts it had not been possible to obtain additional funding to complete the restoration, so facilities were minimal and were first provided by temporary buildings. The return to Blaenau Ffestiniog was achieved at considerable personal cost for some of those involved, too, not to mention the state of the Railway's finances; but there was a physical cost to the Railway, also, for its infrastructure and rolling stock was looking very shabby owing to the lack of maintenance, especially since the Deviation was started.

The first train was hauled by the newest locomotive, *Earl of Merioneth*, with senior driver Evan Davies at the controls; although it rained it was nowhere near as wet as during the opening to Tanygrisiau in 1978. The Company worked hard to ensure that all of those entitled to travel on the first day were able to do so. Travellers included holders of the Centenary of Steam medals issued in 1963 and new medals cast in silver

and bronze designed by Michael Seymour to mark both the restoration and the Company's 150th anniversary. Priced at £150 and £34 respectively, as they were sold as tickets they avoided payment of VAT!

When the Board met on 12th July 1982 '*The clerk reported the sealing of the document relating to one-engine-in-steam operation between Dduallt and Blaenau Ffestiniog.*'

After all the effort, the immediate results were more than a little disappointing. The first full week of services to Blaenau Ffestiniog, also a bank holiday week, saw bookings a little more than 1,500 in front of 1981's bank holiday week and for most weeks subsequently tracked the previous year's figure quite closely, but on six weeks falling below it! Traffic revenue performed a little better but for several weeks barely reflected the 10% fare increase, never mind the extra distance travelled. Sales performance was pretty dismal, only beating the previous year's figure on three occasions, over the August bank holiday period. The opening of a catering competitor in Porthmadog was undoubtedly a factor, as was the poor quality of FR catering at the time – even staff and volunteers transferred their allegiance to the new establishment.

There were some good points during the year. Garraway had noted, on 4th June, that there was heavy traffic from BR and all carriages except one were in traffic. The direct connection at Blaenau Ffestiniog had generated 1,123 bookings during the four weeks to 12th June, compared with 324 in 1981. The Red Star parcels service started on 9th August and the first parcel was carried the next day, although that was the exception rather than the rule. A strike on BR in July, though, affected transfers at Blaenau Ffestiniog, losing the FR two excursions and a large party booking plus ordinary traffic, and cost the FR, in Garraway's estimation, £2,000 in lost receipts.

The layout and facilities at Blaenau Ffestiniog taxed the Board when it met on 12th July; it was thought important for the FR to control the exit/entrance for sales purposes. Better signs were needed, too. Discussions had taken place with BR about a joint island platform, a proposal that had been originally refused by BR because it would hinder the operation of its parcel service, which needed road access, despite such traffic being minimal and declining. Schemes for a museum, cafeteria, booking office, shop and shelter to be located above an island platform were drawn up but neither platform nor associated development was proceeded with.

The Society magazine continued to exercise the Board; Smith and Broadbent were deputed to raise again the matter of editorial control, '*using the example of the ignored request to avoid reference to the Blaenau station as Blaenau Central*': that was its legal name, of course. In the event Dick Hardy, as the Company's nominee on this occasion, raised the issue at the Society's Board meeting on 18th August; after some debate, agreement seemed to have been reached that in cases of disagreement the editor and Wollan should agree wording to their mutual satisfaction: only for Financial Secretary Bryan Chicken to point out that errors of fact should be corrected but querying if matters of opinion should be censored. There was no clarification and the matter was left unresolved.

Society Director Norman Pearce reported this to the Company on 3rd September as a division of opinion, leaving the Board to decide that as informal approaches had been unsuccessful Smith should now make a formal approach. In the report of this meeting given to the Society this brief minute was expanded, reporting Wollan's view that the magazine was inevitably read as the prime source of Company policy and news equally to its dissemination of Society news. '*It is not the Daily Mail*', he had said '*and no more freedom from the responsibility of representing Company policy through its editorials should be expected than is exercised by a volunteer performing duties on the footplate or in the guard's van.*' It was agreed, according to the content of this report, that the Society Board had a corporate responsibility to determine magazine editorial policy and stand by it.

Paul Dukes reported that 11 people were employed at Boston Lodge, three down on complement. The locomotive programme included new tyres for *Linda* and *Blanche* and a new driving axle for *Mountaineer*. £52,300 would be spent on fuel during the year. More waste-oil processors were needed, he said, and his target was to keep expenditure to £50,000 in 1983.

Wollan reported that projected income in 1983 was at present £860,000, with expenditure of £890,000, excluding capital, interest and repayment of loans. Garraway revealed that the current account went into credit for the first time in 1982 on 13th September; he had not reported on banking activity since the end of 1981.

The Festiniog Railway Light Railway (Amendment) Order 1982 was made on 13th October. By it, the Company was permitted to automate the Stwlan dam road and Glan-y-pwll level crossings, without the requirement to '*erect or maintain a lodge or gate*', and to enter into agreements with railway companies. This last article was intended to give proper status to the travel business that had grown out of the BR ticket agency taken on when Minffordd BR became unstaffed in 1964; whilst it did give approval to agreements with railway companies, particularly specifying the British Railways Board and its shipping subsidiaries, it did not sanction agreements with hoteliers, airlines, travel agents and others which might be required to run a travel agency.

Reporting the year's expected surplus, Wollan proposed allocating £10,000 to a 2½% pay rise, backdated to 1st January. When discussing the surplus projected in the 1983 budget the Board agreed that a 3½% rise could be offered from 1st January 1983.

Following consultation with the Society on the post-Blaenau 'future of the Railway' two items of reorganisation were reported to the Board on 12th November. Responsibility for civil engineering was to be transferred to the permanent way department and a Volunteer Resource Manager was to be appointed, both expected to be implemented by the year-end. The possibility of separating the marketing function from the traffic department was considered and the need for a marketing 'man' agreed.

This would be a good place to end this book except for the need to mention two significant events that took place shortly after.

The first was the official opening to Blaenau Ffestiniog that took place on 30th April 1983. George Thomas MP, Speaker of the House of Commons, performed the duty as his last public function before retiring. On this occasion, a bright day, too, there was much speech making, a silver band, a male-voice choir and large crowds. It put the seal on building the Deviation and restoring the Festiniog Railway to Blaenau Ffestiniog.

The second was the retirement of Allan Garraway from day-to-day involvement with the Company as from 30th April, although he remained as acting General Manager until his successor, David Pollock, took up his appointment in August. He then acted as a consultant for the Company until 1986.

At the 18th March Board meeting, Routly had noted that it was the last that Allan Garraway would attend, the minutes recording:

> *'The board expressed their great appreciation of Mr Garraway's 32 years working on the railway, first as a volunteer, from 1955 as manager and from 1958 as general manager.'*

In the circumstances this tribute might not have impressed Garraway too much, but it is well to remember that for many years he *was* the Festiniog Railway and he laid the foundations for a return to a position of pre-eminence in the world of railways that had been established in Spooner's time.

Unaudited Traffic and Revenue data, 1979–83

(From Allan Garraway's Reports)

Year end	**1979**	**1980**	**1981**	**1982**	**1983**
Journeys	363,842	360,209	319,794	335,353	292,428
Bookings	203,977	207,785	185,397	197,782	173,376
Fares	£377,038	£442,914	£440,939	£512,545	£436,287
Sales	£179,802	£208,252	£206,776	£200,541	£187,534

The board and its officers on 20th March 1986, on the occasion of Allan Garraway's retirement. Front, from left: Dick Wollan and Allan Garraway; centre: Dick Hardy, Bill Broadbent; Hugh Eaves, Ed Nicholson and Alan Pegler; rear: Martin Barradell, Robin Scott, Les Smith, Andy Savage, Trevor Bailey and John Routly.

FR archives

and looking back 35 years to the start . . . .

The Old Bull Inn, Barnet, 8th October 1951. Amongst those attending the second meeting that led to the FR's revival were Vic Mitchell (1st left), John Bate (3rd left), Allan Garraway (6th right), W.K. Nelson (4th right), F. Gilbert (3rd right) and Bill Harvey (2nd right).

FR Society Archive

Postscript
1984~2005

Although the story told in this book ends in 1983, the Festiniog Railway has not stood still and has made great advances on many fronts, highlights of which are briefly described here.

When the FR was restored to Blaenau Ffestiniog it was in a pretty poor way. Generally it looked scruffy and it still owed a considerable debt to the bank. Despite this it exuded the confidence of knowing it could overcome great odds to achieve its objectives.

David Pollock took up his appointment as General Manager in this environment on 4th August 1983. The accounts for the year were to show a gross turnover of £840,272 and an operating loss of £45,898 after £22,807 interest had been paid to the bank. At the end of the peak-season services in September seven positions, including the entire three-man building department, were declared redundant, followed at the end of daily running in October by that of the Catering Manager. After several resignations, staff employed settled at 40 full-time and 5 part-time, down from 51 and 6 respectively.

Plans to address the financial situation came to fruition in October 1987, with the launch of a scheme that released some of the Company's unissued share capital, where £1 stock could be obtained subject to the linked purchase of a £250 4% debenture. The reason for this issue was to reduce the Company's short-term borrowings significantly, increasing profits which would be reinvested in a programme of preserving and promoting the Railway's heritage; amenity improvements at Blaenau Ffestiniog and Porthmadog; further covered accommodation at Boston Lodge and provision of a volunteer hostel at Minffordd.

The prospectus for the issue revealed that the Company had received gifts and grants totalling

A regular feature of the last 10 years has been the vintage weekends, with gravity trains of increasing length, here approaching Tan-y-bwlch with Dave High at the helm on 25th June 1994, always a popular attraction.

All photographs in the Postscript are by the author unless otherwise stated.

£1,273,127 since 1954, the donor list being:

Gifts:	
The Society	£245,834
The Trust and others	£204,642
Grants:	
Wales Tourist Board	£379,335
Manpower Services Commission	£186,094
Mid-Wales Development Board	£75,010
European Economic Community	£134,320
Others	£47,892

The issue did not reach its £400,000 target but did raise over £250,000, enough to pay off the overdraft and other borrowing. The 4% interest rate was not intended to be attractive and many debenture holders have not claimed it, but the passage of time and the arrival of low commercial interest rates eventually made it very attractive and caused the issue to be closed.

An indication of the scheme's success in improving the Railway's day-to-day finances was demonstrated by the £61,111 profit made in 1991 including £22,207 interest received. However in 1992 the balance had swung the other way and £6,266 overdraft interest had been paid. Thereafter overdraft interest has been paid every year.

Most of the enhancements proposed by the debenture issue were dealt with from 1989, when the Railway was awarded grants totalling £430,000 from an EEC fund called the National Programme of Community Interest, allocated to promote tourism in Dyfed, Gwynedd and Powys, and a Wales Tourist Board development fund.

These grants financed what Pollock called the InCa (INcreased CApacity) project and they brought improvements throughout: platform buildings and canopy at Blaenau Ffestiniog; new toilets and café extension at Tan-y-bwlch; carriage storage and maintenance facilities at Boston Lodge; catering improvements and a canopy at Harbour Station; a permanent way diesel locomotive, three carriages and the boiler for a new double Fairlie.

The significance of Robert Francis Fairlie as a locomotive engineer – his double bogies are used on electric and diesel locomotives around the world – was emphasised on 1st May 1986, when Type 4 47 645 was named Robert Francis Fairlie: Locomotive Engineer, *complete with FR 150th anniversary crests, at Blaenau Ffestiniog. The FR's service train carried an appropriate headboard.*

The first sign of brightening the trains' appearance was the repainting of Prince, *seen on Cae Mawr, in authentic historic livery for the 150th anniversary in 1986.*

In 1986/7 Merddin Emrys *was the subject of a substantial overhaul; its lines were improved and some heritage features applied, rounded tank tops and Victorian livery, thanks to some private sponsorship.* David Lloyd George, *operational from 22nd July 1992 but completed in 1993, was built with a heritage outline. On 4th April 1993 both locomotives crossed at Minffordd.*

From 1989 attempts were made to soften the lines of Earl of Merioneth, *seen crossing* David Lloyd George *at Minffordd on 16th June 1996. In 2003 the company decided that* Earl of Merioneth*'s tanks would be renewed to a traditional appearance when the locomotive is next overhauled.*

To highlight the 'Mountain Prince' service the livery of several carriages was changed from 1987, as seen here with Blanche *in August that year.*

Right: *A single Fairlie,* Taliesin, *was returned to the FR's fleet in 1999. Although designed as a visual replica of the 1876-built locomotive it is slightly larger. Blaenau Ffestiniog, 25th March 2000.*

The latter item arose after cracks had been found in *Merddin Emrys*'s boiler; whilst a repair had been carried out there was some uncertainty whether it would last. The new locomotive built around the boiler was completed in 1992 and named *David Lloyd George*. Its appearance, though, owed much to the 19th century and nothing to the 20th, certainly nothing to the 1979-built *Earl of Merioneth*! It was slightly larger than *Merddin Emrys*, which had, thanks to support from a sponsor, had its traditional appearance restored during an overhaul carried out in 1986/7. It, too, had been given a historic livery, following the precedent set by *Prince* in 1986.

David Lloyd George was not the only new locomotive to emerge from Boston Lodge, for from 1988 a subscription scheme had raised the funds to build a new 0-4-4T single Fairlie called *Taliesin*, replacing the 1876-built locomotive of the same name that had been dismantled in 1932. Using a mixture of employed and volunteer labour the new *Taliesin*, built to a slightly larger scale than the original, was completed in 1999.

The carriages were built at Carnforth to provide the highest standards of comfort, including insulation and gas-fired heating. They were operated with two existing vehicles uprated to the same standard and a 1990-built observation saloon/driving trailer to provide a set that could operate all year round, thus increasing capacity. At the time of publication there are only a few weeks in January and February when no public services are advertised; during that period there might be some services operated for the benefit of coach parties over part of the line, depending upon the activities of the permanent way department.

From 1995, the FR benefited from a strategic development scheme put in place to encourage investment and work creation after following the closure of Trawsfynydd nuclear power station. The Railway secured a 100% grant of £500,000 for works at Blaenau Ffestiniog (second platform road, signalling, improved pedestrian access and new booking hall and shop in the Queen's Hotel basement), Glan-y-pwll (carriage storage shed) and Tanygrisiau

Prince *was subject to an intermediate overhaul and some visual improvements in the late 1990s on completion of which it was repainted a slightly brighter shade of red. Minffordd, 17th August 2003.*

Following a boiler overhaul in 1995/6 Linda *appeared in Penrhyn black livery. A wagon was adapted to serve as a tender to further enhance its PQR appearance. Photographed at Cae Mawr on 25th October 1996, when hauling a special train operated for contributors to the overhaul fund.*

Janet Towers watches Planet diesel Conway Castle *haul push-pull stock past her house opposite Capel Nazareth on 30th April 1994.*

Mountaineer at Tanygrisiau c1990.

The loco was painted in War Department grey livery, temporarily, for the 'All our Yesterdays' gala in 1995; Tanygrisiau 29th December 1995.

The lined black livery applied to Mountaineer at the suggestion of the locomotive's supporters; Boston Lodge 8th March 1998.

(signalling). Hindsight might suggest that the signalling schemes were not given due consideration in planning for, after delays of some years caused by changes in requirements, the Tanygrisiau scheme was cancelled and that at Blaenau was suspended after an embarrassing derailment, when the points moved under a train entering the station; it was not possible to recreate the fault during subsequent testing. A simpler scheme was introduced at Tanygrisiau in 2004, the location becoming a crossing place for the first time since reopening in 1978.

At £4.3 million, a record was set by the Millennium Commission grant to the Company announced in October 1995. It was awarded not for the direct benefit of the FR at all, but for the reconstruction of the Welsh Highland Railway between Caernarfon and Rhyd Ddu. The FR's interest in the WHR had become public in 1989, following a secret attempt to secure the trackbed from the official receiver in order to prevent the development of a competitor. After a period of some very strong anti-FR publicity, a partial renewal of the Board led to a change in policy and a commitment to restore the WHR in its entirety, with the addition of a three-mile extension to Caernarfon. The policy adopted was to rebuild the WHR with outside funding and, crucially, no borrowing.

Following a High Court hearing and a public inquiry into an unprecedented competitive LRO application the first section, between Caernarfon and Dinas was opened in 1997. Dinas–Waunfawr was opened in 2000 and Waunfawr–Rhyd Ddu in 2003. A £10.75 million scheme to complete the WHR by Easter 2009 was announced in September 2004, with the news that the Welsh Assembly Government was to contribute £5 million. At the same time a public appeal for £$^1/_2$ million to complete the funding was launched; when the target was passed within a month the target was revised to £1 million, the additional funds being earmarked to match grants to be sought for additional carriages.

Vale of Ffestiniog *was adapted from a 350hp Funkey locomotive acquired in 1993 from the Port Elizabeth Cement Company in South Africa. On 18th April 1998 it was posed at Blaenau Ffestiniog with a similarly liveried Class 59 locomotive that was en route to Trawsfynydd with a rail tour.*

Even after the passage of over 10 years the FR's 1993 'Hunslet 100' gala is still the subject of favourable comment. One of the attractions was the presence of Charles, *the elder of the PQR Hunslet trio, seen on 3rd May with* Blanche *and* Linda.

Blaenau Ffestiniog on 6th May 2001. The station acquired permanent buildings and a canopy in 1990, funded by the InCa (increased capacity) scheme. Further changes were made in 1995.

The FR Society was responsible for obtaining a £375,000 award from the Heritage Lottery Fund in 1999; it financed the construction of a carriage restoration workshop at Boston Lodge and the restoration to a very high standard of 1872-built bogie carriages Nos. 15 and 16, the first restored in original livery, the other in 1920s livery. The HLF project also included the repair of many of the wagons that form the demonstration gravity slate train.

Improvements to the Railway's appearance started in a small way after the creation in 1985 of a volunteer department, whimsically named the '*parks & gardens department*' although there have never been any parks, dedicated to the Railway's gardens. Spreading from horticulture, the department eventually took over responsibility for buildings as well, including maintenance and new works. The most significant of these was the long-awaited volunteer hostel at Minffordd, funded by the Society with the support of a £150,000 grant and completed in 1998.

Changes to the Railway's underlying infrastructure have included a programme of track renewal that will see the traditional double-head and bullhead rail replaced by flat-bottom rail throughout the length of the running line, although heritage interests will ensure the retention of the older materials at strategic locations like Penrhyn station. An automatic crossing loop installation was commissioned at Tan-y-bwlch in 1987; Minffordd was similarly treated in 1989. The loops at Dduallt and Rhiw Goch were decommissioned in 1988 and 1989 respectively, although Rhiw Goch was brought back into use in 1994. Minffordd Quarry Lane crossing was automated in 1991. Despite being dependent on obsolete Strowger equipment, the FR's telephone network has been constantly under review and in 1989 the Railway was licensed as a telecoms provider by Oftel.

The Railway's 150th anniversary in 1986 was commemorated in grand style, with a series of profile-raising events throughout the year. Highlights were a gala weekend in April, operation of demonstration gravity trains, including one that ran from Tanygrisiau to the Cob, the naming of a BR Class 47 locomotive

David Lloyd George *and the push-pull set cross the Cob on 30th December 2000. Probably this picture epitomises the InCa scheme; both loco and carriages were funded by it, the provision of additional heated carriages allowing the FR to expand its operating season considerably, the main restriction on operating expansion now being the need to give time to track maintenance. Since the photograph was taken the carriages have lost their special livery in favour of the standard fleet scheme.*

The pioneer Garratt, K1, returned to the FR from the National Railway Museum for a gala visit before restoration commenced; Minffordd, 1st May 1995.

Two Boston Lodge-built replica Darjeeling Himalayan Railway coaches in use with DHR 'B' class 0-4-0ST No. 19 on the Beeches Light Railway in Oxfordshire, 24th October 2004.

Coach Building may be a lost art . . . . but certainly not at Boston Lodge

The revived 'curly roof van' in an advanced state of construction in the carriage workshop at Boston Lodge on 18th April 2004. The rain strip above the side door is a surviving component from No. 3, the vehicle that rotted away at Portmadoc during the war.

This replica Pickering composite brake was built at Boston Lodge for the Welshpool & Llanfair Light Railway and was photographed at Llanfair Caereinion on 5th September 2004.

Beyer Peacock NGG16 Class No. 138 was overhauled at Boston Lodge and Glan-y-pwll and demonstrated at the latter before being transferred to the WHR; 2nd May 1997.

Vintage trains made up in different combinations are also a feature of the vintage weekends. This particular train was laid on for the trustees' annual inspection on 4th October 2002; it is unlikely to reappear as all original stock will in future appear in either 19th century (No. 16, third from back) or 20th century (Nos. 10 and 15, at the rear) livery.

A series of events to mark the 50th anniversary of the FR's revival was started with commemorative dinner held at Boston Lodge on 26th June 2004, marking the anniversary of the takeover. Chief guest was Alan Pegler, seen with FR Trust chairman John Prideaux and Prince*'s driver, Dave High, holding the headboard.*

A 1950s-themed vintage weekend was held on 24th/25th September 2004, almost the anniversary of the first movements under the current regime. The chief guest was Allan Garraway, making his first visit to the railway for nine years, seen with Prince *and fellow 1951 Bristol-meeting attender Vic Mitchell on 25th September.*

The revised carriage livery, introduced for the 'Mountain Prince' service, was so well received that it spread to the whole fleet. Linda *was painted midnight blue, its first full repaint since 1971, in 1991; at the same time a removable tender cab section was made that can be installed or removed to the driver's preference. Minffordd, 28th August 1992.*

after Robert Francis Fairlie and, thanks to support from the paint manufacturer, the appearance of *Prince* in an authentic historic livery.

Special events then became a regular feature in the Railway's calendar. FR150 was followed by Steam 125 in 1988, Steam Gala in 1990, Hunslet 100 in 1993, All Our Yesterdays in 1995, A Festival of Steam in 1997, RailFest in 1999 and Anything Goes in 2001, all held over the May Day public holiday weekend and coinciding with the Society's AGM. As the FR became more confident in its organisational abilities the events became more ambitious and had more and more attractions. All included the use of visiting locomotives, either working on shuttle services or on '*drive an engine*' shunting activities; the visitors included the WHR's 2-6-2T *Russell*, a number of quarry Hunslet 0-4-0STs, a German Feldbahn 0-8-0T, an Alco contemporary of *Mountaineer* visiting from France and one of the NGG16 class Garratts obtained for the WHR, confined by its size to the carriage shed siding at Glan-y-pwll.

Other events held during the 1990s and afterwards included several featuring friends of 'Thomas the tank engine' and several designed to promote and encourage volunteering. One regular feature in the Railway's calendar is the vintage weekend, first held in 1994 and most years subsequently. This increasingly popular event pays unashamed homage to the Railway's past, with many combinations of vintage stock, including mixed trains, goods trains and gravity trains, laid on for the delight of connoisseur and public alike.

The interest in the FR's heritage, whilst always strongly held by many supporters, came to the fore after the establishment of the FR Heritage Group in 1984. Partially a reaction to apparent official lack of interest in heritage matters during the Deviation/return to Blaenau years, the group's founders thought the time had come to give the FR's heritage due precedence. Later described by former Society magazine editor Dan Wilson as '*the Railway's conscience*', the group has worked to preserve elements of the Railway's past and to raise awareness of it. Needless to say the group's members play a significant role in vintage weekends, in planning and in operation.

The Society took longer to adapt its attitude towards the 'restored' railway. Whilst the restoration was considered to be incomplete, the Company had demanded that all surplus funds be handed over to it to be used as it saw fit. After the Trust became charitable in 1964 many donations had been diverted to it in view of the tax advantages but the Society had no influence over expenditure. Society donations had totalled £49, 213 in 1981 and £29,045 in 1982, so substantial sums were involved. By 1984, Society funds were being allocated to specific projects but the Company was still very much in the driving seat.

The worm started to turn, though, in 1986, after Gordon Caddy was replaced as Society Chairman by Gordon Rushton. The latter had many ideas for taking the Society forward and increasing its influence. He was also concerned about the increasing age of Society members and the decline in membership since the Blaenau-euphoric peak of 6,619 in 1982; it dipped under 6,000 in 1986. He was very much against doing things '*because we always do it that way*' and wanted to encourage '*thinking outside the envelope*', a philosophy he developed after he was appointed General Manager in 1991. A sign that the Company recognised the importance of volunteering to the Railway had been made in 1983, with the appointment, of David Green initially, of a full-time Volunteer Resource Manager.

A stronger volunteer influence emerged from Boston Lodge when a team took on the completion of *Blanche*'s overhaul in time for its centenary celebrations in 1993. Whilst not the first time volunteers had contributed to a locomotive overhaul – they had given much to *Prince*'s 1970s refurbishment – the *Blanche* team was notable for the inclusion of persons involved in operating the locomotive. Similar supporters' teams were formed to care for *Linda, Mountaineer* and *Prince* and then the *Blanche* team took on responsibility for overhauling *Merddin Emrys*.

In some instances work had not been scheduled but was initiated by volunteers when the alternative appeared to be a period of prolonged storage for their chosen steed. They also accepted responsibility for raising the necessary funds. The price the Company paid for the work sometimes affected a locomotive's livery, with *Linda* first appearing in midnight blue and then Penrhyn Quarry Railway lined-black and Mountaineer being turned out in lined-black after a spell in War Department grey, applied for the All Our Yesterdays gala in 1995.

Volunteer input at Boston Lodge was not restricted to locomotive repair and operation. Ron Jarvis, who had led the restoration of carriage No. 16, reconstructed four-wheeler No. 5 at his Llanbedr home, working on No. 6 in parallel. No. 5 returned to service in 1983, leaving No. 6 incomplete owing to his declining health. Now identified as No. 2, the latter was completed by a group from the Society's Lancashire & Cheshire area group that became known as 'Team X', the work being completed in 1992. In 1991 'Team X' had returned brake/third No. 10, out of use since 1955, to service and it continues to play a significant part in the care of the Railway's heritage rolling stock.

A team of younger volunteers known as the 'F Team' (don't ask, they say) with an interest in *Mountaineer* extended their interests to wagons from the mid-1990s and have been largely responsible for the expansion of the slate wagon fleet used in the gravity train.

Livery changes, which started with *Prince*'s appearance in lined-red in 1986 already referred to, also spread to the carriage fleet from 1987, with the launch of the '*Mountain Prince*' named train, on which all seats were reservable. Appropriately launched with *Prince*, the carriages allocated to the service were painted in a red and off-white livery to distinguish the service on which they operated. Passengers chose not to make use of the reservation facility, but the livery was well received and adopted for the rest of the fleet.

A policy of restoring the vintage carriages to authentic liveries was started when No. 5 received LNWR-style royal purple and off-white livery in 1989. It is intended that the FR will in future field two vintage carriage sets, one in 19th century livery as applied to No. 5, the other in 1920s-style Kentish green as applied to No. 10 in 1991. To this end the former has benefited from the addition of a curly-roofed brake van constructed at Boston Lodge in 2003/4.

Apart from visiting locomotives, the newly built *David Lloyd George* and *Taliesin* have not been the only '*new*' locomotives to appear at Boston Lodge during the last 20 years, although the first new face, as it were, was actually a reappearance of *Palmerston* in 1988. Following a change in ownership, it returned to the Railway partially restored and, following the acquisition of a new boiler, it was back in action as a coal-fired machine of traditional appearance in 1993. Mike Hart, then Company Chairman, donated his majority holding in the locomotive to the Trust in 2000.

Gordon Rushton and Andy Savage acquired 2ft 6in gauge Bagnall 0-4-4-0T *Monarch* from the Welshpool & Llanfair Light Railway in 1991 and donated it to the Company the following year. Although it was dismantled and there was talk of it being used on the WHR, no serious restoration activity was started on it and it was sold back to the WLLR in 2003. Rushton bought his own locomotive, Kerr, Stuart 0-6-0T *Sgt. Murphy* in 1992; it was rebuilt as an 0-6-2T and left the FR for the Teifi Valley Railway in 1996, after Rushton had left the Company.

Construction of a Lynton & Barnstaple Railway Manning, Wardle 2-6-2T to be called *Lyd* was started at Boston Lodge in 1995; some components had already been manufactured by the scheme's promoter James Armstrong Evans. Funding is via subscription and

Trains crossing at Tan-y-bwlch, 2nd June 2002. The 'old' signal near the station building is a non-functional replica.

operation of 'drive an engine' activities on the FR. When completed, the loco is likely to be allocated to the WHR as its size will militate against regular use on the FR.

The demonstrable skill in restoring and recreating old carriages, highlighted by the quality of the restoration of Nos. 15 and 16, brought considerable attention to the carriage workshops, new business to the railway and hitherto unheard of exotica to the works. The recreated curly-roof van, already mentioned, whilst built for the railway, was funded by a benefactor with an interest in 19th century vehicles; it incorporated components from No. 3, the vehicle that deteriorated beyond repair at Harbour station during the war and closure period. Other commissions have been two Darjeeling Himalayan Railway-style carriages for former society chairman Adrian Shooter's private railway, a replica Pickering brake for the Welshpool & Llanfair Light Railway and the internal fitting out of a Hungarian bogie carriage for that railway too.

After the idea was proposed that the WHR's prime motive power could be Garratts, obtained from South Africa, it was followed by the suggestion that the FR's own Tasmanian Garratt could be extracted from the National Railway Museum for the same purpose. The WHR Society agreed to take on the project and the locomotive made an appearance at the 1995 gala before being moved to Tyseley for restoration. In 2000 it was returned to Boston Lodge for the work to be completed; trials took place in 2004.

Palmerston and *Lilla*, a Hunslet 0-4-0ST that attended the 1993 gala and stayed, find regular use on shuttles, footplate experience activities, photographic charter trains and vintage trains, all additions to the FR's repertoire, within and without galas, since the early 1990s. By means of scheduled services to Minffordd or Tan-y-bwlch attempts were made to offer something to prospective passengers who were unable to afford the time or the fare for a journey to Blaenau Ffestiniog, but both were eventually accused of abstracting traffic from the main services and were withdrawn.

The grant-aided permanent way diesel locomotive was not the first 'new' diesel locomotive to enter service during the period. That honour had been accorded to a second Hibberd Planet, *Conway Castle/Castell Conwy*, acquired in 1981 and in service in 1986 after an overhaul that included fitting a redesigned superstructure. The PW locomotive entered service in 1990. It had been adapted from a six-wheeled 140hp Caterpillar-engined diesel hydraulic locomotive built for export to Mozambique by Baguley Drewry in 1983 but not delivered due to the civil war; it was named *Harlech Castle/Castell Harlech*. It was followed in 1995 by a locomotive designed for passenger use incorporating Baguley Drewry components made for the same order. Completed at Boston Lodge and named *Criccieth Castle/Castell Criccieth*, it is equipped with a 250hp Caterpillar engine, the first time the FR has ever had a new diesel loco complete with a new engine.

A much larger diesel locomotive entered service in 1998, a 350hp double-bogie machine named *Vale of Ffestiniog*. Built by the South African company, C.H. Funkey & Co, it had been obtained in 1993 with another loco of the same type that was restored for use on the WHR. The adaptation of *Vale of Ffestiniog* was sponsored by National Power, the company that operates the Tanygrisiau power station. Usually seen hauling off-peak trains, this powerful locomotive is capable of taking the same loads as a double Fairlie if required.

The FR's penchant for adapting technological advances was demonstrated when *Conway Castle* and *Criccieth Castle* were equipped for working in processor-controlled push-pull mode with the all-year-round carriages. The strategy was intended to reduce crewing requirements and to save time by eliminating the need to run-round at termini. The systems are constantly under review and have been upgraded several times.

Another form of solid-state technology was introduced to the unlikely environment of the vintage trains in 2004. The 'Talking Train' is a tool that allows the railway to market its vintage stock whilst also informing its users of its history and surroundings. Usually consisting of either *Taliesin* and 19th century liveried stock or *Prince* and 1920s-liveried stock the train operates a return trip to Tan-y-bwlch, at the same fare as the return to Blaenau Ffestiniog to avoid any risk of abstraction. Passengers use a state-of-the-art handset that, when the appropriate buttons are pressed, can tell them about the locomotives and rolling stock and lineside structures and environment. The initiative was financed by the society.

Despite the success of the debenture issue and the grants awarded, the Railway's finances showed little change from earlier years and more redundancies were made in 1991 and 1995. After peaking at 47 in 1997 full-time staff employed fell to 39 in 1999 before rising to 61 in 2001 and 80 in 2002. In this last year a loss of £300,000 was recorded, resulting in several redundancies during the autumn.

Palmerston *returned to the FR in 1988 and restoration to working order completed in 1993. Unlike* Prince, *it remains coal-fired. The Cob, 2nd May 1994.*

There have been several changes in the Company's general management during the last 20 years, David Pollock's replacement by Gordon Rushton in 1991 having already been mentioned. In 1996 Alan Heywood took charge, managing the travel Company at the same time. He returned to concentrate on the travel business, being replaced by Society Chairman, Ken Allen, as Chief Executive in 2000. After a period of some trauma felt throughout the Railway, he left in 2002, being replaced initially by Peter Randle and then by Paul Lewin, a volunteer since the age of 15.

The Board, too, has changed. Bill Broadbent retired as the Society's nominee director in 1984 and was replaced by Andy Savage. Mike Hart, a former volunteer, replaced the Earl of Lindsay in 1989; Les Smith retired in 1992, being replaced by Michael Schumann, and John Routly was replaced by George Nissen when he retired in 1993; Mike Hart became Chairman. Mike Colville became the Society's nominee in 1998, replacing Andy Savage; he took on responsibility for finance after Hugh Eaves resigned in 1999; he was replaced as a Director by Society Chairman Ken Allen in 2000. Colville and Allen resigned in 2002, Andrew Hayward replacing the former and Michael Whitehouse (his father had published *Festiniog Railway Revival* in 1963) the latter. Mike Hart had stood down as Chairman in 2000 and was replaced by Nissen; Michael Whitehouse became Chairman in 2003, George Nissen retiring from the Board after the 2003 AGM. To strengthen the Board Malcolm High, Helen Waters and Michael Whitehouse were appointed non-executive Directors in 2002, the latter being replaced by John Ewing, the first WHR Society nominee, in 2003. Malcolm High retired after the 2004 AGM and was replaced by Nigel Burbidge, the auditor and a Boston Lodge volunteer.

The Society became a registered charity in 1997; as well as being able to benefit from tax reclaims on donations it started another new revenue stream at the same time, earning commission from an affinity credit card. Having gained full control of its financial contribution to the Railway, it started to develop a new relationship with it, where the Railway had to justify its requests for support, and on occasion was persuaded to approve Society initiatives too.

The Trust, owning as it does the majority of all classes of stock, is still the ultimate arbiter of the Railway's policy. Sir Osmond Williams Bt, a local dignitary and landowner, had been appointed a Trustee in 1979, joining Bill Broadbent, Trevor Bailey, Pat Garland and John Routly. Bailey died in 1991 and was replaced by John Prideaux. Garland's place was taken by Robert Riddick in 1990 and Michael Schumann replaced Sir Osmond in 1995. A new system of appointment was put in place by 31st December 1998, when Routly and Broadbent retired. Instead of appointments being in Alan Pegler's gift, the Company and Society each have a nomination and the others are independent appointments, to be made after a consultative process. Peter Jordan (then Society Chairman) and the Hon Sir William McAlpine Bt (independent) replaced Broadbent and Routly, and Prideaux became Chairman. Gareth Williams replaced Jordan in 2003.

Throughout this era the FR maintained and enhanced its prominent position in what has become known as the 'heritage railway industry'. The exhibition of a train comprising of *Prince*, No 15 and the curly-roof van in action at 'Railfest', the celebration of 200 years of steam locomotives at the National Railway Museum, York, in May 2004 gave the railway the opportunity of demonstrating its 'chutzpah' to a largely new audience, and attracted new visitors to Wales as a result.

The Railway had been through a period of trauma and financial crisis between 2000 and 2002, but as this is written in 2005 is generally in good heart. The Trust has learned that it cannot abandon responsibility to the Company Board and the Company Board has learned that it has to be kept informed about what is happening at Porthmadog and be prepared to act when necessary. The Society has to learn to see the broader picture, that it represents all its members, and to use its hard-gained influence with wisdom.

~ Appendices ~

Appendix 11 – Alternative proposals for crossing the dam at Tanygrisiau 206
Appendix 12 – Summary of tickets issued; eight weeks 1970/71 207
Appendix 13 – Winter Programme 1969/70 208
Appendix 14 – Grant Applications to the Wales Tourist Board 1973–1993 208
Appendix 15 – Estimate included with 1972 LRO Application 209
Appendix 16 – Extract from drawings LRO Amendment 1968 210
Appendix 17 – Financial details to end of May 1972 211

~Appendix 11~

Llyn Ystradau Deviation – alternative proposals for crossing the dam at Tanygrisiau

This paper deals with Festiniog Railway Company's alternative proposals for crossing the Ystradau Valley at Tanygrisiau dam in the light of correspondence with the Central Electricity Generating Board.

Summary of Previous Correspondence

The works described in this paper have become necessary on account of the reservoir constructed by the Central Electricity Generating Board on the former track of the Festiniog Railway. A proposal to reconstruct the railway on the present route was first sent to the board in May 1963. As a result of a meeting and subsequent correspondence, the following design features were fixed to govern any railway on or near the dam.

(1) That a roadway must be maintained over the dam, with the railway, if any, set into it in the manner of a tramway. A previous scheme to divert the south valve house road is not acceptable.

(2) That there would be no objection to a bridge over the spillway provided the necessary hydraulic requirements were met.

(3) That blasting was heavily restricted near the dam.

(4) That the board would prefer a level crossing over the lower access road, rather than any bridge which might obstruct large loads going to or from the power station.

A scheme conforming with these conditions was first submitted to the Board in our letter of 2nd May. This has now been adopted by the Festiniog Railway Board as their official scheme, and is known as Scheme A.

Scheme A

The proposed works would consist of the following, going towards Blaenau Ffestiniog:

1. A viaduct of prestressed concrete... This would consist of six prestressed concrete spans carrying the railway and supported by piers bonded to the spillway structure. The track is slung between the main beams on light prestressed concrete crossgirders. Each beam is topped by a single tubular steel handrail, while part of the deck is timbered to provide a walkway.

2. From the spillway viaduct to the north end of the dam, the road and railway would share the dam, the railway being set into the road in the manner of a tramway. Except for short sections at each end, the track on this stretch would be level, and the new road surface would be some six inches above the existing level. Certain alterations will be needed to the covers of the cable drawpits on the dam. These will be rebuilt at the new levels, and those which are in the line of the rails will need to be replaced by special steel covers constructed with the flangeway in them. It is proposed to use bituminous material between the rails on the tramway section in order to facilitate the replacement of the rails as this falls due. Rail life should exceed 30 years.

3. A level crossing over the lower access road at the north end of the dam. Since it is necessary for the railway to attain its original height at Cwmorthin road bridge, and since the ruling gradient for the whole line is 1 in 80, it is necessary to raise the road some three feet above its present level at the crossing point. We understand that 1 in 11.4 is the steepest road gradient acceptable at this point to the CEGB. Based on these figures, approximately 110 yards of the road will need to be raised. ... In general, the existing features (gates, kerbs, etc) would be replaced as they are now but at the new level. It will be necessary for the level crossing to be protected by a signalling device. The simplest arrangement would be a system of traffic lights operated by a treadle on the railway, and set at danger to the railway at all times except when a train is approaching, at which time the road danger signals would light up. All signalling and other safety precautions on the railway are subject to rigorous inspection by the Ministry of Transport...

Visually, Scheme A would make almost no difference to its surroundings. The spillway viaduct has been designed as low as possible so that the railings on it can continue the horizontal line of the dam parapet over the bridge while still providing a safe barrier.

Apart from the viaduct, there would need to be signals at the crossing, and possibly some handrails at that end of the dam. However, the visual effect of these would be negligible in the vastness of their surroundings.

Scheme A has a number of disadvantages:

(1) The train service would be suspended whenever the CEGB require to use the dam for operational or maintenance purposes.

(2) Tramway type track is not ideal for use by the Festiniog Railway which, on account of this and the road crossing, would be subject to a substantial speed restriction.

(3) The need for all users of the dam to conform to the Ministry of Transport's safety requirements.

(4) The impossibility of opening the dam to the public.

(5) The difficulty of providing adequate road clearance at the Cwmorthin road bridge.

Scheme D

[This designation may be an error in the original duplicated document.]

To avoid the real or potential drawbacks inseparable from the use of the dam, an alternative scheme has been considered, taking the railway across the valley downstream of the dam. With this route, it would be possible to avoid any alteration to the existing dam and roads, and hence any mutual interference between the activities of the generating board and the railway company.

Coming from Portmadoc, the railway would pass over the end of the dam south of the spillway, and continue a further 400ft along the hillside before crossing the spillway channel on a high concrete or steel bridge. It would skirt the hillock in the middle of the valley and run on to the landscaping beside the dam. From here there would be a second concrete or steel bridge over the Ystradau river, and finally a bridge over the road, returning the railway to its old formation at the original level. (This has the advantage of making it technically possible to reconstruct Cwmorthin road bridge with increased clearance.) ... There need now be no restriction in either width or height of the roadway under this bridge, since the rail level can be fixed to provide any reasonable clearance.

Particular thought has been given to the appearance of this route. Most of the line downstream of the dam would be concealed by the trees which have already been planted there, and this can be assisted by planting on the railway bank itself. Peat, and soft material from elsewhere on the railway route, can be used for soiling the slopes of all embankments. The only conspicuous features would be the three bridges. These have been designed on simple, clean lines to reflect the relatively light loads they are required to carry. At each bridge the abutments would be of local stone, and the rest of the structure in white concrete. It is intended that the bridges should become a positive addition to their surroundings, which they stand in no danger of dominating.

Design Loadings

All structures on the deviation will be designed for a 6-ton axle load, giving a maximum of 18 tons in 6ft, and of 1 ton per foot run between couplings for any item of rolling stock.

~ *Appendix 12* ~

Llyn Ystradau Deviation – Summary of tickets issued; eight weeks of summer service 1970/71

Portmadoc	**1971**		**1970**	
1st class ordinary all stations	7,509		11,564	
1st class economy all stations	1,330	8,839	-	
1st class off peak all stations	1,594		1,723	
	10,433		**13,287**	
3rd class ordinary Dduallt	27,923		39,655	
3rd class ordinary Tan-y-bwlch	3,189		3,204	
3rd class ordinary other stations, privilege tickets, members	7,474		8,354	
3rd class economy all stations	6,914	45,500	-	51,213
3rd class off–peak all stations	10,503		6,869	
	56,003		58,082	
Parties *	4,699		5,823	
Portmadoc total	**71,135**		**77,192**	
Tan-y-bwlch	17,295		16,455	
Minffordd	2,634		2,633	
Penrhyn	1,385		1,134	
Guards	2,937		3,904	
TOTAL	**96,386**		**101,318**	

* Parties were not encouraged during the 1971 peak; there was a corresponding increase in party traffic earlier in the season.

~Appendix 13~

Winter Programme 1969/70

Permanent Way

Location	Work done	Remarks
Gwyndy Bank	Patched	Full relaying deferred pending sort out of flat bottom rail and more time
TyB bridge – bottom points	25 lengths resleepered and ballasted	Fishplates still to have attention – difficulties over supplies
Plas Halt – Crossing	20 lengths rerailed double head	Not completed
Bothy	50 lengths resleepered and ballasted	
Cemetery – Boston Lodge	34 lengths rerailed double head	
	72 lengths resleepered	
Capel Nazareth	New bridge installed, track reinstated	To be lifted and tamped
Dduallt top points	Relaid on new alignment with headshunt and tracks realigned	

S&T

Strengthening of overhead route Penrhyn – Dduallt
Duct and cabling put in at Penrhyn and Tan-y-bwlch
Preparations for colour light signals at Minffordd and Tan-y-bwlch
Reinstatement of overhead lines after theft
Minffordd catch points put into operation
Work in connection with provision of GPO phone at Boston Lodge

Electrical

Reorganisation of electrical supplies to and within Boston Lodge
Provision of low voltage handlamp installation and battery chargers
Night storage heaters at Boston Lodge
Night storage heaters at Portmadoc and improved train charging leads
Improvement of wiring to Harbour station
Provision of alternative mobile generator for PW
Power supplies for colour light signals.

~Appendix 14~

Grant Applications made to the Wales Tourist Board 1973–1993

Year	Amount Awarded	Purpose
1973	£36,350	Harbour Station
1975	£43,120	Unspecified
1978	£50,000	Unspecified
1978	£18,000	Deviation
1980	£9,600	Unspecified
1981	£100,000	Unspecified
1985	£83,200	Rebuilding Merddin Emrys, improvements to Harbour station toilets and weather protection (platform canopies)
1987	Application rejected	Construction of 100-seat heated three-car push-pull train with public address system and disabled facilities
1989	£80,000	Development of station facilities and building a new carriage
1993	£9,250	Purchase of a passenger diesel locomotive
1993	£30,800	Development of a 32-bedspace volunteer hostel at Minffordd and construction of 2ft gauge passenger diesel

Data released by the Wales Tourist Board under the terms of the Freedom of Information Act.

~Appendix 15~

Estimate included with 1972 LRO Application

1. Railway (No 4)

Length 1 mile 5 furlongs 6 chains

Gauge 1ft 11in (60cm)

Construction of Railway

Earthworks	Cubic yards	Price per cubic yard	£	
Cuttings – rock	11,000	£6	66,000	
Earth and loose rock	8,000	£4	32,000	
Total	**19,000**	**£10**	**98,000**	
				£98, 000
Embankments – 21,000 cu yds				
Bridges – one				20,000
Accommodation works – bridge over pressure pipes				15,000
Tunnel – one – 310 linear yards (4,500 cu yds)				60,000
Culverts and drains				10,000
Metalling of roads and level crossings				12,000
Fencing				2,000
Gatekeepers' houses at level crossings				NIL

Permanent Way

	Miles	furlongs	chains			
Single	1	4	8	@ £5,000 per mile		
Double			8		9,000	

Permanent way for sidings and cost of junctions		NIL
Stations, buildings and other works		NIL
Plant, including signalling and telegraphic apparatus		3,000
Contingencies at 10%		23,000
Total for construction of railway		**£252,000**
Land and buildings to be acquired 1 acre @ £20 per acre	£20	
Compensation to landowner for disturbance	£300	
	£320	£320
Land to be obtained by easement 6 acres		
Total cost of construction and of acquisition of land (and buildings)		**£252,320**
2. Preliminary expenses		£680
3. Rolling stock		NIL
4. Generating stations or substations		
5. General charges		
6. Interest on capital during construction		
7. Sundries		

NOTE The whole of the above construction work has arisen from the compulsory acquisition by the Central Electricity Generating Board of former land earthworks and track of the Festiniog Railway Co between Dduallt and Tanygrisiau. Compensation for loss of profit resulting from severance has been settled. The amount to be charged to capital will be, therefore, reduced by £100, 000

Amount to be charged to capital £153, 000

~*Appendix 16*~

Extract from drawings accompanying the Light Railway Amendment Order 1968

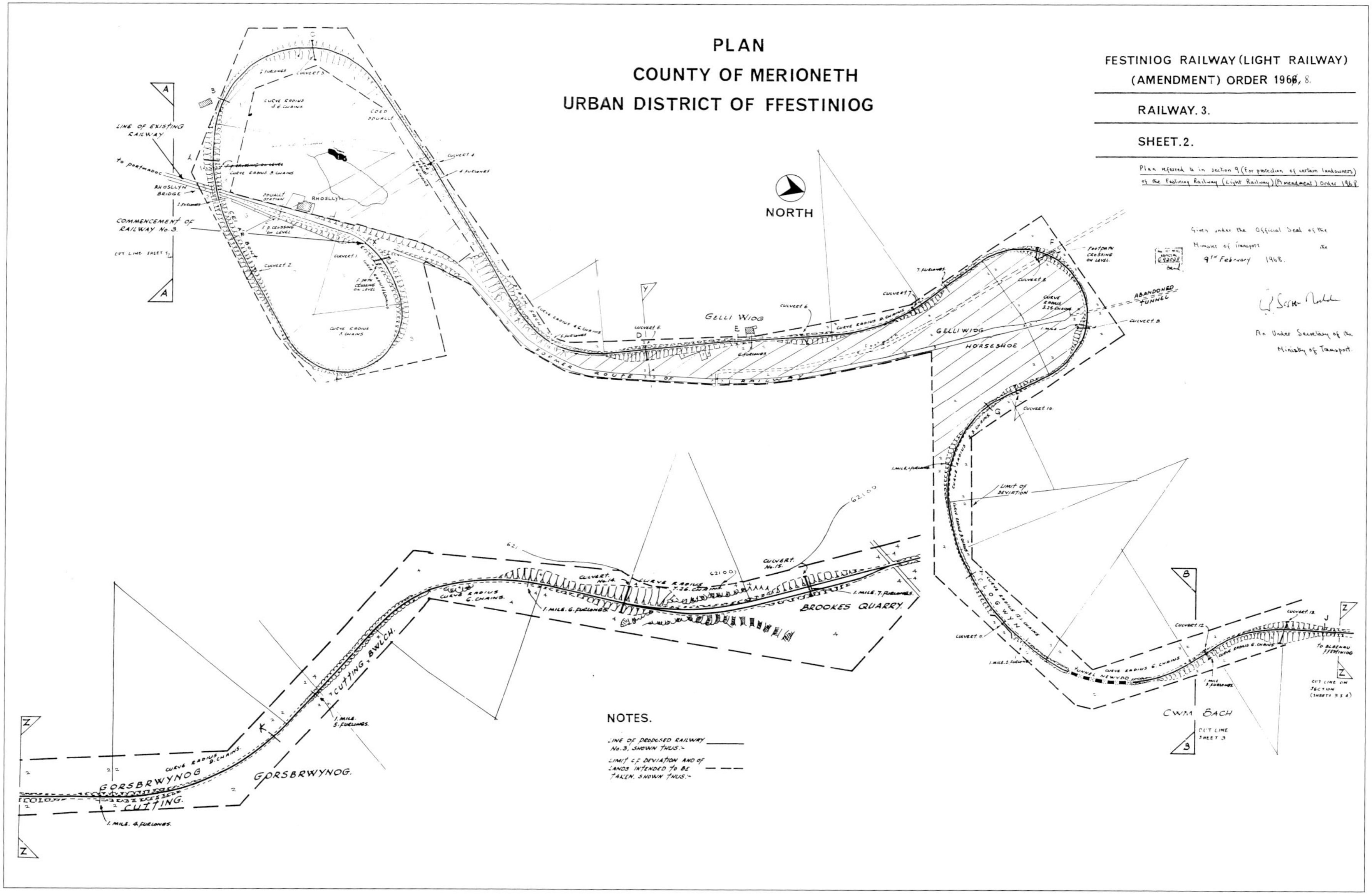

~Appendix 17~

Financial details to end of May 1972

Receipts	1972	1971
Fares	£14,162	£12,783
Railway Letter Service	£459	
Sales	£9,702	£7,758
Mail order	£96	£68
Area groups' sales	£950	£79
Agency	£906	£405
Sundries	£5,517	
Ex KB3	£30,000	
Expenditure	**1972**	**1971**
Wages	£17,985	£17,946
Loco maintenance	£595	£372
Carriage maintenance	£416	£952
Rolling stock sundries	£1,053	£628
Buildings	£696	£856
PW	£1,722	£2,385
S&T	£73	£224
Electrical	£116	£361
Operating	£993	£964
Traffic	£315	£258
Publicity	£546	£10
Office etc	£754	£575
Insurance	£350	£56
Electricity etc	£505	£454
Rents etc	£434	Not comparable
Lorry	£75 cr	£415
Deviation	£1,465	£432
Capital, including Glan-y-mor	£460	£83
Other		£340
Legal	£5	
Bank charges	£292	
Sales, agency, RLS	£7,156	
Contract work	£1,848	
Total (excluding No. 2 account)	**£37,704**	**£28,435**

~ Index ~

A

Active forty 63
Act of Parliament,1832 175
Act of Parliament (Hydro Scheme) 103
Afon Cwmorthin 72,89,103
Afon Cwmorthin bridge 89
Afon Ystradau 103
Alco 37
Allen, Ken 204
Aluminium coaches 57,59,64
Aluminium Company 128
Anderson, Paul 36
Andrew Barclay & Company 41,42
Anglian Building Society 70
Anniversary, 150th 195
Anniversary, reopening 18
Annual convention 63
Archivist, FR 47
Army Railway Squadron 27,44,143,144
Arup, Ove 159
Assistant Treasury Solicitor 129
Association of Minor Railways 94
Association of Railway Preservation Societies 94, 152,155
Automatic crossing 195

B

Bailey, Trevor 10,33,106,107,109,184,204
Bala 44
Bala-Blaenau Ffestiniog branch 16
Ball, Air Vice-Marshal Sir Ben 71,74,78
Ball, Lady 152
Banda, Dr Hastings 42
Bank interest 185
Banwy Bridge 14
Barn cutting 60
Barraclough, Leslie 18
Barradell, Martin 45,47,48,58,129,131,184
Bate, John 33,184
Bates, 'Blaster' 64
BBC TV 39
Bellamy, Bill 110
Beyer, Peacock & Company 27
Blackburn, B.J. 35
Blaenau Ffestiniog 89,98,144,156,159, 160,168,169,172,176,179,182, 186,190,194
Blaenau Ffestiniog, GWR station 45,89
Blaenau Ffestiniog, LNWR yard 45,89
Blaenau Ffestiniog (Central Station) LRO 1981 171,172
Blaenau Ffestiniog opening 179
Blaenau Ffestiniog station scheme 159,172
'Bluebell' 142
Blue Peter 91
Boiler Inspector 33
Bolton, Maurice 39,45,54
Bonus, Allan Garraway 39
Borth-y-gest 37
Boston Lodge 8,182,186
Boston Lodge landslide 14
Boughey, Fred 7,12
Bourne, Developer 39,40
Bourne, Graham 36,37,39,40,41,99
Bridges, pressure pipe 70
British Electricity Authority 103,105, 111,112,113,117,121
British Railways 63,80,121,179
British Railways' Southern Region 131
British Steel 70
British Transport Commission 17,110
Broadbent, Bill 7,8,10,33,39,42,45,49, 52,59,63,64,72,77,78,80,82,89, 91,92,95,130,138,143,144,170,184
Bron-y-Garth hospital 86
Bron Turnor 78,91
Bron Turnor Crossing 15
Bryn Mawr 16,80
BR Agency arrangement 18
BR Engineering 56
Buarth Melyn 82,88,135,145
Budget 27,51,79,82,88,89,95,96,99
Budr 45
Buffet cars 89
  Charles Spooner 89
  Samuel Holland 89
  William Madock 89
Building department 63
Bullock & Turner Ltd 47
'Bunny hutch kiosk' 42
Burbidge, Nigel 204

C

Caddy, Gordon 152,180,200
Caernarfon 47,193
Campbell's barn 132
Campbell's private siding 19,136
Campbell, Colonel 106,132,136,138
Capel Nazareth underbridge 52,53,191
Carnegie Trust 63
Carnforth 190
Carpgate Company 65
Car park 69
Catchpole, Keith 94
Caterpillar engine 203
Central Electricity Authority (CEA) 127
Central Electricity Board (CEGB) 13,65,66,70,71,127,128,129,206, 132,136,137,141,142,149,152
Central Electricity Board (CEGB) Easement 144
Cei Mawr 13,30,144,169
'Centenary of Steam' medals 181
Chace School 36
Chicken, Bryan 93,180
Chief Executive 91,99,151
Citrine, Lord 106,121
City Press Agency 97,99
Coaches
  Aluminium coaches 59
  Bogies 16
  Buffet Cars 7,12, 89
  Hungarian bogie 202
  Livery 10,16,42,46,47,53,91,201
  livery, varnished 16
  No. 10 54
  No. 12 89
  No. 13 10
  No. 14 7,12,72,89,101
  No. 15 68,202
  No. 16 54,68,202
  No. 17 23
  No. 18 23
  No. 19 27
  No. 20 23,71
  No. 23 27
  No. 24 9,10,12
  No. 25 27
  No. 26 12,91,94,123
  No. 30 74
  No. 31 82,86
  No. 32 82,86
  No. 37 59,76
  No. 38 76
  No. 100 12,14,16
  No. 101 12,54
  No. 103 42,89
  No. 104 72,158
  No. 105 38
  No. 110 86
  No. 116 68,89
  No. 117 86,91
  No. 118 86
  No. 119 95,101,167
  No. 120 100,101
  No. 1 van 14
  Observation Car 7
  Pickering brake 202
  Pullman car 'Eunice' 54
  Roller Bearings 13
Cob, the 144
Colville, Mike 204
Combermere Abbey 100,155
Company Clerk 77
Compressor 137

Congratulatory letter 180
Consequential Loss Insurance 36
Cookes Explosive Plant 9
Countryside Commission 151
Court Circular 80
Creamer, Harold 36,40,63
Creau 18
Croesor wagon 10
Cuneo, Terence 12
Cwmorthin bridge 96,98,144,146,147
Cwmorthin river bridge 146

D

'Drive an engine' 200
Daily Mail 182
Daily Telegraph 48,144
Dallison, J.H. 142
Daniels, Robin 118,135,145
Dant, Nigel 57
Darjeeling Himalayan Railway 202
Davies, Aneurin 74,98,132.135-137,140, 144,180
Davies, C.E. 14,103,104
Davies, Evan 161,181
Davies, Rhys 98,132,135-136,140
Dduallt 40,42,43,46,56
Dduallt Manor 132
Debenture, 4% 185
December Gales 36
Dee & Mersey Group 96
Department of the Environment 63
Department of Trade & Industry 68, 69,88
Dependent's Income Insurance 45
Derailments 49,68,91
Deudraeth RDC 35,104
Development Board for Rural Wales 100,150,151,155,171,175
Deviation 46,47,60,96,98,103-150,152
Deviation Compensation 150
Deviation junta 48
Deviation tunnel 143
Dinas 193
Dingle/Midge embankment 142
District Traffic Supervisor, BR 128
District Valuer 86
Dobson, John 7
Dol-y-moch 129
Dolrhedyn 77,131,132,142,146, 165,169
Dorfil Road footbridge 98
Down Your Way 49
Draft Accounts 1964 15
Dragon/New Moon cutting 142
Duffws 13,45
Dukes, Paul 8,49,63,77,155,172,182
Dulake, T.S. 121
Duncan, Martin 155
Dyffryn Ardudwy 10
Dyson Bell & Company 111

E

'Early bird train' 100
East Anglian Group 46
East India & Sports Club 94
East Midlands Group 63
Eaves, Hugh 73,74,88,91,96,100,151, 159,172,184
Economic Forestry Group 16,35,58,68
Edmund Crow Ltd 68
EEC grant 175
Ellis, Clough Williams 41,59,93,132
English Speaking Union 40
Equity & Law Life Scheme 70
European Economic Commission 153
European Economic Community 78,159, 169,172,175
Evans, James Armstrong 201
Evans, Robert 121
Evershed, Dennis 13,132
Evershed, Norman 58,129,131,132
Ewing, John 204

F

Fairbourne Railway 44
Fairlie, Robert Francis 186,200
Fairlie event 48
Fares 15
Fare increases 158
Faulkner, Bill 33
Feature film 85
Festiniog Railway (Light Railway) (Amendment) Order 1975 78
Festiniog Railway (Light Railway) (Amendment) Order 1982 182/3
Festiniog Railway Preservation Society 27, 106
Festiniog Railway Society 151,153,158, 160,179,195,200
Festiniog Railway Special 10
Ffestiniog UDC 13,41,48,104,105,131,136
Fiennes, Gerry 40,63,140,143,153
Fire, Cei Mawr 169
Fire patrols 58
First sod, Deviation 132
First train 181
First train for Dduallt 35
FitzGerald, Sir William MC QC 127/8,129
Flange lubricator 36
Foot-and-mouth disease 40,137
Forest Lodge 131
Forestry Commission 58
Fox, Gerald 13,104,129,132,133
Freeman, Fox & Partners 113,127
FR Heritage Group 200
FR industrial relations 80
Fuel consumption 51
Funkey, C.H. & Company 203
'F' Team 201

G

Ganolfan 69
Garland, Pat 204
Garnedd 138
Garnedd tunnel 27,39,64
Garnock, Viscount 40, 47,49,65,70,89, 93,100,143,175,179,204
Garratt Fund 34
Garraway, Allan 7,27,94,97,155,170, 180,181,183,184,199
Gelliwiog 77
Gelliwiog shuttle 74,77
Gilbert, Fred 103,104,184
Gilbert & Sullivan 10
Girdlestone, Phil 161
Glan-y-don slate tip 86
Glan-y-mor 27,71,100
Glan-y-pwll 71,72,86,159,180,182,190
Glanmeirion 78
Glyndyfrdwy 10,44
Golding, H.W. 136,141,146
Goods Wagons
    Four-wheeled van 10
Goss, Roger 69
Government pay policy 98
'Go with Noakes' 91,95,134,149
GPO, cable duct 33
Grants 185/6,195,208
Gravity working 26,185
Great Central Railway 9
Great Little Trains of Wales 94
Great Northern Hotel 94
Great Western station 13
Greaves & Sons, Messrs J.W. 103
Green, David 201
Greenacres caravan site 37
Greene, Sydney 49
Green Shield Stamps 115
Group Five Engine Association 73
Guardian newspaper 149
Gurley, Norman 157,170
GWR Blaenau site 80
Gwyndy bank 16
Gwynedd County Council 69,72,74,77, 85,146,149,172
Gysgfa 27,68

H

Hafod-y-llyn 53
Halifax Building Society 78
Halsall, John 39,47
Halsall, Katy 47
Halstead, Donald and Partners 142,144
Harbour Station 9, 66,71,75,78,86,90, 96,100,186
Hardy, R.H.N. 'Dick' 94,96,99,182,184
Hard labour, 10 years 10
Harman, Lord Justice 128
Harris, Bob 10,74
Harrison, John 40,41,61

Harrison, Nell 40
Hart, Mike 201,204
Harvey, D.W. 184
Hayward, Andrew 204
Headech, Alan 73
Headhunting 100
Heritage Group 200
Heritage Lottery Fund 195
Heywood, Alan 7,48,52,61,63,155
High, David 185,199
High, Malcolm 204
Highgate crossing 30
HMS Pinafore 10
Hobbs, H.P. 142
Holliday & Edwards 70
Hollingsworth, Brian 103,124,145,150
Hoole, Bill 11,37,86
Horse dandy 34
Hostel, volunteer 30,34,195
House of Lords Select Committee 112
Howes, Fred 10,36,145,155
Howes, Ken 85
HRH Princess Margaret 145
Hughes, Peter 135,145
Hunslet Engine Company 9,42,45,48
Hunslet mines loco 74

I

Ian Allan Ltd 13
Ilott, Major Michael 54, 64
InCa 186
Ingham, Paul 61
Inland Revenue 153
Interest-free loan 35
Isallt 33,34
Isle of Man 33,44
Isle of Man Railway Company 79
Isle of Man Steam Railway Society 33

J

Jackson, Doug 97
Jarrah sleepers 53
Jarvis, Ron 44,201
Johnson, Peter 63,97,169,179
John Player Tobacco Company 44,60,61
Joint BR/FR station 89
Joint Publicity Committee 69
'Jolly good fun' 90
Jones, Bessie 39,40
Jones, Eddie 9,66
Jones, Will 39,40
Jones mobile road crane 70,90
Jones road crane 90
Jordan, Peter 204
Joseph, Michael 69,72

K

Kenneth Brown, Baker, Baker 66
Kent, A.H. 128,129,130,131
Kylchap cowl 11

L

Ladies' toilets 86
Laidlaw Drew Ltd 47,59
Laker, Freddie 97
Lambert, Arthur 93,155,171
Lancashire & Cheshire Group 96, 201
Lands Tribunal 63,65,124,128,142
Lands Tribunal Act of 1949 126
Langsdale, Miss 9,12,14,27,39
Leeds Metal Traders 16
Legacy 88
Leicester Chronicle 91
Leicester Group 63
Lester, Ron 36,49,63
Letter stamps 16,48,167
Lewin, Paul 204
Lewis, Bunny 63,91,141
Lewis, Michael 15
Life Pass 18
Light Railway Order 42,66,78,129,131, 138,139,144,140,171,172,175, 182,183
Lindsay, Earl of 204
Little Wonder café 86,182
Liverpool Daily Post 48
Liverpool Garden Festival 179
Livesey & Henderson 40,124,127,131, 135,142
Llanbedr 201
Llanberis Lake Railway 64,103
Llanfrothen & Penrhyndeudraeth District Committee 34
Llanuwchllyn 44
Llechwedd Coed 36,41
Llechwedd slate caverns 63
Lloyds Bank 68
Llyn Conclog 103
Llyn Cwmorthin 103
Llyn Ystradau 91,94,98,130,133,149,164
LNWR yard 45
Loan account 96
Loch Aber Power Scheme 128
Loch Triog 128
Locomotives
- *Ashover* 171
- Baguley Drewry diesel 203
- Battery-electric 145
- *Blanche* 7,10,18,23,49,51,52,54, 59,63,65,66,69,72,73,74,89, 91,95,98,101,155
- *Conway Castle* 203
- *Criccieth Castle* 203
- *David Lloyd George* 188,190,195,201
- *Dot* 27
- *Earl of Merioneth* (I) 7,34,37,45, 49,52,53,62,63,68,73,74,80
- *Earl of Merioneth* (II) 151,152,153,166,181,188
- Feldbahn 0-8-0T 200
- *Flying Scotsman* 10,65
- Garratt K1 27,33,89,202
- *Harlech Castle* 203
- Hunslet 0-4-0ST 200
- *Jane* 146
- *Lilla* 202
- *Linda* 7,23,34,52,54,56,60,65, 68,72,73,76,78,80,85,98,161, 169,200
- *Livingston Thompson* 63,68,151
- *Lyd* 201
- *Mary Ann* 54,91,167
- *Merddin Emrys* 7,18,23,34,51,53, 56,62,65,68,69,79,93,96,98, 123,134,152,153
- *Moelwyn* 9,15,54,87,152,166,169, 188,190
- *Moel Hebog* 77,90,158
- *Moel Tryfan* 53
- *Monarch* 201
- *Mountaineer* 37,39,45,48,49,51, 52,56,57,63,64,72,73,79,80, 91,96,101,123,133,152,158, 192,201
- NGG16 class Garratts 198,200
- Orenstein & Koppel 65
- *Palmerston* 33,35,40,201,202,203
- *Prince* 7,15,47,73,133,152,158, 159,165,180,187
- *Princess* 49,171
- *Russell* 200
- *Sgt. Murphy* 201
- *Taliesin* 68,189,190,201
- The Simplex 19
- *Tyke* 9
- *Upnor Castle* 45,46,55,75,86
- *Vale of Ffestiniog* 154,169,193,203
- *Vale of Rheidol* No. 8 69
- Visiting Alco 200
- *Volunteer* 7,73

London, Brighton & South Coast Railway 152
London & Counties Bank 65
London Area Group 10
Lowe, C.R. & Company 109
Lynton & Barnstaple Railway 16,202

M

Maenofferen Quarry 39
Maenofferen Slate Company 56
Maentwrog 105
Manpower Services Commission 82,85, 96,145,146,148,149,150
Manx underframes 80
Marchant, Bob le 135,145
Marston, C.N. 136,141
Marston, Peter 180
Massau, Tony 36
Matisa tamper 74

MBE, Allan Garraway 155
McAlpine, Sir Alfred & Company 88,131,132,145,149,151,169
McMillan, Moyra 27
McMullen, Colonel D. 40,128,131
McNaughton, Colonel I. 144
Membership decline 201
Merionethshire County Council 44, 106
Metalastik suspension 16
Midland Area Group 10,15
Midland Rolling & Haulage Company 68
Millennium Commission 193
Minack Chronicles 69
Minffordd BR 18
Minffordd goods shed 16,30,94
Ministry of Transport 35,39,106,139
Miss World 74
Mitchell, Vic 184,199
Moelwyn Tunnel 85,89,100,115,116, 118/9,145,146,148,150,165
Morfa Mawddach 44
Mortgage 85
Moseley Hall hospital 86
Mozambique 203

N

Nabarro, Gerald 105
Nant Gwernol extension 56
Narrow Gauge Railway Museum 27, 34
National Eisteddfod 34
National Parks Commission 104,127
National Power 203
National Programme of Community Interest 186
National Railway Museum 77,86,89,151,202
National Union of Railwaymen 49,74,80,89,99,179
National Westminster Bank 70,74,88, 90,148
Nelson, W.K. 184
Newborough Estate 45
New tourist car 74
Nicholson, Ed 184
Nissen, George 204
Noakes, John 91,95,134,149
North Staffordshire Group 54,59
North Wales Hydro-Electric Power Scheme 103
North Wales Hydro-Electric Power Bill 110
North Wales Power Company 103
North Wales Quarrymen's Union 106
North Western Region 129
Nottingham Castle 60

O

Oakeley Slate Quarries 103,159
Observation Car 100 14
Official opening 183
Oftel 195
Oil firing 47,56,59,63,72,73,77,78, 142,145,150
Olver, Major Peter 77,91,98,141,142, 145,148,150,179,180
One-engine-in-steam 149
Operating loss 185
Ordnance Survey, Deviation 121
Orenstein & Koppel 65
Ormerod, Lord Justice 128
Outside contract 64
Overdraft 40,74,152,179
Overtime 98
Owen, Jack 15

P

Parker, Peter 97
Parks & gardens deptartment 195
Parry, Lord 169,179
Pattern loft 59
Payne, Dave 91
Pay claim 98,160,172
Pearce, Norman 42,160,183
Pearson, Lord Justice 128
Peat, Marwick & Mitchell 140
Peckett Ltd 7
Pegler, Alan 9,10,12,39,42,48,49,65, 74,77,107,113,117,126,131,136, 153,170,199
Pen-y-bryn Halt 40
Penlan 80,90,96,151,154,156,158,159, 169,172
Penrhyn debt 37,45,52
Penrhyn Quarry 7,8
Penrhyn rail 13
Penrhyn station 16,30,34,179
Pension provision 45,85,169
Penstock pipes 149
Pen Cob Halt 40
Permanent way 45,53,62
Permanent way trolley 26
Pithiviers 37
Plas Halt 36
Plas Tan-y-bwlch Estate 91
Polish bogies 73
Pollock, David 183,185,204
Porter, Alan Lowry 103
Porthmadog - Ffestiniog structure plan 90
Portmadoc coaling stage 69
Portmadoc UD Council 10,104
Portmadoc Women's Institute 48
Portmeirion Board Meeting 44
Portmeirion 78
Port Maintenance Troop, RE 483 9
Power Station bridges 90
Pratt, John 77
President of Malawi 42
Prideaux, John 199,204
Princess Margaret, HRH 78,79
Princess of Wales 175
Prince of Wales 47,48,49,95,97,175,179
Pritchard, Megan 54
Project Engineer, Deviation 140
Property development 65
Public inquiry 193
Pullman 16
Purley 36
Push-pull 77
Putnam, Andy 171

Q

Quarry Lane 195
Quarry Tours Ltd 63
Queen's Hotel 48,190
Queen's Jubilee tour 88

R

RailFest 204
Railway Inspectorate 128
Randle, Peter 204
Ransom, John 37,38,48,175
Redundancies 185
Redwing Company 65
Red Star parcels 179,180
Rees, Dewi 92,98
Regional Development Scheme 69
Registered Office 10
Rendel, Palmer & Tritton 124
Rhiwbryfdir 86
Rhiw Goch 16,33,42,70,71,74,77
Rhiw Plas 14,53
Rhoslyn bridge 132,140,141,144
Rhoslyn House 137
Rhyd Ddu 193
Richards, Major S.L. 37
Riddick, Robert 204
Roberts, John 'Borth' 10,41
Robertson, Colonel J.R.H. 40,41,128, 129,131,132,133,141
Rock Services (Midland) Ltd 143
Roller bearings 13
Ronald, David 9
Rouse, David 9
Routly, E.J. 40,42,63,65,69,70,72,74, 77,80,82,88,89,90,91,93,96,97, 100,135,137,143,149,151,169, 172,179,183,184,204
Royal Engineers 8,9,16,23,27,44,128,143
Royal Engineers 24th Eng. Group 124
Royal visit 79
Rudd, Ian 72
Rushton, Gordon 200,201,204

S

S&T department 160
Sands, Ann 8

Rheilffordd Ffestiniog

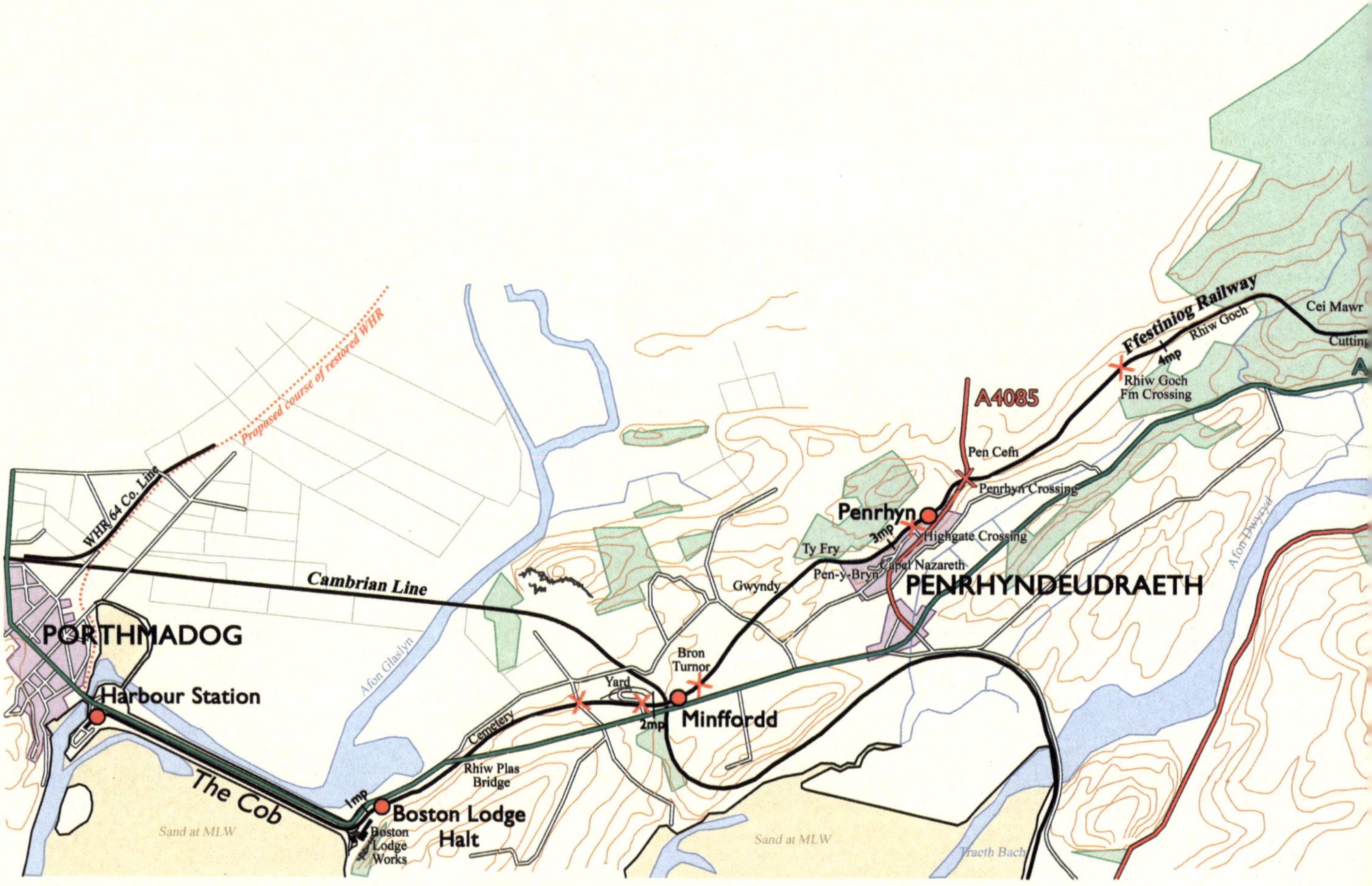